For All The Saints

A Calendar of Commemorations for United Methodists

Clifton F. Guthrie

Editor

Volume V
The Daily Office
A Book of Hours for Daily Prayer
After the Use of The Order of Saint Luke
Dwight W. Vogel, General Editor

Order of Saint Luke Publications
Akron, Ohio

FOR ALL THE SAINTS:
A Calendar of Commemorations for United Methodists

Copyright © 1995 by The Order of Saint Luke
All rights reserved

ISBN 1-878009-25-7

This book is printed on acid-free paper that meets the
American National Standards Institute Z39.48 Standard

Produced and manufactured in the United States of America by

Order of Saint Luke Publications
P. O. Box 22279
Akron, Ohio 44302-0079

Production Editing: Timothy J. Crouch, O.S.L.

The Order of Saint Luke invites people throughout the church to use these resources. We also solicit comments based upon their use. Please direct all comments and suggestions to the publishing office.

You are free to reproduce the materials contained herein, providing the copyright is not held by another publisher, for use in the church or by chapters in the Order by including the following credit line and copyright notice:

References marked "UMH" refer to *The United Methodist Hymnal: Book of United Methodist Worship,* © 1989 by The United Methodist Publishing House. References marked "UMBOW" refer to The United Methodist Book of Worship, © 1992 by The United Methodist Publishing House.

Scripture quotations, unless otherwise noted, are from the New Revised Standard Version of the Bible, copyright © 1989 Division of Christian Education of the National Council of the Churches of Christ in the United States of America. Used by Permission.

Every effort has been made to acknowledge sources and to trace copyrights. If any rights have been inadvertently infringed upon, we as that the omission be excused and agree to make necessary corrections in subsequent editions.

Contents

Acknowledgements

A project like this naturally involves a large number of persons, many of whose names appear on the contributors pages and many of whose do not. All are saints in my eyes for their willingness to give freely of their time and expertise. Particular thanks go to Dan Benedict who wisely saw the need for such a volume. Timothy Crouch, as Director of Publications for the Order of Saint Luke, supported its development and did the hard work of readying the book for publication. Chris Visminas graciously provided the drawings which accompany the major commemorations. Thanks are also due to Dwight Vogel, Don Saliers, Hoyt Hickman, Karen Westerfield Tucker, Grant Sperry-White, Ken Rowe, and Lester Ruth, conversations with whom have lent shape to this sanctoral cycle. It is impossible to measure or overvalue the encouragement and help I received from Ulrike Guthrie, my spouse and live-in professional editor, who with Tom, our son, deepens and improves the text of my life.

Clifton F. Guthrie
The Annunciation, 1995

Introduction

*To lead a moral life one does not need a theory about how one should
live, but a flesh and blood existent.* Edith Wyschogrod[1]

As our lives in contemporary North America become ever more complex
and confusing, we are intrigued by lives which are lived with unusual purpose
and clarity, utterly transparent to a reality beyond themselves. Saints
intrigue us religiously because so rarely anymore do we find people of such
conviction that what they believe about God shapes their entire existence.
They intrigue us morally because while we seem to be running out of answers
for how to heal the deep rifts that exist between us over wealth, power, and
gender, saints somehow pick a way through the rifts and build bridges over
which others can travel. While few of our traditional religious and political
leaders carry any real moral authority among us any longer, there is no end
to the shrill voices making unending pronouncements about what we should
do or be — but they are thin voices carrying a thin message: be nice to others,
don't smoke or eat fat, and recycle your newspapers. When it comes to
knowing how to live what we lack are not voices, but wise guides. We want
a form of living that will stretch our moral and religious imaginations . . . and
carry us along. So saints are catching our attention once again.

To pay close attention to the lives of saints is not to engage in nostalgia for
a pre-modern faith in which relics, miracles, and Church authority protect us
from encountering the deep questions of contemporary life. Rather, it is
precisely the encounter with these questions in a postmodern environment
that has led some persons to a reappreciation of what the saints have to offer
us. Academic ethicists are gradually giving up the Enlightenment project of
finding the right moral *theory* that will give us a formula on how we should
live — giving it up because after many generations of trying they are no closer
to finding the 'right' theory and because there is scant evidence that such
theories are finally of much use. Edith Wyschogrod has argued that while
traditional ethics based upon moral theory may tell us how we ought to live,
it has proven inadequate in actually *helping us* to live morally. What
academic ethicists are rediscovering, of course, is something we have known
all along: that we are less influenced by abstract arguments than by the moral
examples of other people — our mothers and fathers, our friends and
neighbors, our oppressors and mentors. Or, as Wyschogrod says, "To lead a
moral life," we need a "flesh and blood existent." Saints are flesh and blood
existents of life lived well before God.

Saints' lives can have a curious effect on us. The more we believe ourselves
surrounded by their witness (Hebrews 12:1), the more we find ourselves
unwittingly attracted to the idea of following their path. It is hard to read
much about Francis of Assisi, for example, and not find ourselves being

tempted, if only for a fleeting second, to drop everything and serve God and neighbor as he did without reservation. And while the vast majority of us will not (and probably should not) do this literally, we may be gently spurred through his example to engage in some volunteer work among the poor or be moved by the sight of the sun, moon, and stars to sing the praise of God. Whether famous, like Francis, or known only to us, like a favorite aunt or godparent, saints change us simply by existing. "No," Austin Farrer insisted, "there's no getting round the saints."[2]

Martyrs, Confessors, and Calendars

The first calendars of saints were local creations. A Christian community would gather at the tomb of a martyr on the anniversary of his or her death to sing hymns and to celebrate the Eucharist.[3] Hence, the idea of having a "feast" was early attached to the remembering of the saints. Gradually, the circle of those remembered after death in this way grew to include "confessors"—those who had confessed Christ during a time of persecution but who had not been killed. As the numbers of such martyrs and confessors grew, the local bishops took control and regularized the process whereby a name was added to a local list of commemorations.

While the Peace of Constantine brought an end to most "red" martyrdoms (martyrs by blood), the rise of Christian monasticism brought with it the concept of "white" martyrdom — dying for Christ through ascetic practice or extraordinary Christian service. The category of confessor was enlarged to include bishop, priest, or monk for men, and for women, virgin or widow. In Roman Catholicism this typology largely remained intact until reforms introduced within the last century. Kenneth Woodward points out the inherent clergy and male bias in this typology, not to mention its suggestion ". . . that the idea of sanctity continues to be identified at root with forms of renunciation as expressive of the love of Christ."[4] Clearly, one of the challenges in the creation of any contemporary sanctoral calendar is to make it fully representative of the many forms of life in which heroic Christian service can be manifest.

As the church became more centralized in Rome, so, of course, did the process of making saints. The dates of important New Testament figures were also gradually added to calendars, and because their death dates were generally lost to history they were placed on the calendar as convenient, sometimes on the date of the translation (removal and reburial) of their relics or on the date of the dedication of a notable church built in their honor. During the Middle Ages, when there was a popular explosion of the cult of saints, Rome responded by drawing up increasingly complex rules to control the process (the fear was that people would venerate saints who were heretics) and made the distinction between the *sancti* (the saints) who were papally canonized and the *beati* (the blesseds) who were only locally venerated.[5]

Today, all Roman Catholic saints must go through a lengthy and difficult process before their names are added to the liturgical calendar.

But even as the process for officially making saints has become more centralized, local communities of faith are still responsible to initiate the process for considering any specific person for Roman Catholic sainthood. Furthermore, the saints which any local church actually chooses to celebrate varies from place to place. The enduring local character of sanctoral calendars is testimony to the fact that Christianity as it has spread through the world is not a uniform but organic experience taking on the flavor of the culture it inhabits.

This local character is also evident in the recently expanded calendars of the Episcopal Church (*Book of Common Prayer*, 1979), the Lutheran churches (the *Lutheran Book of Worship*, 1978), and the Uniting Church of Australia (*Uniting in Worship*, 1988). They all give evidence of a new boldness of traditionally reticent Protestant traditions to name from within their particular histories lists of persons, "flesh and blood existents," whose commemoration enlarges their practice of Christian faith.

Methodism, Wesley, and the Saints

Underlying many of the major developments in United Methodism in the past decade — a new hymnal and book of worship, revisions in our Discipline's social and theological statements, disagreements over the meaning and practice of baptism and ministry — is a general agreement that United Methodism needs to rediscover its particular identity in the midst of a secular and pluralistic age. For this reason alone, the time to begin identifying a list of saints of our own is long overdue. To propose a calendar of saints days for use within The United Methodist Church may at first seem an odd thing to do, something strangely out of date and entirely too 'high church' for the mainstream Protestant religious tastes of most church members. But while the enthusiastic reception of such a calendar by the majority may not happen for many years, if ever, the tradition of recognizing saints is becoming more familiar and attractive to an increasing number.

Contemporary Methodist treatment of Wesley himself is a strong indication that we already sense what it means to look to the example of a person's life with God as a source for interpreting our own life and faith. When we retell the story of his life — his journey from the Oxford Holy Club to his failure in Georgia to his experience of assurance at Aldersgate to his first efforts at outdoor preaching to the formation of the bands and classes to his decision to ordain clergy for America — we do so with the sense that this is what it means to be 'Methodist.' John Wesley's story is our story, not just in the sense that our experience of God is similar to his, but that his story tells us who we are and from where we came.

At the same time, Wesley's story is not exhaustive of what it means to be United Methodist today. Although it is less common now, there was a time when the stories of many of the heroic and dedicated lives of Methodist preachers and leaders were lifted up for the edification and example of the church. Thumbing through early editions of the *Methodist Magazine* or *Quarterly Review* reveals the regularity with which pictures, extended narrative accounts, and lengthy obituary notices sang the praises of well-known figures. In the mid-nineteenth century a *Methodist Almanac* was published that at least for three years contained a calendar in which the names of famous Methodists (and some other notable persons like U.S. presidents) were remembered on their death or birth dates.[6] Although this was far from being a sanctoral cycle, it was taken for granted that the stories of worthy persons were understood to be an important source of Methodist self-understanding.

Wesley himself had a high regard for the saints. Several scholars have noted that although he makes little mention of other liturgical dates like Christmas and Easter, he often describes All Saints' Day in his journal as a day very near to his heart. In 1748, for example, he wrote, "Nov. 1. Tues. — Being All Saints' Day, we had a solemn assembly at the chapel, as I cannot but observe we have had on this very day for several years. Surely, 'right dear in the sight of the Lord is the death of his saints.'" Laurence Hull Stookey sees this as evidence that the earliest Methodists used this date to commemorate those of their number who had recently died.[7] Wesley is also known to have read about the lives of the saints, and as an Anglican priest inherited and used the 1662 *Book of Common Prayer* that included not only the feast days for the Apostles and other New Testament figures but over sixty other commemorations listed as 'black letter days.'

There is further evidence of Wesley's regard for the saints in his *Collection of Forms of Prayer for Every Day in the Week*. Here he concludes many of his morning and evening prayers with references to the hope of being united with those who have already died in the faith. For example, for Thursday mornings he suggests this prayer:

> . . . unite us all to one another by mutual love, and to thyself by constant holiness; that we, together with all who went before us in thy faith and fear, may find a merciful acceptance in the last day.[8]

More interesting still is that in his fifty-volume *Christian Library* project, Wesley included an "Office of the Saints" in *Devotions for Every Day of the Week, and the Great Festivals*. In this abridgment of John Austin's *Devotions in the Ancient Way of Offices*, Wesley retains a prayer during the afternoon office for God to grant us the "grace to imitate [the saints] here, and to rejoice with them in Thy kingdom hereafter."[9] The evening office puts the question:

> Are we devout already, as the saints of God, and chaste, and temperate, and resigned as they?

Do we despise the world with a zeal like their's, and value heaven at the same rate with them?

O that we lived, like you, whose aim was high....

Let us worship and fall down, and kneel, like you, before our Lord and Maker.

We hope assuredly to be with you, and enter into his rest, where you already are arrived.[10]

John Wesley's appreciation for the saints was amplified in his brother Charles' hymns. Geoffrey Wainwright has shown how clearly these hymns testify to the lively sense among the Methodists of the unity of the Church militant with the Church triumphant.[11] Surprisingly strong convictions about the communion of saints are revealed in two verses from a funeral hymn considered by some to be among Charles' finest hymns (it appears in a slightly altered form as no. 709 in the present United Methodist hymnal for All Saints' Day):

> Come, let us join our friends above,
>   That have obtain'd the prize;
> And on eagle wings of love
>   To joys celestial rise.
> Let all the saints terrestrial sing,
>   With those to glory gone;
> For all the servants of our King,
>   In earth and heaven, are one.
>
> One family we dwell in Him,
>   One church above, beneath,
> Through now divided by the stream,
>   The narrow stream of death.
> One army of the living God,
>   To his command we bow;
> Part of his host have crossed the flood,
>   And part are crossing now.[12]

Rattenbury notes that, "The figure of the united family and unbroken army to which death is but a narrow ditch easily bridged, brings home with even greater force the oneness of the two sections — Militant and Expectant — of the Church of Christ."[13] This theme is also present in the second and third stanzas of the hymn, "Happy the Souls to Jesus Join'd:"[14]

The church triumphant in Thy love,
    Their mighty joys we know;
They sing the Lamb in hymns above,
    And we in hymns below.

Thee in Thy glorious realm they praise,
    And bow before Thy throne;
We in the kingdom of Thy grace,
    The kingdoms are but one.

Wainwright detects a "doxological thrust" to the many Wesleyan hymns expressing the communion of saints, leading him to suggest that together they might be seen as a kind of "musical iconography" which, "enact the presence of the saints so that the joy of heaven may be known upon the earth."[15] Indeed, more and more United Methodist congregations are recovering these deep Wesleyan sensibilities and are again making All Saints' Day (often moved to the nearest Sunday) an important part of their liturgical year. During these services, it is common for the names of those who have died in the past year to be read aloud after the *Epiklesis* in the Great Thanksgiving.[16]

But the fact remains that however lively Charles' hymns portray a sense of the communion of saints past and present, and however dear the first day of November was to John, it is difficult to use the Wesleys themselves to legitimate a full-fledged sanctoral calendar. In revising the Anglican services for Methodist use in America, John flatly removed "Most of the holy-days (so called)" [including all the saints' days], because they were, he judged "at present answering no valuable end."[17]

Yet given the evidence of Wesley's high regard for All Saints' day and the saints themselves, it may be that his decision to strike their commemoration from the calendar was more a matter of disagreement with much of Roman Catholic practice surrounding the saints than a disregard for their place in teaching us how to live as Christians. This seems to be borne out in his writings where he clearly states the standard puritan concern: that practices such as praying to Mary and the saints as mediators and the reverencing of icons and relics lead to idolatry.[18] Traditional Catholic theology has sought to avoid accusations of idolatry by making a sharp distinction between the *latria* (praise, worship) that is due only to God and the *dulia* (service, imitation) that is appropriate for saints. But Wesley, like most Protestants, feared that such neat distinctions easily become clouded in actual practice. Arguing that there is no scriptural warrant for claiming a separation between the "mediator of intercession and of redemption," he writes, "He alone 'who died and rose again' for us, makes intercession for us at the right hand of God. And he alone has a right to our prayers; nor dare we address them to any others."[19]

The use of saints as intercessors was clearly objectionable to Wesley. He also was disturbed by the fantastic stories that he commonly found in reading the lives of Roman saints. In his journal entry from November 29, 1762, he writes,

> My fragments of time I employed in reading, and carefully considering, the lives of Magdalen de Pazzi, and some other eminent Romish saints. I could not but observe, 1. That many things related therein are highly improbable. I fear the relators did not scruple lying for the Church, or for the credit of their Order: 2. That many of their reputed virtues were really no virtues at all; being no fruits of the love of God or man, and no part of the mind which was in Christ Jesus: 3. That many of their applauded actions were neither commendable nor imitable: 4. That what was really good, in their tempers or lives, was so deeply tinctured with enthusiasm, that most readers would be far more likely to receive hurt than good from these accounts of them.[20]

Thus, Wesley's objections of these accounts were really two-fold: the outlandish stories attached to some saints tended to obscure their real importance, and therefore they had at best an uncertain benefit for Christian edification.

In spite of the difficulties Wesley found with some practices surrounding the use of saints by Christians, or perhaps as a reaction against those difficulties, Wesley himself gives us two striking examples of how particular saintly persons can be useful exemplars of faith and practice, or, as Wyschogrod says, "flesh and blood existents." Wesley wrote an inspirational account of the last few weeks in the life of Sarah Peters that was printed in the *Arminian Magazine* in 1782. Peters was a close friend and associate of Wesley and had a remarkable ministry among condemned prisoners (see November 13). He wrote of her, "I never saw her, upon the most trying occasions, in any degree ruffled or discomposed, but . . . always loving, always happy." Interestingly, the account is included in his published journal on November 13, 1748 — the day she died.

In 1785, Wesley wrote *A Short Account of the Life and Death of the Rev. John Fletcher*. Wesley's regard for Fletcher was so high that he asked him to be his successor as the leader of the Methodist movement (see August 14). At the end of his *Account*, Wesley writes, "Within fourscore years, I have known many excellent men, holy in heart and life: But one equal to him, I have not known; one so uniformly and deeply devoted to God. So unblamable a man, in every respect, I have not found either in Europe or America. Nor do I expect to find another such on this side eternity." But Wesley does not stop after offering these high words of praise. We are then specifically encouraged to imitate Fletcher's example in the faith: "Yet it is possible we may be such as he was. Let us, then, endeavor to follow him as he followed Christ."[21]

A Wesleyan Approach

Wesley found some popularized accounts of saints wanting, not only because they encouraged the superstitious practices he found objectionable but because they offered so little material actually useful for Christians seeking the example of saints. But as his own writing on Peters and Fletcher indicates, he was convinced that historically reliable accounts of saintly lives are useful devotional reading. Following the points of objection he recorded above in his journal for November 29, 1762, we might propose some indication of what Wesley *would* hope to find in reading the lives of saintly Christians. These four criteria guided reflections on the shape of the calendar presented here.[22]

First, the account of the saint should be as historically accurate as possible, not dwelling on the many improbable stories that accrued to some of the more popular saints. It must be said, however, that it is very difficult to distinguish in practice between what we reliably know of some saints and the stories that accrued to them through the years, nor is it always desirable. This is primarily an issue for those saints from antiquity, saints like Jude the Apostle and Nicholas the Bishop of Myra, about whose lives few facts are known. To press for a strict separation between fact and fiction would strip away from these saints precisely the roles they have played for so many centuries in exemplifying particular saintly virtues. How shall we remember St. Nicholas at all without bringing to mind the many stories which portray him as generous Christmas gift-giver? The Apostle Jude without thinking of him as the patron of lost causes? Part of the beauty and importance of saints is that they cannot be constrained by the left-brained logical thought with which the Western world is so enamored. To live in their presence is to open a space in our faith for the creative and unpredictable side of God's dealings with us.

With the more recent additions, particularly those of the Methodist tradition, we usually have more historical data from which to draw. But even here we recognize that the memories of notable figures are generally turned favorably in proportion to their perceived importance. To record their lives at all is to engage already in an act of interpretation. So while the present volume does seek a Wesleyan bias toward historical accuracy, we recognize that whenever we move from talking about saints in general to making lists of particular saints, we are already in the wonderfully gray area of myth-making.

Second, the saints' lives should show evidence of the love of God and neighbor, or as Paul puts it, the fruit of the Spirit. The virtues of their lives should be those that are genuinely desirable for the Christian life and not merely fascinating; however miraculous or important the deeds of a person might seem it is the quality of the life itself that merits our attention. An effort has been made to distinguish between persons who are historically important and those who can reasonably be considered saints by contemporary United

Methodists. On the other hand, sometimes more historically obscure figures are included for their particularly courageous witness.

The third criterion follows closely upon the second: the deeds and words of our saints should be both commendable and imitable by present day Christians. Two particularly difficult cases comes to mind. Jesse Lee was likely the most important early leader of Methodism after Asbury and is widely known as the "Apostle to New England" for his groundbreaking work there. He is remembered fondly for his keen wit and passionate commitment to Christ, but there is some disagreement about his role in early Methodist attitudes toward slavery. Although he may have personally disliked slavery, he apparently argued for a relaxation of the strong Methodist stance against it so as not to offend rich Virginia Methodist planters. Most people would agree that it is unfruitful and unfair to use moral 'litmus tests' from the present to measure figures from the past. And Lee certainly had saintly characteristics and deep faith and is in many ways an example for us. But it is difficult to see how a contemporary United Methodist Church whose members include people of all races can reasonably be asked to extol his memory on an annual basis.

Anthony Bewley (see September 13), now largely forgotten, was the center of a storm of controversy over his abolitionist activities and was subsequently hung by a mob in Texas. His may be the only case in the calendar of a Methodist having been murdered for religious convictions and his story was compelling and different enough to warrant his inclusion in this trial calendar. But information about his case comes chiefly from an article written from a sympathetic Northern point of view, so further research may eventually lead to a different conclusion about his place on this calendar.

Both Lee and Bewley suggest how much of a gray area surrounds the selection of particular names and the need for the fourth and final criterion derived from Wesley: enthusiasm for particular persons should not not obscure their true story, nor distract from the fact that they are only imitable by us in so far as they were themselves imitators of Christ. Just as we must be sensitive in our selection of saints to our present needs, we must also be honest. We are bound to listen to the judgements of the best historians as to the lives and characters of the saints included here. More important still is the realization that saints do not exist to support our point of view. In their transparancy to Christ they reveal the truth about ourselves in both familiarity and difference, grace and critique.

The Shape of the Calendar

Choosing who should appear on this calendar was the most difficult task of this entire project. Again, we have sought to include those whose lives, as the criteria suggest above, "show evidence of the fruits of the Spirit," and whose lives are "commendable and imitable." This involves making some kind of religious and moral evaluation of highly complex and individual lives, weighing them according to the needs and concerns of the present. The Vatican has a standing institution, the Congregation for the Causes of Saints, whose sole purpose is to investigate and document the lives of those proposed for sainthood and to evaluate them according to set criteria. We did not have such resources at our disposal. But the Roman task is fundamentally different from ours. Whereas canonization is a papal statement that the entire Church is obliged to recognize, assuring believers that a certain person has in fact gone to heaven and can act as a mediator for prayer, here we only suggest that a person appearing on this calendar has lived such a life or exhibited such a particular virtue as to merit our remembrance, our imitation, and our praise to God. However, even this sort of judgment is highly personal. No doubt, our calendar is far from perfect and will require continual modification as the years go on, but we can begin by acknowledging that all saints, however holy, like us had their rough edges.

As already noted, sanctoral calendars were initially local creations, and preserving something of this same local quality has been attempted here. Primary place has been given those names from the traditions that in 1968 joined to form The United Methodist Church (Methodist and Evangelical United Brethren) and those names from the universal Church which stand closest to the stream of tradition represented in contemporary United Methodism. The argument for retaining a local flavor is being tried, of course, by continuing revolutions in travel and communication and by a desire that our prayer life not be too parochial. There is good reason, therefore, to begin thinking of shaping a more 'global' calendar which draws equally from Methodists from across the world. Occasionally, a name on the calendar stretches us in that direction (see, for example, Peter Jones on June 28 or Jashwant Rao Chitambar on July 4). But for now we have largely chosen to retain some of the traditional local flavor of a sanctoral calendar by thinking of it as a calendar for United Methodists living in the United States. This choice ensures that the calendar will be diverse enough to include the wide variety of peoples who now constitute United Methodists in North America without growing unmanageably large.

In choosing non-United Methodist persons who would be on the calendar priority was given to the principal New Testament figures, to those important saints who predate the Reformation, and to those other figures who represent major post-Reformation developments relevant to the development of Methodism. With an eye toward ecumenical prayer we also gleaned from the sanctoral calendars of other traditions, notably those in the *Lutheran Book of Worship* and the Episcopal Church's *Book of Common Prayer* and *Lesser Feasts and Fasts*, and the Roman and Eastern Orthodox calendars. Also of interest is the 'calendar of commemorations' in *Uniting in Worship*, the book of worship for the Uniting Church of Australia (the first church of a Methodist heritage to have such a calendar).

A glance at the calendar shows it to be strongly ecumenical in character. It has increasingly become a common expression of good ecumenical manners for churches to include on their calendars the names of important persons from their sister denominations, even if those denominations do not yet have a calendar of their own. Hence, John and Charles Wesley have appeared already in the Lutheran and Episcopal Calendars, the Church of England's *Alternative Service Book* (1980), and Australia's *Uniting in Worship* (on May 24th, Aldersgate day). This tradition has been continued here. Hence, names like John Woolman (October 7) and Jonathan Edwards (March 22) appear on this calendar.

However, names from non-United Methodist traditions which do not appear on the calendars of their own traditions are also not included here. This is also a matter of good ecumenical manners,[23] although it was a particularly painful decision in that it excluded persons like Dorothy Day and Archbishop Romero who are facing lengthy and possibly inconclusive canonization processes in the Catholic Church. Against this decision weighs the deep conviction that persons like this are not wholly owned by one denomination but belong to the Church universal. Some United Methodists may want to add these names and others to their personal list of yearly commemorations.

In choosing United Methodist names, we thought of ourselves as standing in the river of present United Methodism in America and looking back to the basins, creeks, and streams of people who made us what we are today. Great care has been taken to make the calendar inclusive of women and men from all the peoples which are a part of our history. This means that the calendar is large. Perhaps it contains too many names and will overwhelm the person who picks up this book still unsure about the place of recognizing saints. But if, as liturgical scholar Aidan Kavanaugh has repeatedly emphasized,[24] what we believe grows out of what we pray, then the trial use of this calendar will itself determine the continuing worth of lifting up particular names. It is to be expected that more will be added while others are dropped and that the whole calendar will be questioned and reinvented as the needs of our prayer change.

Prayable Lives

It is hoped that those who do appear on the calendar are persons who have lived lives that are 'prayable.' That is, because they are transparent to the character and intentions of God, their lives prompt us both to render thanks to God and to pray that our lives might become likewise transparent. They are also exemplary, by which is meant both that they are exemplary of the best of Christian witness and that they are examples of people who have lived faithfully within particular social locations. To include so many persons from so wide a range of social locations is not simply an attempt to be politically correct, but to open our prayer life to risk and potential growth.

To say that these persons are exemplary witnesses does not mean that they are necessarily best viewed as having lived lives that should be imitated literally in every respect. Who wants to repeat John Wesley's experience with marriage? Who admires Luther's unpredictable temper? As the case of Jesse Lee points out, every truly human life will be replete with events and character traits which will be difficult to understand or undesirable to imitate in our present culture and personal circumstances. But what makes saints interesting is not finally the particular example they set for us but the source from which they come — God. John Coleman remarks that the attraction of saints, "is their power to lure us beyond virtue to virtue's source."[25] Saints do not pique our interest as examples of a preexisting set of virtues; they have a wholeness in themselves that speaks to us of God.[26]

In the end, whether we find such a calendar helpful or not is probably a matter of our religious imagination. For some of us, the memorializing of the departed faithful will be seen as a distraction to a pure experience of Christ. No matter how carefully the theologians argue the infinite distinction between the worship that is due to Christ alone and the veneration that is due the saints, that distinction can readily get lost in the day to day practice of commemorating the saints. But suggesting that certain people have lived lives that are "prayable" (in the sense of giving thanks to God for their witness and asking that our lives be likewise faithful), is really a rather small and tentative suggestion. The Church has always, both formally and informally, raised up our exemplary foremothers and fathers as persons to whom we owe a special debt of gratitude for our own faith (churches and denominationally affiliated schools, for example, are regularly named in memory of their founders or important forebears). This is precisely, of course, how John Wesley is already viewed by the vast majority of Methodists — he is studied, revered, and imitated. At least one of his experiences, that on Aldersgate street, is already commonly lifted up as exemplary for United Methodists. But the Christian life is larger than Wesley. As Wesley himself understood when he praised the importance of All Saints' Day, the ways in which God's love is made manifest among us in the particularities of our lives are many and varied. The gate and the path may be narrow, but there is a stunning variety in the people who enter it.

Using the Calendar

This is the fifth volume of a *Daily Office* being produced by The Order of Saint Luke. As such, it is but one part of a complete re-visioning of our prayer lives, our ongoing relationship with God. This book may be used as a part of the cycle of prayer envisioned there or as a stand-alone devotional volume for personal or corporate use. It fits most easily and naturally into a setting where the daily office (or some other form of daily corporate prayer) is already being said. Yet it could also be used in a number of other ways. An administrative council might choose to reflect on a saint as a beginning devotion. Groups in retreat settings might find this a refreshing resource for their prayer together. Remembered in the morning, these saints can live with us throughout the day as we contemplate their example of Christian living. Remembered at the end of the day, they can help us learn from our experiences and may occasionally cause us to repent.

Order of Precedence
Each Sunday is first and foremost a celebration of the resurrected Lord. It is therefore not appropriate that such a Lord's Day service be used to commemorate saints (with the exception of All Saints' Day if it has been moved to the nearest Sunday). Other liturgical dates which occur during the week (i.e. Epiphany, Ash Wednesday, Maundy Thursday, the days of Holy Week, and the Ascension) also have precedence over the dates in this calendar. In case of a conflict with a Sunday or Holy Day, saints may be commemorated on the next available date. Occasionally the calendar lists two names for one date. Sometimes this indicates that two persons are to be remembered together, other times it is a simple reflection of the fact that two worthy people happen to have died on the same day. In the second case, it is left to personal discretion whether to choose one over the other, to celebrate them together, or to move one to the next available date. If introducing the practice of commemorating saints to a congregation, it may be wise to begin with the twenty eight major saints' days. In a few instances, minor commemorations of persons whose death dates fall on major saints days are moved up one day, that is, they are remembered on the eve or vigil of their death date.

Major Commemorations
Twenty eight dates on the calendar are considered 'major' saints' festivals or commemorations. These consist of three types: principal figures from the New Testament (the Apostles, Peter and Paul, Mary the Mother of Jesus, Mary Magdalene, etc.), other holy days related to the saints (All Saints' Day, The Annunciation, The Conversion of Paul, etc.) and the two principle founders of Methodism, John and Charles Wesley. Following ancient practice, these dates are fittingly celebrated in a service of Word and Table (see the

"Great Thanksgiving for All Saints and Memorial Occasions," p. 74 in the *Book of Worship*). Hence, scripture lessons, two prayer selections, and artwork which can be useful for meditation or for reproduction in bulletins have been included. The life of the saint being remembered can be used as illustrative homiletic material, although the scriptures remain the primary focus of the sermon. The appropriate liturgical colors are also given for these major commemorations.

Minor Commemorations

On the lesser saints' days the scripture readings of a daily lectionary should be followed, the liturgical colors of the season retained, and the particular saint(s) for the day remembered chiefly in prayer. Specific prayer suggestions are included for each commemoration according to their salient gift or ministry. The list of categories or commons by which saints in the calendar are grouped largely takes its shape from the scriptures which speak of the gifts of the Spirit (Rom 12:6; 1 Cor 12:8, 28-30; Eph 4:11; 1 Pet 4:10f). It is not possible to make these categories conform precisely to the various lists in the New Testament because the lists differ from one another. Martyrs do not appear in the lists, but were early considered to be the first rank among those who have died in the faith (Rev 6:9-11). Prayer suggestions are also included for musicians, whose particular gifts have added so deeply to the worship life of the Church.

In a Service of Word and Table

If a weekday service commemorating a major or minor saint is to conclude with the Eucharist, the presider may wish to include the name(s) of the commemorated saint(s) in the eucharistic prayers. This can be done in two ways. For major commemorations in particular, the celebrant may, as mentioned above, choose to use the form from the *Book of Worship*, "The Great Thanksgiving for All Saints and Memorial Occasions." For minor commemorations, the conclusion of the Great Thanksgiving may be said adding the following underlined words:

> By your Spirit make us one with Christ,
>   one with each other,
>   and one in ministry to all the world,
> until Christ comes in final victory,
> and <u>with *Name* and all the saints</u>
> we feast at his heavenly banquet.

December

(11/30	**Andrew)**
1	Nicholas Ferrar
2	
3	
4	
5	Clement of Alexandria
6	Nicholas
7	Ambrose of Milan
8	
9	
10	
11	
12	
13	
14	John of the Cross
15	
16	
17	John Stewart
18	Thelma Stevens
19	William Wesley Van Orsdel (Brother Van)
20	Captain Thomas Webb
21	**Thomas**
22	
23	
24	
25	*CHRISTMAS*
26	**Stephen**
27	**John**
28	**The Holy Innocents**
29	
30	
31	

January

1	**The Holy Name**
2	
3	Gilbert Haven
4	John Seybert
5	
6	*EPIPHANY*
7	
8	Richard Watson
9	
10	
11	
12	
13	George Fox
14	
15	(alt. date for Martin Luther King, Jr., see April 4)
16	Hiram Rhoades Revels
17	Antony of Egypt
18	**The Confession of Peter**
19	Pseudo-Macarius of Egypt
	John Ernest Rattenbury
20	
21	Agnes of Rome
22	
23	Sarah Ann Dickey
24	Eli Stanley Jones
25	**The Conversion of Paul**
26	Timothy and Titus
27	John Chrysostom
28	Thomas Aquinas
29	
30	
31	John Raleigh Mott

February

March

1	
2	**John Wesley**
3	
4	
5	William McKendree
6	
7	Perpetua and her Companions
8	
9	Gregory of Nyssa
10	Harriet Ross Tubman
11	Thomas Ware
12	Gregory the Great
13	
14	
15	
16	Lucy Rider Meyer
17	Patrick
18	Cyril of Jerusalem
19	Joseph, Mary's Husband
20	
21	
22	Jonathan Edwards
23	Martin and Henry Boehm
24	Ida Bell Wells-Barnett
25	**The Annunciation**
26	Richard Allen
27	
28	
29	**Charles Wesley**
30	
31	John Donne
	Francis Asbury

April

1	
2	
3	
4	Martin Luther King, Jr.
5	George Miller, John Walter, and John Dreisbach
6	
7	
8	
9	William Law
	Dietrich Bonhoeffer
10	
11	Garfield Bromley Oxnam
12	
13	
14	
15	
16	
17	
18	Francis Burns
19	Philip Melancthon
20	
21	Anselm
22	
23	
24	Samuel Wesley
25	**Mark**
26	
27	Peter Boehler
28	
29	Catherine of Siena
	Laura Askew Haygood
30	

May

1	**Philip and James the Less**
2	Athanasius
3	Thomas Coke
4	Monica
5	Olof Gustav Hedström
6	
7	
8	Julian of Norwich
9	Gregory of Nazianzus
10	
11	
12	
13	
14	
15	
16	William Nast
17	Harry Hosier
18	Jacob Albright
	Mary McLeod Bethune
19	
20	
21	
22	
23	
24	William Edwin Robert Sangster
25	The Venerable Bede
26	
27	John Calvin
28	
29	
30	
31	**The Visitation**

June

July

1
2 Anna Howard Shaw
3
4 Jashwant Rao Chitambar
5 Richard Whatcoat
6 John Hus
7
8
9
10
11 Benedict of Nursia
12
13
14
15
16
17
18
19 Macrina the Younger
20 Belle Harris Bennett
21
22 Mary Magdalene
23
24 Thomas à Kempis
25 James the Elder
26 Charles Albert Tindley
27
28 Johann Sebastian Bach and George Frederick Handel
29 Mary and Martha of Bethany
30 Susanna Wesley
31

August

1
2
3
4
5
6 *The Transfiguration*
7 John Mason Neale
8 Dominic
9
10 Laurence
11 Clare of Assisi
12
13 Florence Nightingale
14 John William Fletcher
   Maximilian Kolbe
15 Mary
16 Charles Grandison Finney
17
18 Francis John McConnell
19
20 Bernard of Clairvaux
   William Booth and Catherine Mumford Booth
21 Georgia Harkness
22
23
24 Bartholomew
25
26
27
28 Abba Moses of Scete
   Augustine of Hippo
29 Maggie Newton Van Cott
30
31 John Bunyan

September

1
2
3   Samuel Checote
4   Albert Schweitzer
5
6   James Bradley Finley
7
8
9   Mary Bosanquet Fletcher
10
11   Isabella Thoburn and Clara Swain
12
13   Anthony Bewley
14   Holy Cross Day
15
16
17
18   Dag Hammarskjöld
19
20
21   **Matthew**
22
23
24
25   Peter Cartwright
26   Freeborn Garrettson
     and Catherine Livingston Garrettson
27   John Dickins
     Alejo Hernández
28
29   Michael and All Angels
30   Jerome
     George Whitefield

October

1	
2	
3	
4	Francis of Assisi
5	
6	William Tyndale
	Jennie Fowler Willing
7	John Woolman
8	
9	
10	
11	
12	
13	
14	
15	Teresa of Avila
16	Thomas Cranmer
17	Ignatius of Antioch
18	**Luke**
19	
20	
21	
22	
23	**James of Jerusalem**
24	Sarah Crosby
25	
26	
27	
28	**Simon and Jude**
29	
30	
31	

November

1	**All Saints**
2	Phoebe Palmer
3	Richard Hooker
4	
5	
6	
7	
8	
9	
10	Leo the Great
11	Martin of Tours
	Søren Kierkegaard
12	
13	Sarah Peters
14	
15	
16	Margaret, Queen of Scotland
17	Philip William Otterbein
18	Hilda
19	
20	
21	Anna Oliver
22	
23	Clement of Rome
24	Eliza Garrett
25	Isaac Watts
26	Sojourner Truth
27	
28	John Dempster
	James Mills Thoburn
29	
30	**Andrew**

Common Prayers

Evangelists (Missionaries)

Holy and merciful God, in your love for the world you raised *Name* to be *an* evangelist[s], *a* herald[s] of the good news: strengthen and guide those entrusted with the proclamation of your Word that as they make known your redeeming love we may heed and receive their glad tidings, through Jesus Christ our Lord, who lives and reigns with you and the Holy Spirit, one God, now and forever. Amen.

[RBA]

Strong Word of God, by whom the world was created,
in whom the world is redeemed,
Always send forth heralds like *Name*, to bear the good news,
that your saving way may be made known in every place and time,
in every land and to every people,
for your sake and for the sake of the world. Amen.

[RBA]

Healers

Blessed and most merciful God, you have shown us your compassion by raising up healers like *Name* to bring us the remedies that bring salvation: Grant also to us in this generation the same gifts of your power, that not only our bodies but also our souls may be made whole by the medicine of your heavenly grace, through Jesus Christ our Lord, the great Physician, who lives and reigns with you and the Holy Spirit, now and forever. Amen.

[Gelasian Sacramentary; alt. TJC]

Jesus, Son of David, Wellspring of health and salvation,
we give you thanks for the healing ministry of *Name*, your disciple[s].
Have mercy on us, and make us well by faith,
that throwing off the cloak of our sorrows
we may follow you on the way. Amen.

[CFG]

Leaders

Almighty God, in whose kingdom servants are leaders, we give you thanks and praise for the memory of your servant[s] *Name*, who sensed the flow of your desire for the world and called us to new ways of worship and being: Let our will be caught by the tide of your love that creation might be renewed and all your people live in peace, through Jesus Christ our Lord, who lives and reigns with you and the Holy Spirit, one God, now and forever. Amen.

[CFG]

Pillar of Cloud and Pillar of Fire, you always raise among your imprisoned people leaders of burning vision like *Name*. Part the dead waters of the past and bring all your people to a new land of promise, through Jesus Christ our Lord. Amen.

[CFG and DTB]

Martyrs

Martyr Master, as we commemorate *Name* who was [were] obedient to death for the sake of the gospel, grant that we may be bold to obey you in life and in death so that whether we live or die we are yours, in Jesus Christ our Lord, who lives and reigns with you and the Holy Spirit, one God, now and forever. Amen.

{DTB}

Fearless Jesus who suffered a baptism of blood,
as we celebrate *Name* who confessed your name in the face of the spiritual forces of wickedness and death-dealing scorn, renew in us our baptismal promise
> to reject evil,
> to resist injustice and oppression
>> in whatever forms they present themselves,
> and to openly confess you as Savior and Lord. Amen.

[DTB]

Musicians

Almighty God, who gave to your servant[s] *Name* the gift of music and the heart for praise of you, the triune God: Grant that your whole church may delight to sing your praise and to daily participate in the song of all creation, through Christ and by the power of the Holy Spirit. Amen.

[DTB]

God of sound and sense,
    as we commemorate *Name* who glorified you in the gift of music,
    so may we fix our faith and affections upon you, and
    make melody and song our delight in your majesty and mercy. Amen.

[DTB]

Pastors and Bishops

Gracious God, our Shepherd, we thank you for raising up *Name* as a [bishop and] pastor in your church. Remembering *his/her* faithfulness and care, fill all shepherds of your church with truth in doctrine, fidelity in Word and Sacrament, and boldness and vision in leading the people, through Jesus Christ our Lord, who lives and reigns with you and the Holy Spirit, one God, now and forever. Amen.

[DTB]

Good Shepherd of the flock, we thank you for faithful bishops and pastors like *Name* who teach and defend the faith. By your Word call them from maintenance to mission, from ease to vision, and from fear to courageous leadership. Amen.

[DTB]

Preachers

God our Creator and Redeemer, anoint from among your people zealous and faithful preachers like *Name* and give us ears to hear the gospel that your image may be fully restored in us, through Jesus Christ our Lord, who lives and reigns with you and the Holy Spirit, one God, now and forever. Amen.

[CFG]

Loving and patient God,
  how beautiful are messengers like *Name* who bring good news.
Stir us and your whole church to enact the gospel
    wherever we encounter bad news
    and to always rejoice in the power and freedom of your Spirit. Amen.

[DTB]

Prophets (Reformers)

God our Hope, in troubled days you send your Spirit upon daughters and sons, the young and the old, and fill them with visions, dreams, and reforming zeal: Make your will known to us again, as you did through your prophet[s] *Name*, that all your people may call upon you and be saved, through Jesus Christ our Lord, who lives and reigns with you and the Holy Spirit, one God, from generation to generation. Amen.

[CFG]

Purify us with your holy fire, O God,
    and send us prophets in our day like *Name*
        whose voice called for cleansing and honesty.
Turn our hearts toward others in repentance.
Refine our devotion and service to be pleasing to you
    as when we first loved you.
For your mercy, we revere you,
    through Jesus, our redeemer. Amen.

[DTB]

Saints

Gracious God, by the holy example of *Name* you have drawn us more deeply into the mystery of your way with the world: Grant that as living members of the family of saints we might be made perfect in love and join their ceaseless life of praise, through Jesus Christ our Lord, who lives and reigns with you and the Holy Spirit, one God, from generation to generation. Amen.

{CFG}

Witnesses in faith, in prayer, and in deed,
holy in life, perfected in love,
with us on earth, around us in heaven,
your faithful saints point to the Way:
    Praise be to God, for the memory of *Name*,
    and for saints who are with us, even today. Amen.

[RBA]

Teachers

God our Teacher, from whom comes all true knowledge: So bind your words to our lives and write them on the tablets of our hearts, that we may not be swayed by false winds; and grant us faithful guides like your servant *Name*, that our path to you be made straight and sure through Jesus Christ our Lord, who lives and reigns with you and the Holy Spirit, one God, now and forever. Amen.

[CFG]

Holy Sophia [Wisdom],
you have befriended us with *Name*
    who waiting patiently beside your doors
        grew rich in the knowledge of your ways
        and found in you an intimate friend.
So teach all your children your way and your truth,
    that finding you we may find life. Amen.

[CFG]

November 30
Color: Red

Andrew

All the gospels and the book of Acts mention Andrew, the brother of Simon Peter. In both Matthew and Mark, Jesus calls Andrew, together with Peter, as the first of his disciples: they left their fishing "immediately . . . and followed him" (Mt 4:18-20; Mk 1:16-18). Thereafter, Andrew is merely a name in the lists of the twelve. The sole occasion in which he appears along with the apostolic 'inner circle' of Peter, James, and John is in Mark, where the four question Jesus concerning the destruction of the Temple in Jerusalem (Mk 13:3). Only in John does Andrew have a slightly more independent and developed role. John introduces him as a disciple of John the Baptist. His hometown, we are told, is Bethsaida. The Baptist sees Jesus and says to Andrew and another, unnamed disciple, "Look, here is the Lamb of God." Curious, the two follow Jesus who invites them to his lodgings. Shortly after this visit, Andrew finds Peter, tells him they have "found the Messiah," and brings his brother to Jesus (1:35-42).

John mentions Andrew on two further occasions, both of which involve him in a somewhat similar mediating role. Andrew is the disciple who, prior to the feeding miracle, brings Jesus the lad with "five barley loaves and two fish" (6:9). Also, Andrew, together with Philip, takes his master the message that some Greek pilgrims in Jerusalem "wish to see Jesus" (12:20-22).

Later church tradition neglected Andrew. Even the Christian imagination found little soil here for the flowering of legend. The church historian Eusebius notes Andrew's missionary field as Scythia; one tradition has God revealing to Andrew that John should write his gospel; and in the apocryphal *Acts of Andrew*, we find him preaching for over twenty-four hours whilst being crucified. The familiar association of Andrew's martyrdom with an X-shaped cross does not appear until the 13th century. At sometime during the 8th century, Andrew was recognized as patron saint of Scotland. Our sharpest image of Andrew, therefore, remains a simple gesture made with ready conviction and authority: introducing brother Peter to Jesus. A humble role, perhaps, but hardly insignificant.

A. P. R. Gregory

Deuteronomy 30:11-14
Psalm 19 (*UMH* 750)
Romans 10:8b-18
John 1:35-42

Almighty and eternal God, who called your servant Andrew to lead others into the company of your blessed Son: Grant that we may follow his example and lead all humanity into your holy Church, to the honor and glory of your Name, through the same Jesus Christ our Lord, who lives and reigns with you and the Holy Spirit now and unto ages of ages. Amen.

[Gelasian Sacramentary; alt, TJC]

Jesus, Holy Word come near us,
    Save us from abstractions,
    Pluck us from our sea of words,
    Befriend us with gentle companions like Andrew,
    and let us meet you here and now. Amen.

[CFG]

December 1
Nicholas Ferrar (1637)
See Common of Leaders, Saints

Born in 1592, Farrar was the founder of the Christian community located on the estate of Little Gidding in Huntingdonshire, England. Prior to establishing the community, Ferrar had been an exemplary scholar at Cambridge (Clare Hall), spent several years traveling extensively throughout Europe, and had served as a member of Parliament and as Deputy-Treasurer of the Virginia Company.

Despite Ferrar's involvement in political and business ventures, he appears to have preferred a prayerfully-ordered, contemplative life. The manor at Little Gidding was purchased in 1625 by Ferrar's mother to provide such a retreat, and was soon occupied by numerous members of the Ferrar family, by several of their friends, and by their respective servants. Under Ferrar's direction, the estate's buildings (including a chapel) were renovated, a school was organized for the resident children (which later included children from the surrounding area), and a dispensary established as a center from which to distribute necessary food and medicine to sick and poor neighbors. Ferrar was ordained a deacon of the Church of England by Bishop William Laud on Trinity Sunday, 1626.

The occupants of Little Gidding were devoted to an austere and disciplined life of prayer and work. On weekdays, short services of hymn singing, psalm readings, and Gospel lessons occurred hourly from 6 a.m. to 8 p.m., with leadership shared by male and female members of the community. Ferrar devised a lectionary system by which the whole of the Psalter was completed each day and the four Gospels were read in their entirety each month. The group gathered daily in the chapel for matins, the litany, and evensong according to the *Book of Common Prayer*. In addition, every night, two members of the community kept watch from 9 p.m. to 1 a.m., and during those four hours they were expected to recite, by alternating verses, all one hundred and fifty Psalms.

Writings from the community, which remained in existence for at least twenty years, survive in the form of recorded conversations or stories produced from what became known as the "Little Academy," a discussion group organized to address matters intellectual, devotional, and moral. The literature and prayer of this community, in turn, inspired the creation of a poem by T. S. Eliot: "Little Gidding," the last of his *Four Quartets*.

K. B. Westerfield Tucker

December 5
Clement of Alexandria (220)
See Common of Pastors and Bishops, Teachers

Clement was converted to Christianity in his youth and set out to learn about the faith from the best of contemporary teachers. He was deeply influenced by a certain Pantaenus, the head of an informally organized school at Alexandria, a great center for learning and culture. Clement succeeded Pantaenus and instructed pupils in the Christian faith at the school until he was forced to flee the city when persecution broke out against the Christians under Septimius Severus in 202 A.D. It is possible that he remained a lay person throughout most of his teaching ministry, although he was ordained a presbyter at some point before his death.

Second-century Egypt was a stronghold of Gnostic Christianity, and its spokespersons had claimed the Greek philosophical tradition in support of Gnostic interpretation of Christian teachings. Clement's great achievement was to dispel the fear of Greco-Roman culture and learning which had engulfed orthodox Christians, reclaiming their intellectual heritage for their enrichment in the faith. Throughout his work he cites Plato, Homer, and the Greek tragedians as freely as he does the New Testament and Septuagint, presenting philosophical learning as the Gentiles' guide to Christ even as Paul presented the Torah as the custodian for the Jewish people. He enabled the gospel to speak to the well-educated, and gave orthodox Christianity intellectual integrity.

According to Clement, the Word of God "first exhorts, then trains, and finally teaches."[1] He thus wrote first his *Exhortation to the Greeks*, presenting Christianity as the true piety lauded by the philosophers. In a second book, the *Instructor*, he portrays Christ as the soul's trainer, the "bridle of untamed colts," and sets forth a comprehensive Christian ethic according to which Christians are to enjoy the good gifts of the Creator, but to use them with moderation, detachment, and regard for God and neighbor. In the third of the trilogy, the *Miscellanies*, Clement lays out Christian teachings in the language of the philosophers, and points the way to becoming a "true Gnostic," a person who knows God and imitates God's goodness.

Clement's ministry encourages Christians today to face boldly the challenges to faith posed by science, secular philosophy, and religious pluralism. He urges believers to embrace education and use all the intellectual resources at one's disposal in order to arrive at a response which embodies both fidelity to Christ and intellectual courage.

D. A. deSilva

December 6
Nicholas (c. 342)
See Common of Pastors and Bishops

Nicholas is the historical figure who begins the trajectory of legend and popular tradition that ends in his complete transformation into Santa Claus. Sadly, little is known of Nicholas save that, during the fourth century, he was bishop of Myra, capital of the province of Lycia in Asia Minor. Thereafter, even sober details lack evidence. He is said to have suffered torture and imprisonment during the persecution instigated by the Emperor Diocletian and to have attended the Council of Nicea. None of the early lists of bishops present at the council, however, includes his name. In the sixth century, the Emperor Justinian dedicated a church to Nicholas, along with St. Priscus.

The transformation of Nicholas' memory takes place in the West. In 1087, the delighted citizens of Bari in Italy claimed to have acquired Nicholas' remains. Western enthusiasm for Nicholas drew on the first account of his life, written some two hundred years before the saint's relics arrived in Italy. This work contains a crucial legend in which Nicholas saves three girls from prostitution, following their father's bankruptcy. To provide them with dowries, Nicholas makes three nightly visits, each time throwing a bag of gold into their window. This story inspired representations of Nicholas holding the three bags. It is possible that the bags were later mistaken for children's heads, inspiring Nicholas' association with a grotesque story in which he resurrects three murdered children pickled in a brine-tub. Once established, the link with children leads through the Dutch St. Nicholas (Sinte Klaas), who each year distributed gifts or rods according to moral desert, to the American Santa Claus.

Nicholas is also patron saint of sailors and, according to some, of the unjustly judged. If we connect the latter with the Nicholas' traditional concern for children, we may entertain an image resistant to both the sentimentalism of "Santa Claus" and the authoritarian moralism of the saint that provides rods for naughty children. Representing the unfairly or harshly judged is surely a fit task for the patron saint of the young.

A. P. R. Gregory

December 7
Ambrose of Milan (397)
See Common of Pastors and Bishops

Ambrose was born in 339 to an aristocratic family in Trier, a city of Gaul. His father was prefect of Gaul, and Ambrose followed in his politician father's footsteps, becoming governor of Liguria and Aemilia, whose capitol was Milan. This northern Italian city contained an ancient Christian community which by the last quarter of the fourth century was wracked with fighting between the Nicene and Arian churches of the city. When the Arian bishop of Milan died, the assembly to elect a successor was torn by conflict. While Ambrose was appealing for peace, a quiet voice was heard, "Ambrose for bishop." His personal resistance to his elevation to the bishopric proved unsuccessful. With the backing of both the Nicene and Arian churches he was baptized (it was not uncommon then to wait until late in adulthood for baptism), ordained priest, and consecrated bishop of Milan. His speedy move from the governorship to the episcopate demonstrates the fluid boundary in the fourth century between the offices of civil and ecclesiastical power.

Ambrose was known as an outstanding preacher and author. He is perhaps best known for his converting influence upon Augustine, whom Ambrose baptized on Easter Day, 387. His writings *On the Mysteries* and *On the Sacraments* provide invaluable insights into how Christians in Milan thought about the meaning and practice of Christian initiation and the sacraments. Ambrose demonstrated his commitment to a life of discipleship by giving away much of his personal wealth to the poor. He fearlessly defended the Nicene Christians of Milan against the personal whims of the emperors and empresses of his time. He exhibited great personal courage in refusing to capitulate to the Empress Justina's demand in 385 that the Arians of Milan be given a basilica for their use.

Ambrose is also famous for his hymns, some of which have entered the stream of worldwide Christian hymnody. One example is the morning song, "O Splendor of God's Glory Bright" (*UMH* 679). Ambrose is unusual in that although he died on April 4, 397, he is commemorated on this, the day of his consecration as bishop in 374.

G. S. Sperry-White

December 14
John of the Cross (1591)
See Common of Saints

Juan de Ypes was born into poverty on June 24, 1542 at Fontiveros, near Avila, Spain. He was educated by the Jesuits at Medina del Campo (where he worked as a nurse to support himself), and later went to the University of Salamanca, as a novice of the calced (shoe-wearing) Carmelite order. At Salamanca he studied theology and was ordained a priest in 1567. He became active in the reforms of the Carmelite order led by Teresa of Avila, and in 1568 became one of the first two men to become discalced Carmelite friars. To show his dedication to the ideals of the Teresian reform he took the name Juan de la Cruz (John of the Cross). John became a leader in the reform movement and held important positions within the reformed Order. In December of 1577, the reform was halted and John was arrested by his fellow Carmelites. When he refused to renounce the reform he was held in solitary confinement for nine months. He escaped, however, and migrated to a reformed monastery in southern Spain, where he spent his time writing and working as a spiritual director. He died in obscurity on this date in 1591, at Ubede in Andalusia.

John of the Cross is known for his mystical writings which include *The Ascent of Mt. Carmel, The Dark Night of the Soul, The Spiritual Dialogues between the Soul and Christ, The Living Flame of Love,* and *Thorns of the Soul.* These works reveal a depth of spiritual experience and insight expressed in wonderfully poetic language.

Thomas Merton wrote of John of the Cross:

> If we read the saint carefully, and take care to weigh every word, we will see that he is preaching a doctrine of pure liberty which is the very heart of the New Testament. He wants us to be free. He wants to liberate us not only from the captivity of passion and egoism, but even from the more subtle tyranny of spiritual ambition, and preoccupation with the methods of prayer and systems for making progress. But of course, one must first be *called* to this contemplative freedom.[2]

G. S. Sperry-White

December 17
John Stewart (1823)
See Common of Evangelists

Born the son of free blacks in 1786, John Stewart remained in his native state of Virginia until the age of twenty-one. When he left home to move to Ohio, Stewart began his long and difficult personal journey through a spiritual wilderness. Robbed of all his possessions, dependent on alcohol, and alternately dissolute and remorseful, he finally became so despondent that he wanted to end his life. As he contemplated death he thought he heard a voice call his name. He saw no one, but was able to turn back and begin his process of conversion.

Stewart attended nearby Methodist camp and prayer meetings, and entered a period of deep reflection. While in private prayer, he again thought he heard a voice, this time directing him to "declare my counsel faithfully." For a time, he struggled against the call and finally fell ill. Confronting death once again, he vowed to commit himself to mission work among the Indians, and to follow his calling to the northwest.

With neither money nor credentials, Stewart began work among the Wyandot Indians of Ohio in the winter of 1816. Faced with strong resistance by the Wynadots, envious accusations by other Christians, and recurring charges by dishonest whites that he was a runaway slave, Stewart persevered with courage and determination. The Quarterly Conference licensed the "missionary pioneer" in 1818, and the following year, the Ohio Conference established an official mission to the Wyandots. By the time he died in 1823, Stewart had converted numerous Wyandots and had been adopted into their nation.

The last words he spoke to his wife on his deathbed remain as his testimonial and creed, to encourage all who strive to find the truth: "Wife," he said softly, "be faithful."[3]

S. H. Hill

December 18
Thelma Stevens (1990)
See Common of Prophets

"Let's call this meeting to order," Thelma Stevens would say. Long after a stroke deprived her of clear thinking, Stevens carried on habits developed during a lifetime devoted to serving God. Stevens (b. 1902) worked to overcome barriers that divide and separate people.

Propelled by the memory of witnessing a Mississippi lynching, Stevens made a commitment to spend her life working to eradicate racism. She studied New Testament and sociology at Scarritt College. She learned that Jesus rejected the external authority of Jewish tradition in favor of an inner moral consciousness guided by "his sense of the presence and spirit of God."[4] Stevens rejected teachings of church and culture about the sanctity of segregation, replacing them with a belief, confirmed by her experiences in black communities of Nashville and Augusta, that all persons are children of God who deserve to be treated with equality, dignity, and respect.

For 28 years from 1940 to 1968, Stevens headed the Department of Christian Social Relations of the Woman's Division of the Board of Missions of The Methodist Church. Because the gospel of Jesus taught racial inclusiveness, Stevens called Methodist women to work to end discrimination in the military, schools, government, business, and in The Methodist Church.

Guided by multiracial consultations, Stevens outlined for Methodist women appropriate next steps for dismantling racism. Women of the Woman's Society of Christian Service and the Wesleyan Service Guild laced their meetings with Bible study and prayer. They adopted a Charter on Racial Policies. Community surveys and local discussions uncovered problems and pain. International, interracial teams of women toured the U.S., leading workshops on racism. In times of racial crisis, Stevens initiated seminars on race that brought community leaders to deal with heated passions, anger, inequity, and rumor. Quietly and often surreptitiously, Methodist women carried on interracial work in local communities all over the nation.

Theologian Walter Muelder once invited Stevens to spend a day describing churchwomen's work with social issues. In conclusion he asked, "What is the theological base by which you did this?" Stevens replied,

> The only thing I know is that these are the kinds of things that Jesus told us about, that he lived out when he was in the world. I can read the gospel and these things come clear to me. . . . [Mission begins] at the point that every human being is a full human being. You just don't patronize people. You help them become fully conscious of the fact that they are full human beings.[5]

A. G. Knotts

December 19
William Wesley Van Orsdel, "Brother Van" (1919)
See Common of Evangelists

Originally from Gettysburg, Pennsylvania, Van Orsdel came to Fort Benton, Montana in 1872. Arriving on June 30, he preached that afternoon in a local saloon where he received the nickname "Brother Van" which stayed with him the rest of his life.

For forty-seven years, Brother Van set the tone for Methodism in Montana. He held a service almost every day and traveled some 15,000 miles a year. One historian has observed, "For the small Methodist constituency in Montana to maintain a college, a hospital, and a children's home and school during the frontier days was all but impossible, and yet Brother Van through faith, prayer, persistence and sacrifice somehow managed to convince the people that it could be done."[6]

He was loved by the Indians of Montana who gave him the name Great Heart. In 1873, they took him on his first buffalo hunt, an event reproduced in a painting by the cowboy artist Charles M. Russell. Russell, affectionately recalling in a letter the first time he met Brother Van, wrote in his rough prose, "I have met you many times sinc that, Brother Van, sometimes in lonely places, but you never were lonsun or alone, for a man with seared hands and feet stood beside you and near him there is no hate, so all you met loved you."[7]

As a presiding elder, Brother Van always credited the growth in his district to the pastors and people. He reported to the annual conference, "You, brethren of the ministry and laity, with your wives, are the victors. You have been instruments, under God, to bring about the results."[8] As a boy, Brother Van had heard President Lincoln deliver the Gettysburg Address and he frequently repeated Lincoln's phrase, "under God." His colleagues in the annual conference showed their respect for him by electing him a delegate to General Conference six times.

Brother Van was particularly fond of a song by W.A. Spencer called "Harvest Time" which became a favorite of Montana Methodists.

> The seed I have scattered in springtime with weeping
> And watered with tears and with joy from on high,
> Another may shout when the harvesters' reaping
> Shall gather my grain in the sweet by and by.
> > Over and over, yea, deeper and deeper,
> > My heart is pierced through with life's sorrowing cry,
> > But the tears of the sower and the songs of the reaper
> > Shall mingle together in joy by and by.[9]

B. W. Coe

December 20
Captain Thomas Webb (1796)
See Common of Preachers

A rough-hewn English army officer and enthusiastic preacher, Captain Webb was a pioneer in the planting of Methodism in America. Born in 1725, he became a lieutenant and came to America in 1758 to fight the French. He lost his right eye to a musketball at the Battle of Montmorency in 1759. He married Mary Arding of New York in 1760 and they had a son, Charles. When his wife suddenly died he returned to England depressed and contemplating suicide. Upon hearing a Moravian preacher by the name of Cary, however, he had a vision of Christ and was converted in 1765. A few days later he met the Methodists and soon had his first preaching experience in Bath: when the scheduled preacher did not arrive, he stood up and shared the story of his life and conversion.

When he returned to Albany in 1766 he held prayer meetings and preached more often, gaining a hearing in Albany and on Long Island. Learning of the fledgling Methodist society led by Philip Embury, he startled the small gathering by appearing in sword and regimentals. He joined them as a preacher of a simple doctrine of forgiveness and an inward witness of the Spirit, attracting such a crowd that the society had to move to the now famous Rigging Loft.[10]

Webb raised money for the first chapel on John Street and also helped organize the Methodist society in Philadelphia, preaching the first Sunday sermon in the chapel which would become St. George's church. His pioneering work took root in New Jersey, Long Island, Pennsylvania, and Delaware. Returning to England in 1772, Webb assisted Wesley for awhile and helped convince him to send more missionaries to America. In 1773 he traveled to America a third time and remarried.

The consensus among early Methodists was that Webb's preaching was strange (he often spoke of his personal visions and revelations) but effective. John Adams heard him and was deeply impressed. Wesley wrote of him, "The Captain is all life and fire; therefore, although he is not deep or regular, yet many who would not hear a better preacher flock together to hear him. And many are convinced under his preaching, some justified, a few built up in love."[11]

Caught in the turmoil of the revolution, he was accused of being a spy and was put in prison where he took on the work of a chaplain. He eventually made it back to England and became a leader among Methodists in Bristol.[12]

C. F. Guthrie

December 21
Color: Red

Thomas

Thomas was among the twelve whom Jesus called and commissioned to heal the sick and proclaim the gospel. Though all four gospels mention him, John's gospel alone features him as a speaker interacting with his fellow disciples and Jesus. In three vignettes we catch a glimpse of Thomas and perceive through the evangelist's characterization the earnest, struggling faith of this early follower of Jesus.

Jesus learns that Lazarus is ill and announces his intent to return to Judea. The disciples are astonished since only a little earlier the Jews had threatened to stone him (John 10:31). Jesus assures them that the trip is necessary: Lazarus must be awakened. Thomas speaks up, "Let us also go, that we may die with him" (11:16). Though some see cynicism in Thomas's words, we should rather admire his courage and devotion to Jesus.

Later, Jesus comforts his disciples in a "Farewell Discourse" (John 14), assuring them that his departure to the Father will not end their fellowship. They know the way to the place where he is going. But Thomas is puzzled and asks, "Lord, we do not know where you are going. How can we know the way?" (vs. 5) His query elicits the celebrated words, "I am the way, and the truth, and the life. No one comes to the Father except through me." Thomas's understanding may be clouded, but his desire to "journey" with Jesus is clear.

The final scene follows the resurrection. Thomas is absent when Jesus appears to the disciples on Easter day. He disbelieves their witness and demands tangible proof of the risen Lord. From this episode we have come to link the epithet "doubting" with Thomas's name, but the crux of the story is its finale. Jesus appears a week later and offers his hands and side to Thomas and bids him not to doubt but believe. Thomas's confession, "My Lord and my God," is the climax of the fourth gospel. He believed, and his faith, sometimes courageous, sometimes confused, sometimes wavering, is much like ours as we follow the risen Christ.

According to Eusebius, Thomas carried the gospel to Parthia. The apocryphal Acts of Thomas gives a legendary account of mission work and martyrdom in India. According to the Acts he worked in India as a carpenter and builder and so in Roman Catholic tradition he is the patron saint of builders and architects.

N. C. Croy

Habakkuk 2:1-4
Psalm 126 (*UMH* 847)
Hebrews 10:35-11:1
John 20:24-29

Holy Triune God, Thomas recalls our journey toward faith.
  As he asked to see you, by baptismal faith bring us to yourself.
  As he refused secondhand experience, by the means of grace
      bring us to the true joy in Christ.
  As he confessed you triumphantly, so open our lips to say,
      "My Lord and my God." Amen.

[DTB]

Lord Jesus, like Thomas we were not in the room
  with the apostles on the day of resurrection.
  Like Thomas our faith cries out to you for sight.
  Like Thomas, we long for more than rumors.
Help us to believe where have not seen and to have life in your
name. Amen.

[DTB]

Stephen

According to the book of Acts, Stephen was one of the seven men chosen to distribute food fairly in the Jerusalem church (Acts 6:1-6), and is thus remembered as one of the first deacons (those set aside to serve) of the Church. However, he is primarily remembered in the church's calendar because of his martyrdom. Stephen was stoned when his lengthy denunciation of the ruling council moved it to murderous rage (Acts 7:54-60).

Stephen was considered the protomartyr (or the first martyr) by universal agreement in the patristic church. He is thus the first entry in a triumphal parade of martyrs which has marched through every Christian age. As Eusebius notes, punning on Stephen's name, Stephen was the first to win the martyr's crown (*stephanos* in Greek).[13] The feast of Stephen in the earliest existent calendars literally began a series of commemorations of other biblical martyrs in late December. This assemblage was recognized by later commentators, who labeled these martyrs *comites Christi*, companions of Christ in death.

The commemoration of Stephen insures that a sharp edge always remains on what it means to be a witness (*martus* in Greek) for Christ. Stephen shows that Jesus' command at Acts 1:8 ("You will be my witnesses") might mean direct conformity to Christ in death. To witness to Christ might mean to die as a sacrifice to powers who try to squelch prophetic voices.

Stephen therefore corrects any overly self-indulgent Christianity. He offers a different witness to Christ, namely, that to be a person "full of faith and the Holy Spirit" (Acts 6:5) sometimes leads to being the most despised and lowest of people.

L. Ruth

2 Chronicles 24:17-22
Psalm 17:1-7, 15 (*UMH* 749)
Acts 6:(1-7), 8-7:2a, 51-60
Matthew 23:34-39

God of mercy, in baptism you call us to share your cross and passion. In the hour of extreme demand when our flesh and heart would fail, be our strength and portion forever, through Jesus Christ, who lives and reigns with you and the Holy Spirit, one God, now and forever. Amen.

[DTB]

Lord Jesus, when the teeth of rage and resistance threaten us,
fix our vision on you at the right hand of God.
With Stephen, make us free to yield ourselves to you
  and to ask for mercy upon those who would destroy us.

[DTB]

John

"This is the disciple who is testifying to these things and has written them and we know that his testimony is true" (Jn 21:21).

Since the second century, church tradition has held that the Apostle John, the son of Zebedee and brother of James, authored the Fourth Gospel late in his life. Bishop Irenaeus expresses the view most clearly with his words, "Afterwards, John, the disciple of the Lord, who also had leaned upon His breast, did himself publish a Gospel during his residence at Ephesus in Asia."[14]

According to the New Testament, the Apostle John was a fisherman, called to discipleship by Jesus along with his brother James. In the course of Jesus' ministry, John was one of the privileged three to join Jesus in significant moments during his ministry. Along with Peter and James, John watched Jesus bring Jairus' daughter to life, witnessed Jesus transfigured on the mountaintop, and accompanied Jesus as he prayed in the Garden of Gethsemane. It was to John, his beloved disciple, that Jesus entrusted the care of his mother as he was dying on the cross. At the report of Mary Magdelene, he outran Peter to see the empty tomb, and was the first to recognize the risen Jesus at his appearance near the Sea of Tiberius.

Perhaps the most significant aspect of the tradition of Johannine authorship is that, in the words of Clement, it was John who gave the church a "spiritual Gospel."[15] Distinct in language and imagery from the other three Gospels, the Evangelist provides a story of Jesus that stirs our hearts and imaginations. Indeed, the eagle is a fitting symbol for John's Gospel, as its prose often soars with poetic richness. For this reason, John has traditionally been invoked as a patron saint of authors and theologians. It is John's Jesus who has a theological discussion with a Samaritan woman, who weeps at the death of his friend, and who mystifies Pilate at his trial. It is also John's Jesus who urges his followers to "love one another as I have loved you. No one has greater love than this, to lay down one's life for one's friends" (Jn 15:12f).

C. C. Grant

Exodus 33:18-23
Psalm 92 (*UMH* 811)
1 John 1:1-9
John 21:20-25

Everlasting God, in the Word made flesh, we have seen your glory,
full of grace and truth. We rejoice today with John, your evangelist,
who declared the mystery of the Incarnation and wrote of Jesus
with the eagle's view. Evermore bring us to believe in your son
and to have life in his name. Amen.

[DTB]

God of many names, bring us again and again to know eternal life
   by the One who is
      bread from heaven,
        light of the world,
          gate for the sheep,
            resurrection and life,
              the way, the truth, and the life,
                the true vine.

[DTB]

The Holy Innocents

The Holy Innocents or Innocent Infants are those children of Bethlehem slain by Herod as he tried to remove Jesus as a contender for king of Israel (Mt 2:13ff). Their feast comes as a hard slap to the face, reversing any excess of sentimentality created by Christmas. The Innocent Infants remind us that from the beginning of God's work in Christ, forces of violent evil were already at work in opposition to him. The shadow of the cross loomed even over the manger of Bethlehem.

The feast of the Innocent Infants was celebrated in the early church not as an extension of the Nativity story but as a commemoration of martyrs. Indeed, in some churches, the Innocent Infants were grouped together in the calendar with other biblical martyrs, e.g., Stephen, John the Baptist, James, Peter, and Paul.

Almost every patristic treatment of the Infants recognized them as martyrs. These early sources balanced the remembrance of Herod's cruelty with an understanding that God through Christ stands victorious over all evil and rewards those who have suffered unjustly for Christ. Early authors portrayed the Innocent Infants as playing with palms and crowns before the heavenly altar[16] or as having joined the blessed choir of martyrs.[17] On this basis the Innocent Infants were not to be pitied.

In our own time the Innocent Infants can offer a broadened vision of martyrdom. Perhaps it is not sufficient to shake our heads in sadness as we see innocent children today victimized in war, in physical and sexual abuse, in drive-by shootings, and in an avalanche of other violent evils. The Infants call the church to name these children, too, as martyrs, denouncing the evil forced on them as against Christ and proclaiming the hope that God is victorious over such injustice. The Innocent Infants remind us that the shadow, and the victory, of the cross looms over the mangers of today.

L. Ruth

Jeremiah 31:15-17
Psalm 124 (*UMH* 846)
Revelation 21:1-7
Matthew 2:13-23

Sovereign Lord, who keeps our tears in a bottle and records our laments in your book: gather into your arms of mercy all innocent victims and beat back the machinations of tyrants, for the sake of Christ our Savior who lives and reigns with you and the Holy Spirit, One God now and forever. Amen.

[DTB]

Refuge and Redeemer, when the rage and darkness of the world comes with senseless wasting of lives, you make victims your dearest prize and enable us to see their feet standing before the throne and before the Lamb. Amen.

[DTB]

January 1
Color: White

The Holy Name

The raucous celebration of the new year was as much a problem for ancient Christians as it is for Christians today. Writers such as Augustine and a variety of church councils promoted fasting and prayer as a counterbalance to pagan feasting, sacrifice, and orgies. Eventually the Roman church made January 1 into a feast celebrating the Anniversary (Latin: *natale*) of the Mother of God, perhaps under the influence of Byzantine Christian usage. By the sixth century in Spain and Gaul, January 1 came to commemorate the circumcision of Jesus (Lk 2:21), and this association continued in several Western liturgical traditions. In the West, a feast on January 1 celebrating the name of Jesus dates only from the fifteenth century; it was connected with the growth of devotion to the name of Jesus, particularly among the Franciscans.[18] But liturgically, the feast primarily derives its meaning from its association with the celebration of the Incarnation on December 25.

Luke records that the angel Gabriel appears to Mary announcing that she will bear a son. Mary is instructed to name him Jesus (Lk 1:31). The name itself was a common Jewish name, the Greek form of "Joshua," meaning "God saves," or just, "savior." In Matthew, the charge to name him Jesus comes to Joseph through an angel in a dream, along with the etymological reference, "for he will save his people from their sins" (Mt 1:21).

United Methodists can find hymnic expression of the theme of this day in Edward Perronet's "All Hail the Power of Jesus' Name" (*UMH* 154, 155). A more daring move would be to recover some of the ancient association of this feast with the Incarnation cycle and with Mary. Thus United Methodists could reflect upon the meaning of the new year in the context of the Incarnation, which Christian understand as the action of a loving, gracious God in the created world of history and years.

G. S. Sperry-White

Numbers 6:22-27
Psalm 8 (*UMH* 743)
Galatians 4:4-7 or Philippians 2:5-13
Luke 2:15-21

Almighty God, who gave Jesus a name above every name: Grant that his mind
indwell our affections throughout the new year and that our choices and
actions may honor him, who lives and reigns with you and the Holy Spirit, one
God, now and forever. Amen.

[DTB]

At your name, Jesus, our knees bend and our tongues confess you as our Lord.
 At your name, Jesus, our fears flee away.
 At your name, Jesus, temptation and evil lose their power.
 At your name, Jesus, disease turns to health.
 At your name, Jesus, our sin is forgiven.
 At your name, Jesus, there is no condemnation.
 At your name, Jesus, self-preoccupation yields to our true center.
 At your name, Jesus, the boundless grace of God is released.
 At your name, Jesus, all rulers, powers, and authorities in heaven
  and on earth attend to the wisdom and purpose of God.
Praised be your name.

[DTB]

January 3
Gilbert Haven (1880)
See Common of Prophets

Bishop and abolitionist, Haven was born in Malden, Massachusetts on September 19, 1821. From his conversion to Methodism in 1839 until his death he struggled to articulate the social consequences of his religious beliefs. As an undergraduate at Wesleyan University, Middletown, Connecticut, he taught Sunday school in Cross St. A.M.E. Zion Church. He later taught and then headed a Methodist boarding school in upstate New York.

Passage of the Fugitive Slave Law in 1850 potentially implicated the entire nation in the moral contradiction of slavery to American democracy. One of these fearless minority who decried this act as intolerable was Gilbert Haven, a churchman who, understanding the hypocrisy of racism, delivered his famous "higher law" sermon:

A government therefore, which endorses slavery, which orders the recovery of those who have escaped from its dreadful dungeon, ought to be met with one general burst of execration, one united prayer and effort for the repeal of its wicked enactment, and the deliverance of those so unrighteously bound. . . .

Should we be called upon to assist in the execution of this law, we must refuse.[19]

Haven entered the Methodist ministry through the New England conference in 1851 and pastored several churches in his home state. When Lincoln issued his first call for troops in the Civil War he volunteered as a Chaplain. After the war, as editor of *Zion's Herald*, New England Methodism's weekly newspaper, and after as bishop, Haven attracted national attention by his firm expression of the belief that if all persons were equal before the Lord, they could not be unequal in society or politics. He also stood unsuccessfully against the tendency to separate churches and conferences on racial lines.

Haven's radical egalitarian views shocked his contemporaries. Even though his supporters managed to elect him bishop, no northern conference wanted his leadership. Ironically, yet providentially, he was sent to the mission conferences established by the northern church in the south for blacks. Haven's home was in Atlanta and his people were entirely black. Reassigned to Liberia in 1876, he contracted malaria from which he never fully recovered, dying on this day in 1880. Benjamin Tanner, editor of the *Christian Recorder*, an A.M.E. weekly, observed of him, "He was of the few that made public opinion rather than followed it; and happily . . . he made it on the side of the poor . . . and the ostracized."[20]

K. E. Rowe

January 4
John Seybert (1860)
See Common of Pastors and Bishops

A pioneer missionary, John Seybert was elected bishop in 1839, the first Evangelical Association leader to hold that office since Jacob Albright who died in 1808. Seybert was born on July 7, 1791 in Mannheim, Pennsylvania into a German Lutheran family. Although he was a confirmed Lutheran, he recalls in his journal that, "my life, from youth up was one of wickedness, though my parents tried every possible means to check and control me. Neither coaxing nor scolding, neither kindness nor sternness availed."[21] But his early life was plagued by misfortune and trouble. A year after his father died in 1806, his mother deserted her sons to join a religious cult and John had to raise his younger brother.

When he was nineteen, however, John attended an Evangelical Association revival held in Mannheim by Matthias Betz. He recalls how, "Before he was half-way through, I was thoroughly convinced that he was a true servant of Jesus Christ. I was also convinced that I was no Christian, but a sinner who richly deserved the wrath of God. Then and there I received a wound from the sword of the Spirit and a stroke from the hammer of the Word, from which I never recovered, and the effects of which will continue with me through all eternity."[22] Two months of penitential struggle followed before, bending over a trough of water to wash his tears, he felt forgiveness through Christ.

Ordained deacon in 1821 and elder in 1824, Seybert was elected twice to be presiding elder (1825 and 1834). His tirelessness, his conservative personal habits, and his strict but fair style of relating to other clergy often lends comparison with Francis Asbury. In spreading the gospel primarily to the American Midwest and Canada, it is estimated that Seybert traveled over 175,000 miles on horseback, preaching 9,850 times while making 46,000 pastoral visits and 8,000 prayer and class meetings, not to mention the 10,000 calls upon the sick and afflicted. Consumed by his vocation, he never married. In a sermon on Job, he relates the trust in God which guided him through his struggles in life:

The devil hates no one so much as those Christians who are so entirely swallowed up in God. . . . Oh my brethren and sisters! Whatever you do, press deeply into God. Watch and pray, submit yourselves wholly unto the Lord, and trust him in the greatest adversities.[23]

T. Rand

January 8
Richard Watson (1833)
See Common of Teachers

Richard Watson was the first systematic theologian of Methodism. He attempted to bring order to John Wesley's theology in his monumental *Theological Institutes* and helped translate Wesley's theological emphases to a new generation.

Watson was born on February 22, 1781 at Barton-on-Humber, Lincolnshire, England. The seventh of eighteen children, he was a precocious child and avid reader. He began to preach at age fifteen after the sudden death of his maternal grandmother, a devout Methodist. He withdrew briefly from the Wesleyan Methodists in 1800 over a doctrinal dispute and joined the Methodist New Connexion in 1803. He returned to the Wesleyan ministry in 1812.

While Watson is chiefly noted for his theological work, he had a great interest in missions. He served as a general secretary of the Wesleyan Missionary Society from 1821 to 1825 and helped draft its constitution. His reputation as an interpreter of Wesleyan doctrine grew after publishing a pamphlet refuting statements made by Methodist scholar Adam Clarke about the Trinity that seemed to many, including Watson, to be heretical.

Watson completed his *Theological Institutes* in 1829. It was well received and became an essential part of the Methodist preacher's library. An apologetic work, its intent was to reinterpret Methodism for the changing cultural situation of the early nineteenth century by bringing together scriptural revelation with human experience. Fighting both Calvinist predestinarianism and the Pelagian gospel of self-help, Watson stood in the stream of Wesley's mediating Arminianism. Watson's theology was thoroughly rational and sometimes dry, but like Wesley, he always strove for a practical divinity. The *Institutes* were designed to help train a new generation of preachers and missionaries, a purpose which it nobly fulfilled in both America and England well into the nineteenth century. It was included in the 1868 *Discipline* of the Methodist Episcopal Church as the primary theological text of the course of study.

He also wrote a biography of John Wesley, edited a *Theological and Biblical Dictionary,* and scriptural commentaries, numerous articles and a book for youth, *Conversations for the Young; Designed to Promote the Profitable Reading of the Holy Scripture*.

Ill for much of his last three years, Watson died in 1833 and is buried near City Road Chapel in London.

J. B. Weakley

January 13
George Fox (1691)
See Common of Leaders

A radical among radicals, George Fox, the founder of the Society of Friends, belongs to the left wing of 17th century Puritanism. Born in 1624, Fox left his village home in Leicestershire at eighteen and began a lifetime of traveling: first, in search of a personal awakening; then, after 1646, to preach the godly life as he now understood it. Fox found enthusiastic hearers among folk disaffected with the political and religious solutions of Cromwellian England. Together with other itinerant preachers, men and women, he established congregations first in the north and midlands, then in the south-west. By 1660, when the monarchy was restored, the "Quakers," as they were nicknamed, seemed a significant enough threat to merit vigorous persecution.

A robust critic of hierarchical church order, ordained ministers, and set forms of worship, Fox emphasized personal responsibility and an immediate experience of the Spirit. This, the inner illumination given by Christ, and not creeds, or even scripture, is the source and test of true faith. Radicalism in social matters accompanied the theological challenge: the early Quakers rejected forms of social deference such as honorific titles, oath-taking, and military service. Even before the return of Charles II, such beliefs and practices put Fox and his friends in jail. He responded to the intensified persecution of the Restoration with brilliant organizing, setting up systems of local meetings and mutual support. He also traveled to Ireland, the Caribbean, and North America. Shortly before Fox's death the Toleration Act of 1689 ended the assault upon Quakers and other Puritan groups. The courage and integrity of persecuted Quakers helped lead to public disgust against the trials, imprisonments, and beatings.

Fox warns us against vicarious religion: no one can discharge for me my responsibility to God; I cannot appeal to ministers to excuse my sloth for the Spirit is offered to me also. Margaret Fell, who married Fox in 1669, described how his preaching shook the foundations of comfort:

> I stood up in my pew and I wondered at his doctrine.... He [said] 'The Scriptures were the prophets' words and Christ's ... and what they spoke they enjoyed and possessed.... You will say, Christ saith this, and the apostles say this; but what canst thou say?' ... And I cried in my spirit to the Lord, 'We are all thieves, we have taken the Scriptures in words and know nothing of them in ourselves.'[24]

A. P. R. Gregory

January 16
Hiram Rhoades Revels (1901)
See Common of Leaders, Saints

Revels, a Methodist preacher and politician of African- and native-American descent, was born to free parents in Fayetteville, North Carolina, September 1, 1822. Revels was forbidden by law to attend southern schools but Indiana and Ohio institutions gave him both grade school and seminary education. Graduating in 1845 from Knox College, Galesburg, Illinois, Revels was one of few American blacks who received a college education prior to 1860. He was ordained by the African Methodist Episcopal Church in 1845.

During the Civil War, Revels recruited blacks for the Union Army and became chaplain of a black Mississippi regiment. Though a pre-war dispute had led him into Presbyterian ministry, he returned to the A. M. E. Church after the war. In 1868 Revels joined the Methodist Episcopal Church declaring, "the grand old Church . . . could do more than any other Church . . . for the colored people of America."[25]

Wary of compromising his ministerial duties, Revels cautiously entered Reconstruction politics as a Natchez, Mississippi, alderman, becoming a state senator in 1869. The Mississippi legislature elevated him to the U. S. Senate in January 1870, placing Revels, a black southerner, in the seat that the Confederate president Jefferson Davis had once occupied. Retiring from the Senate in 1871, he became president of Alcorn University, Oakland, Mississippi, a newly established school for blacks.

Leaving politics, he devoted himself again to the ministry, pastoring several churches in north Mississippi. Before and at the General Conference of 1876, he joined a protest against racially segregated annual conferences in the South. The Conference washed its hands of the whole debate, ruling the issue of separate conferences, congregations, and schools a local matter. By his death on this date in 1901, few M. E. congregations remained integrated.

Revels cautioned that legislation sanctioning segregation would depart from the earliest attitude of Methodists toward African-Americans. The "Mother Church," he wrote, "came among them to do good — she showed no pride and offishness toward. . .their color and previous condition of servitude, but treated them kindly and affectionately, taking them by hand and conducting them into the same fold or church with themselves."[26] Like John Wesley, Revels believed God calls the Church not to model itself after the world but to model true community for the world.

T. J. Bell

January 17
Antony of Egypt (356)
See Common of Saints

Antony was born to affluent Christian parents who farmed along the Nile river village of Coma in Upper Egypt. At age twenty, shortly after the death of his parents, he entered a village church and heard the saying of Jesus to the rich man: "If you would be perfect, go and sell all that you have and give to the poor, come, follow me and you will have treasure in heaven." Seized by these words, he sold the farm, gave his money to the poor, and moved to the edge of town to live among local hermits and ascetics.

Directed by the wisdom of older hermits, Antony was schooled for a life of discipline and solitude. Over time, Antony moved further and further away from the village, into the wilderness of the desert. His days were occupied with prayer, fasting, and the recitation of scripture. In 286 Antony entered a period of absolute solitude at Pisper at a desert fort near the Red Sea. For some twenty years, he fought the demonic powers and overcame the forces of evil on their own turf: the interior life of the self.

In 306 he emerged from the desert to a flock of followers seeking his wisdom and guidance. He moved to Alexandria where he earned an income gardening and making mats, all the while encouraging persecuted Christians under the tyranny of Maximinus. It was during this time that he met Athanasius from whom most of our biographical information about Antony is based. In his *Life of Antony*, Athanasius, the devoted disciple, describes his master Antony as one restored to the glory of original creation.

During the middle ages, Antony became the embodiment of the spirit of early monasticism. He was a patriarch to monks and was very popular among medieval Christians. Sayings attributed to Antony were collected and taught. Like darts, they pierce reality with the sting of insight and discernment:

A certain philosopher asked St. Antony: Father, how can you be so happy when you are deprived the consolation of books? Antony replied: My book, O Philosopher, is the nature of created things, and any time I want to read the words of God, the book is before me.[27]

Antony died in 356, well over 100 years of age. According to the legend, he left his only possessions, his mantle and a sheepskin tunic, to his favorite student, Athanasius.

J. S. Hudgins

The Confession of Peter

The commemoration of the Confession of Peter marks the beginning of the Week of Prayer for Christian Unity. The origins of this feast, which appears to have been celebrated from at least the mid-fourth century, lie in the celebration of the Chair (Latin: cathedra) of Peter. This reflected the pre-Christian practice of commemorating dead relatives just before the beginning of the new year (which at that time took place on March 1) by leaving an empty chair at the table. Only later was the feast interpreted to refer to the *cathedra* occupied by the bishop of the Roman church.[28]

The idea of praying for the unity of the body of Christ is, of course, nothing new. In modern times, the idea of devoting a week to such prayer has its roots in two rather different sources. Since its preparatory meeting in 1920, the Faith and Order movement had advocated a Week of Prayer for the Unity of the Church concluding on Pentecost. Since 1916, an Octave of Prayer for Unity had been observed by Roman Catholics; its origins lay in the work of the Anglican Friars of the Atonement (who first celebrated the octave in 1980, the year they were to become Roman Catholic). Largely because of the work of the Roman Catholic ecumenist Paul Couturier in "decentralizing" the theme of the octave, Faith and Order shifted the date of its week of prayer to that of the octave (Jan. 18 - Jan. 25). Since 1966, materials for the Week of Prayer for Christian Unity have been produced jointly by the World Council of Churches and the Vatical Secretariat for Promoting Christian Unity.[29]

United Methodists can find value in marking the beginning of the Week of Prayer for Christian Unity by commemorating the confession of Peter: "You are the Christ, the Son of the Living God" (Mt 16:16). The remainder of the Gospel reading for today confronts the reader with some of the thorniest issues in ecumenical dialogue: the meaning of apostolicity and authority. However United Methodists answer those questions, Peter's reply to Jesus places them in their proper framework: confession of Christ's lordship.

G. S. Sperry-White

Acts 4:8-13
Psalm 23 (*UMH* 754, 137)
1 Peter 5:1-4
Matthew 16:13-19

God of hope, who moved an impetuous and imperfect Peter to be the first among those to confess Jesus as Messiah, so move us, that having inherited and joined this confession, we may boldly unite in witness to your saving grace, through Jesus Christ, the Son of the Living God, who lives and reigns with you and the Holy Spirit, one God, now and forever. Amen.

[CFG]

Chief Shepherd,
   You see in us what we ourselves do not yet see,
   You move us to risk beyond our knowing,
      Restore us and lead us,
         we who stand on the rock of Peter's testimony,
      Anoint us until we overflow,
      Prepare for us a table of unity,
         that we may dwell in your house together,
         through Jesus Christ our Lord. Amen.

[CFG]

For All The Saints/49

January 19
Pseudo-Macarius of Egypt (fourth century)
See Common of Teachers

"I read Macarius, and sang," wrote John Wesley in his journal on July 30, 1736. The author of *The Fifty Spiritual Homilies* and the *Great Letter* is unknown to us by name. Although Wesley like many others thought the author was Macarius, an Egyptian monk who is remembered on this day, today scholars suggest that Syria, perhaps Mesopotamia, was this person's home. Recent authors have viewed Macarius as a writer who inhabited both the Syriac and Greek-speaking worlds. Through the *Homilies,* Macarius has influenced Orthodox, Roman Catholic, and Protestant thought since the fourth century.

The writings attributed to Macarius contain the rich biblical imagery common to many Syrian Christian authors. In addition, the similes and metaphors the *Homilies* contain reveal their writer's wide experience in the world. Several authors have noted the emphasis Macarius lays upon the human heart as the field upon which the battle for salvation is waged. Macarius writes often of the work of the Spirit in the heart, a theme which spoke to Wesley and entered the stream of Wesleyan theology.

Another striking feature of the *Homilies* is their eschatological perspective. As much as he stresses the present experience of the Spirit's working in the heart, Macarius also reminds his hearers that the gift of the Spirit involves a disciplined waiting for the revelation of God's glory at the end time.

So to all God-loving souls, I mean, true Christians, there is the first month, Xanthicus, which is called April. This is, indeed, the day of resurrection in which, by the power of the Sun of Righteousness, the glory of the Holy Spirit rises up from within, covering and warming the bodies of the saints. This is the glory they interiorly had before, hidden in their souls. For what they now have, that same then pours out externally into the body . . . . It clothes the naked trees; it opens the earth. This produces joy in all animals. It brings mirth to all. This is for Christians. Xanthicus, the first month, the time of the resurrection in which their bodies will be glorified by means of the light which even now is in them hiddenly, this is the power of the Spirit who will then be their clothing, food, drink, exultation, gladness, peace, adornment, and eternal life. For the Divine Spirit, whom they were considered worthy even now to possess, will then bring about in them every beauty of radiance and heavenly splendor.[30]

G. S. Sperry-White

January 19
John Ernest Rattenbury (1963)
See Common of Teachers

Torch bearer of Wesleyan faith and practice, J. Ernest Rattenbury (b. 1870) was nurtured on the rich food of British Methodism. He was ordained at the age of twenty-three, entering the vocation of his father and grandfather who were both Wesleyan Methodist ministers.

Rattenbury devoted the strength of his early years to service in England's great mission halls. A crowning personal achievement, he opened Kingsway Hall in West London, which quickly became an important center of evangelism in England. Throughout his long life, Rattenbury strove to overcome the "false antithesis" between altar and pulpit, sacrament and gospel. To this end, he observed that Holy Communion, which he called "the Protestant Crucifix," was the central devotion of the Evangelical Revival.[31]

Holding tenaciously to a faith both sacramental and evangelical, Rattenbury stated, "However much certain groups of Christians may have unduly stressed the Sacraments," he stated, "it is entirely objectionable to proclaim the Gospel as if it excluded sacraments."[32] He also wrote extensively about religious experience, including *The Testament of Paul: Studies in Doctrines Born of Evangelical Experience* (1930) and *The Conversion of the Wesleys* (1938). In the 1930s he helped form the Methodist Sacramental Fellowship to preserve the centrality of the Eucharist in Methodist piety. His correspondence in the 1940's along with his published works gave impetus to the founding of The Order of Saint Luke, which still embraces many of the same ideals as the Methodist Sacramental Fellowship.[33]

Written in 1948, Rattenbury's last major book, *The Eucharistic Hymns of John and Charles Wesley* revealed a compelling Eucharistic theology derived primarily from Daniel Brevint's work, *The Christian Sacrament and Sacrifice* which emphasized the "real presence" of Christ in the Eucharist.

In his mature years, Rattenbury found the summation of his own scholarly work and devotional life in one verse of a Wesley hymn that he had learned as a child:

> Five bleeding wounds He bears,
> Received on Calvary;
> They pour effectual prayers,
> They strongly speak for me:
> Forgive him, O forgive! they cry,
> Nor let that ransomed sinner die.[34]

A. P. Grant

January 21
Agnes of Rome (304)
See Common of Martyrs

Agnes was a young Christian virgin (probably 12 or 13 years of age) martyred in Rome during the persecution under Diocletian. A popular saint, her cult grew quickly and she was placed on the sanctoral calendar of many churches in both East and West. The many martyrolgies and stories about her often conflict in detail.

Despite her young years, it is said that she taught and encouraged other young women. There are also indications that she was so desirous of martyrdom that her parents had to confine her to their home. She was brought to trial before the governor, perhaps by unsuccessful suitors. The governor attempted to scare her into marrying one of any number of young men by threatening her with torture. She steadfastly refused, insisting that she was already the bride of Christ.

One story explains the governor then ordered her to be taken to a brothel and raped by its patrons (this was often done to women martyrs). All but one of those who came to rape her, however, lost their desire because they were so awed by her appearance. The one young man who did attempt to take her was killed instantly. The governor had her brought before him again after this incident and asked how she killed the youth. When Agnes claimed that God had sent an angel to protect her, the governor challenged her to prove the truth of the claim by reviving the young man who had been killed. In response to Agnes' prayer, he was brought back to life.

Upon the young man's resuscitation, she was accused of doing magic and was burned to death. It is said that she was seen praying from the time she entered the flames until she died. Other stories claim that she died by the sword. Her relics are reported to be buried beneath the basilica named for her built next to the Via Nomentana, not far from Rome. Her emblem is a lamb because of the similarity of her name with the Latin *agnus* (lamb).

L. H. M. Hoover

January 23
Sarah Ann Dickey (1904)
See Common of Teachers

Sarah Dickey, born in 1838, was a member of the United Brethren Church and in 1893 was the first woman to be fully ordained in that tradition. A Northern white woman who devoted her life to educating African-American children in Mississippi, Sarah spent her childhood moving around Ohio living with various relatives and family friends. During this period her own education and religious upbringing were badly neglected so that she could barely read by age sixteen. Despite her own ignorance, Sarah resolved to become a teacher and began to attend school regularly while still paying for her room and board with domestic work. Three years later she successfully passed a test that earned her a license to teach.

For the next several years, Dickey alternately taught and studied, including a nineteen-month job in Vicksburg at a mission school. A recurring dream throughout this period gave her a sense of divine guidance and providence. In the early version of the dream, Sarah wandered through deep woods on a path to a meadow, but a wall around the meadow prevented her from entering. During her time in Vicksburg, however, the dream changed. The wall disappeared and she suddenly found herself in the meadow. From that time, Sarah knew that God wanted her to work among Black people and she felt that she should go to Mount Holyoke Female Seminary to prepare herself.

After her graduation from Mount Holyoke in 1869, she went back to Mississippi, and by 1875 she was ready to start her own school in Clinton. The Ku Klux Klan threatened her and the white people of Clinton ostracized her socially, but she persevered and succeeded in establishing Mt. Hermon Female Seminary. For many years she provided the only education available to African Americans in the area. After her death in 1904, the American Missionary Association took over the school. The school lingered on for another twenty years but finally could not survive without Dickey's hard work, initiative, and faith.

Dickey's life serves as a model of faith and perseverance in expressing God's love for the downtrodden. Despite seemingly insurmountable obstacles including lack of money, widespread hostility, and even physical intimidation, she did the work that God called her to do. In the process, she did her part to improve the situation of the newly freed slaves in the South.[35]

H. Hill

January 24
Eli Stanley Jones (1973)
See Common of Evangelists

Jones, a renowned missionary to India, popular writer, and influential Methodist leader, was born in 1884 in Clarkesville, Maryland. As a teenager, he responded to an altar call during a Methodist revival meeting. According to his testimony, however, he did not *experience* his conversion until a service two years later. Of that first service, he said, "I fumbled for the latchstring of the Kingdom of God, missed it . . . [and] took church membership as a substitute."[36]

He was educated at City College, Baltimore, and Asbury College, in Wilmore, Kentucky. He was teaching at Asbury College when the Board of Missions of the Methodist Episcopal Church asked him to go to India in 1907.

Jones was instrumental in defending the importance of an indigenous proclamation of the Gospel in mission work. His Christian Ashram at Lucknow was a community committed to an indigenous expression of the Gospel, mutual spiritual responsibility, racial and caste equality, and economic sharing. He wrote, "Christianity must be defined as Christ, not the Old Testament, not Western civilization, not even the system built around him in the West, but Christ himself and to be Christian is to follow him."[37] A careful student of Indian culture, his message was influential among the upper and lower castes and he became, in effect, a missionary to all of India. His first book, *Christ of the Indian Road* (1925), was translated into thirty languages.

His strong calling to mission work led him to turn down the office of bishop after his election by the 1928 General Conference. He said, "If I go on and receive the consecration to the office of bishop my evangelistic work as I have carried it on is practically at an end. I see very clearly now the issue before me, and I do not feel that any price I could pay would be great enough to cancel that."[38] He went on to publish many other widely read books, including, *Christ and Human Suffering* (1933), *The Christ of the American Road* (1944), and *How to be a Transformed Person* (1951). He died on January 25, 1973.

M. W. Stamm

The Conversion of Paul

The conversion of Paul, the "Apostle of the Gentiles," took place within a few years following the crucifixion of Jesus, when he was still known as "Saul," a Jew of the tribe of Benjamin, a Pharisee, and a fervent opponent of the movement known as "the Way." According to the Acts of the Apostles, Paul approved of the stoning of Stephen. Following Stephen's martyrdom, Paul embarked upon a journey to Damascus to arrest some Christians there and bring them to Jerusalem for condemnation. It was on the road to Damascus that Paul was suddenly encountered by the risen Christ. This conversion experience is related three times in Acts (9:1-19; 22:5-16, and 26:12-18). Although each of these accounts is narrated in a slightly different manner, the same basic sequence of events is consistently reported: Paul sees a great light and hears a voice saying, "Saul, Saul, why are you persecuting me?" Upon asking, "Who are you, Lord?", he hears the reply, "I am Jesus whom you are persecuting." With that, Paul is directed by the risen Lord to continue on his journey. Now, rather than arresting followers of "the Way," he begins his ministry of proclaiming the Gospel.

Paul himself recounts his conversion in Galatians recalling his "earlier life in Judaism" wherein he took to "violently persecuting the church of God" (1:13). He emphasizes that God "called me through his grace," and "was pleased to reveal his Son to me, so that I might proclaim him among the Gentiles" (1:15, 16). Thus Paul refers to himself as an "apostle," as he "was sent neither by human commission nor from human authorities, but through Jesus Christ and God the Father, who raised him from the dead" (1:1).

Paul's missionary activity contributed to the rapid growth of Gentile Christianity from Asia Minor westward. His letters have been formative for Christian theology and practice and his life bears witness to the transformative power of the gospel. A former enemy of the gospel, Paul himself was martyred under the Emperor Nero. It is this saint who, knowing the love of God which called him out of enmity into grace, wrote:

Who will separate us from the love of Christ? Will hardship, or distress, or persecution, or famine, or nakedness, or peril, or sword? As it is written, "For your sake we are being killed all day long; we are all accounted sheep to be slaughtered." No, in all these things we are more than conquerors through him who loves us (Rom 8:35-37).

M. F. Foskett

Acts 26:9-21
Psalm 67 (*UMH* 791)
Galations 1:11-24
Matthew 10:16-22

God of the height and depth and breadth of mystery,
  so deepen our conversion to the way of the cross
  that we never turn back,
  but always witness to your great love for all people,
  through Jesus Christ, our Lord. Amen.

[DTB]

Lord of every road,
  illumine our self-righteousness
  with your sovereign grace.
  Blind us to the old things,
  enable us to be crucified with you
  in daily gratitude for your call and
  fill us with your Spirit.

[DTB]

January 26
Timothy and Titus
See Common of Saints, Pastors and Bishops

As long-term companions to Paul, Timothy and Titus provided spiritual and intellectual support for the southern European mission of the Gospel. Communications preserved in the Pastoral Epistles, Paul's Letters, and the Church's story in Acts give us a glimpse into their contributions to the early Church.

The early Christian community at Lystra commended Eunice's son, Timothy, to Christian service with Paul. Young Timothy underwent circumcision in deference to his Jewish mother and the Jewish communities in which he would minister (Acts 16:3). Undergoing ordination by laying on of hands (1 Tim 1:18; 4:17; 2 Tim 1:6), he joined Paul for his second and third missionary journeys. As Paul's associate, Timothy's work was crucial in founding churches in Corinth, Thessalonica, and Philippi. He was sometimes sent to deal with particularly sensitive and difficult situations. As Paul commends him to the Philippians, "I have no one like him who will be genuinely concerned for your welfare. . . . Timothy's worth you know, how like a son with a father he has served with me in the work of the gospel" (Phil 2:20, 22). He was appointed by Paul to be the bishop of the church in Ephesus (1 Tim 1:3). Tradition holds that Timothy was martyred in Ephesus by stoning and clubbing under Emperor Nerva after Timothy's objections to the orgiastic worship of Artemis.

As circumcision figured in Timothy's nascent ministry, so it did with Titus as well. The decision that Titus would not undergo circumcision proved a major departure of Christianity from its Jewish roots (Gal 2:1-3). Titus' ministry would touch the lives of the poor and the outcast, eminently seen in his work to collect the contribution for the struggling church in Jerusalem (2 Cor 8:16-17). Acting in a diplomatic capacity as Paul's courier of the "painful" letter to the Corinthian church, Titus' diplomatic efforts elicit Paul's praise: "God . . . consoled us by the arrival of Titus, and not only by his coming, but also by the consolation with which he was consoled about you" (2 Cor 7:6-7). The Epistle to Titus indicates that Paul appointed him as bishop of Crete (Titus 1:4-5).

H. P. Minor

January 27
John Chrysostom (407)
See Common of Teachers, Pastors and Bishops

John Chrysostom, born in Antioch between 344 and 354, received early training in Christian piety and morality from his mother, Anthusa, who was widowed while John was still young. He studied rhetoric in preparation for a legal career, but upon abandoning that goal he was baptized and made a reader in the church. He spent some years in the monastic life, at home and then in the nearby mountains under the guidance of a hermit. John returned to be ordained deacon and presbyter in Antioch, and in 397 he became bishop of Constantinople. His moral exposition of the Bible and his rhetorical skills gained him a reputation as a gifted preacher, for which he later earned the name "Chrysostom," or "Golden-mouth."

In both Antioch and Constantinople, John preached particularly to the needs of urban Christians. With boldness John addressed the challenges of a large, wealthy church that no longer suffered the threat of persecution but suffered internally from a lack of commitment. He was troubled by the great disparity of wealth amid homelessness and poverty and by the distractions of various forms of urban entertainments that tempted many Christians. He sought to bring about renewal by urging personal piety, charity, and reform.

To his congregations John encouraged practices which were inspired by his own experience of the ascetic life. Families should pray together and read the Bible at home. Christians should live simply and share from their abundance with those in need. John preached relentlessly on the need to develop self-discipline, and he modeled for the people a severe and strict lifestyle of renunciation. In one sermon he told them: "But this is easy, to philosophize in words; teach me by your life — that is the best teaching."[39]

His personal austerity and stern prophetic stance produced both ardent followers and strong opposition. His criticism of the wealthy and the powerful are considered to be largely responsible for his ultimate exile in Armenia where he died on September 14th, in 407. As September 14 is Holy Cross Day, he is traditionally remembered on this, the day of the reburial of his remains in Constantinople. In a letter of encouragement to the deaconess Olympias written shortly before his death, he said:

Do you see the resourcefulness of God? Do you see the wisdom? Do you see how marvelous? Do you see the loving kindness and care? Therefore do not be disturbed, do not be troubled, but endure continuously giving thanks to God for all things, praying and praising God. . . .[40]

A. Berry Wylie

January 28
Thomas Aquinas (1274)
See Common of Teachers, Saints

Thomas, the youngest son of a noble family, studied for the priesthood at the Benedictine Abbey of Monte Cassino but shocked his family by joining the Dominican Order, committing himself to the ideals of poverty and study. While on his way to Paris for his training, Thomas was captured by his family and imprisoned for over a year, resisting their attempts — including temptation by a prostitute — to dissuade him from his calling. In Paris his classmates, probably intimidated by his enormous power of concentration and his imposing physical stature, dubbed him the "Dumb Ox," but the Church would later honor him as its "Angelic Doctor."

Girded with the confidence that all truth is of God, Thomas tirelessly devoted his life to seeking and teaching Truth. In a lasting achievement, he disarmed the "secular" science of Aristotle that appeared to threaten Christian faith by carefully combing through Aristotle's works, separating the truths from the errors and demonstrating the compatibility of the new science with Christianity.

Ever the humble teacher, Thomas wrote his most famous work, an enormous summation and brilliant exposition of Christian doctrine, for beginners. His *Summa Theologiae* traces out the workings of God's love in creation and redemption, culminating in friendship with God in love, the *"Visio Dei"* (Vision of God).

He took his own lessons to heart. On December 6, 1273, upon returning from Mass to his work on the last sections of his *Summa*, Thomas caught a glimpse of the inexpressible mystery and grandeur of God and fell silent, leaving his great *Summa* unfinished. He later confided to his secretary and friend Reginald of Piperno, "I can write no more. All that I have hitherto written seems to me nothing but straw compared to what I have seen and what has been revealed to me."[41]

After some initial contestation of his teachings, Thomas was canonized by Pope John XXII in 1323. He was made a Doctor of the Church in 1567, and in 1879, Pope Leo XII proclaimed him the "Common Doctor" of the Catholic Church, the standard of orthodoxy. His faithfulness to scriptural and natural revelation and his respect for the workings of reason and science within Christian faith continue to provide a model for Christians seeking an understanding of their faith.

S. D. Olson

January 31
John Raleigh Mott (1955)
See Common of Evangelists

Lay evangelist, ecumenist, and president of the World Council of Churches, Mott was the most important Methodist ecumenist of the early twentieth century. Born in 1865 in Purvis, New York, his family soon moved west to Pottsville, Iowa, where he was raised until he returned to upstate New York to attend college at Cornell University. During his sophomore year, Mott felt a call to ministry and became involved in the Cornell University Christian Association, the YMCA, and the Student Volunteer Movement. His participation in these organizations planted in him his long interest in ecumenical cooperation.

After college he continued his work with student organizations and is often quoted as saying, "This work among students, first in one's own country and then across the many years throughout the world, was my first love." In his work with students through the World's Student Christian Federation, he traveled to Australia, China, Japan, Korea, the Philippines, South Africa, South America, Russia, as well as to Europe. He chaired the committee which called the Edinburgh Conference of 1910, during which the ideal of world evangelization was pushed and which became the forerunner of the modern ecumenical movement. Mott was also deeply involved in the later 'Faith and Order' and 'Life and Work' Conferences.

The coming of World War I divided the nations among which Mott was working. Will Stewart, his secretary said of him, "It was the Great War which exacted the greatest toll. . . . Even so he did not give up in despair but set at once about saving the fragments."

After the war, he continued his ecumenical efforts, traveling the world as an ambassador for peace, ecumenism, and Christian unity. These efforts culminated in the formation of the World Council of Churches in 1948. Mott was credited for his direct influence upon ten generations of students, from which the World Council's early leadership was largely drawn. In 1946 he was awarded the Nobel Peace Prize. On this occasion he summarized his life as "an earnest and undiscouragable effort to weave together all nations, all races and all religious communions in friendliness, in fellowship and in cooperation." Shortly before his death, Mott reaffirmed a statement he made in 1933: "While life lasts I am an evangelist."[42]

T. A. Rand

The Presentation

The Presentation of Jesus in the Temple, celebrated on the fortieth day after Christmas, belongs to the so-called minor Christological feasts, a category which includes the Annunciation (March 25) and the Visitation of Mary to Elizabeth (May 31). This feast probably has a dual origin. A feast mentioned by the pilgrim Egeria in the fourth century, and referred to in the mid-fifth century as *Hypapante*, or "[Feast of the] Meeting," was celebrated in Jerusalem on the fortieth day after Epiphany. Egeria reports that the sermon she heard on that day focused upon Luke 2:22-39. In Rome, a feast held forty days after Christmas seems to have been intended to replace a pagan procession around the city meant to expiate sins. A candlelight procession was associated with both feasts; thus the name "Candlemas," by which this day has been known in many calendars.

The Gospel reading for today, Luke 2:22-39, comes from the Lukan infancy narrative. It is well known that Luke's treatment of traditional material in the infancy narratives is complex. However, one characteristically Lukan theme that shines through the story of the Presentation is the universal salvation God brings in and through Jesus. Of course, the other side of the coin here is that Jesus was not born into just any people, but that he was born a member of Israel. Simeon proclaims that the infant is "a light for revelation to the Gentiles," but he also announces that Jesus is "for glory to your [i.e., God's] people Israel." (2:32). If the Presentation story has anything at all to say to post-Holocaust Christians, perhaps it is that at the heart of Christian faith is one who was born a member of the people with whom God made an everlasting covenant. The revelation to Gentile Christians celebrated on this day consists at least partially in the reminder that in the economy of the salvation Christians proclaim, the elder sibling is Israel.

G. S. Sperry-White

Malachi 3:1-4
Psalm 84 (*UMH* 804) or Psalm 24:7-10 (*UMH* 756)
Hebrews 2:14-18
Luke 2:22-40

Almighty and everlasting God, we pray that, as your Son Jesus Christ was presented as a child in the temple to be the hope of your people, so may we be presented to you with the will to be faithful and obedient through Jesus Christ our Lord, who lives and reigns with you and the Holy Spirit, one God, now and forever. Amen.

[DTB]

God of promise, Simeon and Anna saw Jesus and welcomed salvation.
 Stir up in us a devotion that
   waits with longing for your deliverance
   for the oppressed and suffering,
    and points us to our redeemer, Jesus the Messiah. Amen.

[DTB]

See *The United Methodist Book of Worship*, 316.

February 4
Cornelius the Centurion
See Common of Saints

Cornelius and the members of his household in Caesarea are remembered as the first Gentile converts to Christianity. According to Acts, the early Church was comprised of only Jewish believers prior to the conversion of Cornelius and his household. Thus Cornelius' conversion signaled God's inclusion of the Gentiles among the followers of "the Way."

Acts relates the story of Cornelius' conversion twice (10:1-44 and 11:4-18). Cornelius was "a centurion of the Italian Cohort . . . a devout man who feared God with all his household; he gave alms generously to the people and prayed constantly to God" (10:1-2). As a centurion, a military officer in charge of 100 foot soldiers, Cornelius must have been a citizen of Rome. His conversion was witnessed and facilitated by the preaching of Peter when, following the direction of an angel of God, Cornelius sent for Peter to come to his house in Caesarea. Before receiving his summons, Peter had a vision wherein he saw a large sheet descending from heaven with all manner of living creatures upon it. Three times upon hearing a voice say, "Get up, Peter; kill and eat," Peter protested saying, "By no means, Lord; For I have never eaten anything that is profane or unclean." Each time the voice answered, "What God has made clean, you must not call profane." Understanding the meaning of this vision only when he received Cornelius' summons to come to the home of a Gentile, Peter realized that "God has shown me that I should not call anyone profane or unclean" (10:28).

At Cornelius' house, Peter said, "I truly understand that God shows no partiality, but in every nation anyone who fears him and does what is right and acceptable to him" (10:34-35). As he continued to preach about Jesus Christ, the Holy Spirit fell upon Cornelius and his household and they were immediately baptized.

According to Acts, Peter's ministry among Gentiles was met with initial resistance by the Jewish believers in Jerusalem. However, upon hearing Peter's testimony directly, "they praised God, saying, 'Then God has given even to the Gentiles the repentance that leads to life' (Acts 11:18). Thus for the early Church, Cornelius' faith and conversion served as a testimony of God's acceptance of all peoples. For the Christian Church today, the life and witness of Cornelius reminds us as well that God indeed shows no partiality, and that the kingdom of God is open to all people.

M. F. Foskett

February 5
Philipp Jakob Spener (1705)
See Common of Leaders, Teachers

As a youth and a university student, Spener retained the Lutheran piety of the Alsatian home into which he was born on January 13, 1635. From Strassburg University where he did undergraduate and theological studies he received his Th.D. degree on June 23, 1664, the same day he married Susanna Ehrhardt, who became a steadfast wife and mother of their eleven children.

Spener served as the senior of the Lutheran clergy at Frankfurt/Main from 1666-86. Here in 1670 he created the "collegia pietatis," small renewal groups. In 1675 his best known work, the *Pia Desideria*, appeared. It lamented church corruption and called for reform not in doctrine, but in life. Six reform proposals were offered: (1) more extensive use of the word of God, (2) establishment of the spiritual priesthood, i.e., more animated lay religious activity, (3) emphasis on a Christianity given to doing as well as to knowing, (4) loving behavior in religious controversy, (5) reform of theological education with a focus on faith and piety as well as academic preparation, and (6) the preaching of edifying sermons that would produce faith and its fruits.[43]

Between 1686 and 1691 Spener was the Saxon court preacher in Dresden. His last pastorate in Berlin (1691-1705) found him involved in considerable controversy with Lutheran Orthodox antagonists and using his influence at the Prussian court in successfully creating Halle University as a Pietist stronghold. There, under the leadership of August Hermann Francke (1663-1727), emerged the educational, social, and missional institutions that effected Pietism's vital worldwide witness.[44]

Spener stressed the Wiedergeburt (the New Birth) and the daily renewal by the Holy Spirit that must follow it. He insisted that three things happen in the New Birth: faith is ignited in the heart; newborn persons have their sins forgiven, are justified, and are adopted as God's children; and an entirely other and new nature is created in them. Faith ought to eventuate in love. "Indeed, love is the whole life of the man who has faith and who through his faith is saved, and his fulfillment of the laws of God consists of love."[45]

K. J. Stein

February 11
Fanny Jane Crosby (1915)
See Common of Musicians

Fanny Crosby, born in 1820, went blind at six weeks of age but her disability did not prevent her from becoming the most prolific writer of hymns in American history. A precocious child who began writing verse at age eight, she eventually became a teacher of grammar, rhetoric, and history at the New York School for the Blind. Her hymnody, which is well represented in *The United Methodist Hymnal* (1989), continues to be a powerful influence on the worship experience of United Methodists.

Crosby began her hymn-writing career shortly after her marriage to Alexander Van Alstyne in 1858 and eventually produced more than eight thousand hymns. It has been noted that "much of the writing was done to order. For Biglow and Main (her publishers) she produced three hymns a week."[46] A lifelong Methodist, she often visited services in missions throughout Manhattan. After one such visit, she came away convinced that no one was beyond redemption. She wrote that it was the duty of the Christian to

Rescue the perishing, care for the dying,
Snatch them in pity from sin and the grave,
Weep o'er the erring one, lift up the fallen,
Tell them of Jesus, the mighty to save (*UMH* 591).

Her most enduring and beloved hymns speak of a personal and heartfelt devotion to Christ: "To God be the glory, great things He hath done!" (*UMH* 98), "Jesus, Keep Me Near the Cross" (*UMH* 301), "Pass Me Not, O Gentle Savior" (*UMH* 351), "Close to Thee" (*UMH* 407), and "I Am Thine, O Lord" (*UMH* 419).

Her deep roots in Wesleyan spirituality are evident in her hymn, "Blessed Assurance, Jesus is Mine" (*UMH* 369):

Blessed assurance, Jesus is mine!
O what a foretaste of glory divine!
Heir of salvation, purchase of God,
Born of his Spirit, washed in his blood.

This is my story, this is my song,
Praising my Savior all the day long.

G. L. Hayes

February 13
Absalom Jones, Priest (1818)
See Common of Pastors and Bishops

Absalom Jones, the first Black priest of the Protestant Episcopal Church, served his people as a caring priest and a leader of the African-American community. Jones was born a slave in Sussex, Delaware in 1746. At sixteen, Absalom was taken to Philadelphia. There he learned to write and began attending night school. In Pennsylvania during Jones' lifetime, "universal freedom" was a prevailing notion among many whites, and a law passed in 1780 in Pennsylvania called for the eventual abolition of slavery.

It was in this context that Jones became an active member in the mostly white congregation of St. George's Methodist Episcopal Church. By 1787, Black membership had increased along with white resentment. One Sunday, white church trustees asked Jones, Richard Allen, and other Black worshippers to move to the newly built gallery, trying to pull them off their knees while in prayer. He then led other Black members out of the church following the service. They would not worship at St. George's again.

That group voted to affiliate with the Protestant Episcopal Church rather than the Methodist Episcopal Church, and on July 17, 1794 the St. Thomas African Episcopal Church was dedicated with Jones as its first ordained priest. Father Jones was known for his frequent visitations, strong pastoral qualities, and constant support of the advancement of Black people. While never forgetting the evils of slavery, he preached a message of liberation without bitterness.[47] In 1793, during a yellow fever epidemic, he and other parishioners cared for the sick. St. Thomas organized schools and mutual aid societies, and in 1799 and 1800, Jones was involved with petitioning the state legislature and Congress to end slavery.[48]

In his Thanksgiving Sermon of 1808, preached on the occasion of the abolition of the slave trade, he said:

> Let the first of January, the day of the abolition of the slave trade in our country, be set apart in every year, as a day of publick (sic) thanksgiving.... We implore thy blessing, O God, upon ... all who are in authority in the United States .... O save thy people from the calamities of war. Give peace in our day.[49]

T. M. Eugene

February 17
Frances Elizabeth Caroline Willard (1898)
See Common of Prophets

Willard was the longtime president of the Woman's Christian Temperance Union (WCTU) from 1879 to her death, and one of the most famous reformers of nineteenth-century America. Born in 1839, she grew to young womanhood in Evanston, Illinois in the midst of a strong, liberal Methodist community that helped her to form a good character, the continuous goal of her life. Her Methodist faith grounded her life and impelled her always outward and onward toward a new social vision.

Willard's teenage wish to "be good and do good" guided her reform career, whether as dean of women at Northwestern University when the school first admitted women in the early 1870's, or as an organizer of the WCTU during the mid-1870's. When she became president of the WCTU, she brought with her into the office her determination to work for a broad range of women's rights reforms, including woman suffrage, women's economic independence, and women's ecclesiastical rights. She believed in and called unceasingly for women's self-development: women's right to be and do whatever they discerned that God called them to do.

For Willard and her organization, the aim of prohibition of the use of alcohol and other drugs, and the elevation of women to a status equal to that of men was a means to the end of creating a new age where men and women could work together as partners in building a world that was just, peaceful, and harmonious — what Willard understood to be the kingdom of God realized on earth. In "The Woman's Cause is Man's" published in 1892 in *Arena*, a reform journal, Willard wrote of her vision of a partnership of women and men, and its basis in their common spiritual nature:

> The noblest way in which to think of men or women is to think first of their more enduring nature, their spiritual part, that which all human beings have in common.... The more we can think of each other on this plane the nobler will be our treatment of each other, because we cannot help reverencing the spiritual for the reason that it is the highest, it is the most enduring, it is the most godlike. All else will some day fall away from us, but spirituality is an undying characteristic.

C. D. Gifford

February 18
Martin Luther (1546)
See Common of Leaders, Teachers

Born into a Saxon miner's home in 1483, Luther received his B.A. degree from Erfurt University in 1502 and his masters degree in 1505. He disappointed his father by forsaking legal studies and becoming an Augustinian monk. Monastic rigor, ordination to the priesthood in 1507, and receipt of a doctor of theology degree as he began his teaching career as a professor of biblical studies at Wittenberg University in 1512, however, did not bring Luther the peace of soul he arduously sought. Troubled by his sin before God, he found no release until in lecture preparation he discovered in Psalms 31 and 71, as well as in Romans 1:16-17, that the righteousness of God is redemptive, not condemnatory, and that salvation comes as we trust the divine righteousness in Christ to cover our sin.

Luther's sermons and many subsequent publications supporting his new "discovery" of the Gospel of salvation by grace through faith ran counter to the medieval church's emphasis on pleasing God as best one could through good works as well as by faith. In his great 1520 treatise "On the Freedom of a Christian," he summarized the paradoxical nature of his theology: "A Christian is perfectly free lord of all, subject to none. A Christian is a perfectly dutiful servant of all, subject to all." By faith we are freed from doing the works of the law for our salvation and we are opened upward to God; by love we are opened downward and outward to our neighbor.

At the Diet of Worms in 1521 Luther, on Scriptural grounds, refused to recant his teachings. Condemned by both the Roman Catholic Church and the Holy Roman Empire, he spent the rest of his life in Wittenberg protected by the electors of Saxony.

In 1525 Luther married a former nun, Catharine von Borah. Six children were born into their happy home.

There are some one hundred volumes in Luther's collected works, including many biblical commentaries. "A Mighty Fortress is Our God" is the best known of his hymns. By the time Luther died, half of modern-day Germany and the Scandinavian countries were following his theological and liturgical reforms.

K. J. Stein

February 20
Frederick Douglass (1895)
See Common of Prophets

In February of 1818 in Talbot County, Maryland, Harriet Bailey, an African-American slave woman, gave birth to a son, Frederick Augustus Washington Bailey. Although born in "the dark night of slavery," this son would become one of the leading lights in the nineteenth-century American abolitionist movement, a celebrated author and a social reformer. After escaping from slavery in 1838, he changed his name to Frederick Douglass, a change symbolic of his new identity. Douglass was no stranger to the physical and psychic indignities of slavery, of course, but he stood firm in his hope. Concerning the importance of hope in his pilgrimage to freedom, he wrote:

> From my earliest recollection, I date the entertainment of a deep conviction that slavery would not always be able to hold me within its foul embrace; and in the darkest hours of my career in slavery, this living word of faith and the spirit of hope departed not from me, but remained like ministering angels to cheer me through the gloom. This good spirit was from God, and to him I offer thanksgiving and praise.[50]

After his escape from slavery, Douglass was hired by the abolitionist William Lloyd Garrison and began an extensive lecture tour in the United States and Europe, exposing the atrocities of slavery and advocating social reform. His literary and rhetorical abilities propelled him into national prominence and he enjoyed a distinguished but turbulent career as a champion of human rights.

One source of considerable turbulence in Douglass' life was his attempt to hold in tension his two "religions": Christianity and Abolitionism. Soon after his emancipation, Douglass moved to Massachusetts and joined the Zion chapel, an African Methodist Episcopal Zion congregation where he would serve as a lay preacher. He was fond of his experience at Zion chapel but felt that his ultimate calling was not to be a preacher but a prophet of abolition. As his belief in the direct intervention of God in human affairs waned, and his repulsion of the wedding of American slavery and American Christianity waxed, his relation to organized Christianity became increasingly strained. He was criticized by church leaders for his religious liberalism which credited human efforts for antislavery successes more than it thanked God. Douglass continues to remind America of the need to close the gap between religious creeds and actual deeds.

B. R. Braxton

February 21
Ezekiel Cooper (1847)
See Common of Preachers, Saints

Cooper was born in Caroline County, Maryland on February 22 1763. Raised an Anglican, at thirteen he joined Methodism after hearing Freeborn Garrettson as he preached to American troops on the Cooper farm during the Revolutionary War.

Cooper began his ministry on the Long Island Circuit in 1785. For the next thirteen years he served several appointments: East Jersey Circuit, Baltimore, and Annapolis, and served a year as presiding elder of the Boston district. Asked by Bishop Asbury to assist with the Methodist Publishing House and help see it through a financial crisis, in 1799 Cooper was elected over his own protests by the Philadelphia Conference and reluctantly became the second book agent of the Methodist Publish House.

Although initially reluctant, Cooper threw himself into straightening out the book concern, digging it out of debt, regulating its sales procedures, and clarifying its publication policy: "To cultivate moral and religious knowledge . . . we confine ourselves to the publication of books and pamphlets, upon subjects of morality and divinity; more especially such as treat on experimental and practical religion."[51] He supervised the move of the publishing house to New York City in 1804 and by the time he resigned in 1808 he could report that the book concern was financially stable. He died in Philadelphia on this day in 1847, having served in the preaching ministry for sixty-two years.

Having wide knowledge of various subjects, Cooper was described as a "living encyclopaedia." He was concerned that Methodists record their history and wrote a plan for an archive that would have required all preachers to collect detailed geographical, historical, and biographical information relevant to their circuits. The monumental work was never finished.

Cooper was a hardworking man who lived a celibate life in service of Christ. He loved to fish, however, carrying with him his tackle and a walking cane which he used as a fishing pole. Once, Cooper was asked if he thought he wasted his time fishing if he did not catch anything. He responded: "Although I caught nothing, while watching my line I have finished the outlines of two sermons."[52]

J. B. Weakley

February 22
Kanichi Miyama (date of death unknown)
See Common of Evangelists

Kanichi Miyama was the first legal Japanese immigrant to the United States to be baptized a Christian. He was also the first Japanese ordained in the U.S.

Miyama was born into a samuri family in Hagi, Yamaguchi Ken, Japan on October 25 1847. As a student he came under the influence of the famous teacher, Yoshida Shoin who favored opening Japan to Western knowledge and influence. Unable to pass an Army physical examination, Miyama traveled to America. Landing in San Francisco with no knowledge of English he enrolled in a class taught by Dr. Otis Gibson, the superintendent of the Chinese Methodist Mission in Chinatown, San Francisco. This relationship eventually led to his baptism by Gibson on this date in 1877. Miyama organized a Gospel Society for Japanese immigrants in October, 1877, from which grew the first Japanese Methodist church in America (now known as Pine United Methodist Church). Miyama was appointed to the congregation in 1884 as an assistant to Gibson.

Ordained deacon in 1886, the next year Miyama became an elder and full member of the then California Conference and was appointed to do Mission work to the Japanese in Hawaii. With support from the meager earnings of the members of the Japanese church in San Francisco, he sailed to Honolulu and began his evangelistic work among the Japanese laborers. He came back to San Francisco once, but returned to Hawaii in 1888 and founded the first Methodist Church in Hawaii with 38 members (now the Harris Memorial Methodist Church of Honolulu). In the conference year of 1888-89, Miyama baptized 155 persons, among them Ando Taro, the Japanese consul general.

Miyama returned to Japan in 1890 and founded the Ginza Church in Tokyo. He went on to found churches in the cities of Nagoya and Kamakura. He was also a great crusader for the temperance movement.[53]

L. E. Suzuki

February 23
Polycarp (155)
See Common of Martyrs, Pastors and Bishops

Outside of the account of the death of Stephen (Acts 7), the story of the martyrdom of Polycarp is the oldest such story extant. Polycarp belongs to the so-called sub-apostolic age: in his youth he had heard the preaching of an apostle, in his case an apostle named John (some have presumed this John to have been the Beloved Disciple, others are less certain). Thus Polycarp belongs to the first generation following the death of the apostles. Polycarp also knew Ignatius, another witness to the apostolic age; the Antiochene bishop and martyr addressed a short letter to him. Polycarp may even have been responsible for collecting (and thus preserving) Ignatius' letters.

Polycarp is best known, however, for the account of his martyrdom. In it, we find the central motif which motivated later women and men to give their lives for their faith in Christ: dying in a death like Christ's as the highest form of discipleship. Certainly, Ignatius said something similar earlier (see October 17). The difference, however, lies in the fact that the *Martyrdom of Polycarp* strives to show that in all things Polycarp's death was parallel to the account of Christ's passion, or "conformable to the gospel" (chapter 1). Thus the story of Polycarp's death served as a model for future narratives of the death of Christian martyrs. The *Martyrdom* also includes a number of polemical features of which the modern reader must be aware, including a strong hint of anti-Judaism (e.g., the Jews of Smyrna urge the Romans to arrest Polycarp), a common feature in early Christian writing.

Particularly striking is Polycarp's prayer of self-offering before he is burned at the stake. Its form and content, many authors believe, may have been very like the prayer he prayed each Sunday at his church's eucharist:

> Lord, almighty God, through whom we have come to the knowledge of yourself, God of angels, of powers, of all creation, of all the race of saints who live in your sight, I bless you for judging me worthy of this day, this hour, so that in the company of the martyrs I may share the cup of Christ, your anointed one, and so rise again to eternal life in soul and body, immortal through the power of the Holy Spirit.[54]

G. S. Sperry-White

Matthias

Matthias was chosen an apostle to replace Judas Iscariot after his betrayal of Jesus. In the account in Acts 1:15-26, Peter suggests that Judas' replacement must be someone who had been with Jesus from his baptism until the ascension and was a witness to the resurrection. Two qualified candidates come forward, Joseph Barsabbas and Matthias (because of this, the early church tradition placed Matthias in the seventy sent out by Jesus to preach even though his name is not mentioned there or elsewhere in the New Testament). The disciples then use the Old Testament practice of casting lots. The two names are written on stones, which, after a prayer for guidance, are shaken together in a bag. The first stone to come out indicates that Matthias is chosen. "Matthias," in fact, means "gift of God," fitting for the one believed by the early Christian community to have been selected by God. He is an example to us that willing witnesses will come forth to serve the Lord in the place of those who turn away.

According to tradition, Matthias' mission field included Palestine, Cappodocia, and Ethiopia. Origen referred to a *Gospel of Matthias*, although no such text has survived. One apocryphal story claims that while in Macedonia, Matthias drank a poison that was supposed to cause blindness. Not only was he unharmed, he healed 250 persons who had been blinded by the poison. In another story he is bound and thrown into prison but the Lord appears in a great light and sets him free. After this, Matthias tells his tormentors, "Ye shall go to Hell alive," and the earth opens and swallows them. As a result of this miracle, many others are then converted.[55]

Tradition also holds Matthias to have been a martyr, although the stories of his martyrdom vary, one claiming that he was crucified and then hacked with a halberd (or ax), another that he was beheaded and stoned. He is remembered on this day in the Episcopal and Lutheran calendars, but his celebration has recently been moved in the Roman Catholic Church to May 14th, between the Ascension and Pentecost, the period during which he was chosen to be an apostle.

S. Webb Phillips

Acts 1:15-26
Psalm 15 (*UMH* 747)
Philippians 3:13-21
John 15:1, 6-16

Gift-giving God, as you guided the Church to see in Matthias the calling of an apostle, so call forth and make evident your gifts in all your people that together we who have become witnesses to your redemption may carry on the work of Christ's apostles, in the power of your Holy Spirit. Amen.

[CFG]

Grower of the Vineyard, when the vine was injured you strengthened it and grafted Matthias among the Twelve: Always grant us such pastors and leaders that the whole may grow and bear good fruit in Christ. Amen.

[CFG]

February 25
Amanda Berry Smith (1915)
See Common of Preachers, Evangelists

Former slave and washerwoman, Amanda Berry Smith achieved international acclaim as a holiness preacher, evangelist, and "singing pilgrim" who traveled throughout the United States, Europe, India, and Africa.

Born January 23, 1837, about 20 miles north of Baltimore, she was freed during childhood when her father purchased his family and moved them north to Pennsylvania. Denied an education because of local race prejudice, the Berry children learned the alphabet from their parents. She went to work as a domestic, and while praying in the basement of the home where she worked, was converted to the Christian faith. She remained a lifelong member of the African Methodist Episcopal Church.

After the Civil War, she moved to New York where she heard John Inskip preach on sanctification and experienced what was then called "the second blessing." When her husband died in 1869 she began her ministry, traveling to New Jersey and throughout the northeast leading revivals, testifying, singing, and preaching at camp meetings.

Once, she shared this testimony of faith:

God saves people so that they will stay saved. When you get 'sealed' it takes the nonsense out of you. . . . How careful God is to protect his sealed ones. . . . Temptations will come even to the sealed ones, but. . . . Remember, God's eye is upon you, and Jesus sees all the fiery darts that are shot at his sealed ones, and catches and quenches them in his own precious blood. We are under the special protection of the divine almighty One when once we are sealed. Hallelujah![56]

She spent most of her public ministry before mainly white congregations. Through her riveting renditions of slave spirituals and traditional hymns and her stirring testimonies about her experiences with God, Smith attracted the attention of such prominent holiness leaders as Phoebe Palmer, Frances Willard, and William Taylor.

In the early 1890's she returned to the U.S. after twelve years as an itinerant missionary in Europe, India, and West Africa, and in 1893 she published her autobiography. Later, she founded an orphanage and industrial school for black children in Harvey, Illinois, a suburb of Chicago. Failing health forced her to retire to Sebring, Florida, in 1913, where she died on this date in 1915.

A. M. Israel

February 27
George Herbert (1633)
See Common of Pastors and Bishops

George Herbert was an Anglican parish priest, poet, and essayist, whose life and writings locate the individual Christian life firmly within the work and prayer of the Church. Deeply devout, though not without spiritual struggles, Herbert's writings affirm the Bible as the true Word of God, the mystery of the sacraments, and the daily, weekly, and annual rounds of prayer and worship prescribed in the *Book of Common Prayer*. The prose description of clerical duties in *A Priest to the Temple, or the Country Parson: His Character, and Rule of Holy Life*, and the poems collected in *The Temple*, are among his most famous compositions. A poem entitled "Praise (II)" from the section "The Church" in *The Temple* has been set to music and sung as a hymn by Methodists in Great Britain and by those now joined with the Uniting Church in Australia:

> King of Glory, King of Peace,
> I will love thee;
> And that love may never cease,
> I will move thee.

> Though my sins against me cried,
> Thou didst clear me;
> And alone, when they replied,
> Thou didst hear me.

> Thou has granted my request,
> Thou hast heard me:
> Thou didst note my working breast,
> Thou hast spar'd me.

> Sev'n whole days, not one in seven,
> I will praise thee.
> In my heart, though not in heaven,
> I can raise thee.

> Wherefore with my utmost art
> I will sing thee,
> And the cream of all my heart
> I will bring thee.

> Small it is, in this poor sort
> To enroll thee:
> Ev'n eternity is too short
> To extol thee.[57]

The seventh of ten children, Herbert was born at the family estate in Montgomeryshire (near the border between England and Wales), but upon the death of his father, moved as a young child first to Oxford and then to London. He excelled academically, and eventually at Cambridge pursued studies leading to the degree of Bachelor of Divinity. Ordination was delayed for several years, as he explored a possible vocation in public service: in 1619 he was elected Public Orator at Cambridge, and in 1624 served as a representative to Parliament from Montgomeryshire. Dissatisfied with secular office, he quickly received ordination and spent the rest of his short life in pastoral and literary service to the Church.

K. B. Westerfield Tucker

John Wesley

Founder of the Methodist movement, priest of the Church of England, keen scholar, brilliant organizer, social reformer, and tireless preacher of the gospel, John Wesley (b. 1703) was the fifteenth of the nineteen children born to Susanna and Samuel. His providential rescue from a fire at the Epworth rectory in 1709 led his deeply religious mother to take even more seriously the task of forming in him the religious and personal habits which made his later work so effective. He was schooled at Charterhouse in London and Christ Church College, Oxford and became a fellow of Lincoln College, Oxford. There he began with Charles the now famous "Holy Club" known for its strict devotion and ministries of compassion. The works of William Law, Bishop Taylor, and Thomas à Kempis deeply shaped his understanding of Christianity as a call to a practical holiness.

In 1736, he accompanied Oglethorpe to Georgia as a missionary where his reforming zeal met with dismal failure. Finding himself in a disastrous relationship and under legal attack, he left the colony under cover of night dejected and religiously confused. He returned to England convinced that he had "the faith of a servant not of a son." But encouraged by Moravian Peter Böhler to "preach faith until he had it," Wesley soon had his famous Aldersgate heart-warming experience on May 24, 1738. That summer he visited the Moravians of Hernnhut and was impressed by their fellowship, their organization into "bands," and their love feasts.

Returning to England and being turned out of numerous parish pulpits, he took up George Whitefield's practice of field-preaching. The crowds responded, some with enthusiastic outbursts, others with threats of violence, but he eventually won many hearers, especially among England's working classes. He formed his converts into societies for "experimental religion" whose only requirement was the desire "to flee from the wrath to come." Smaller classes were developed for more intense training in the faith. To extend his work, Wesley began to send out highly disciplined lay preachers. Gathering them for yearly conferences, he firmly supervised Methodism's phenomenal growth. In his many writings, Wesley created a highly original theological synthesis both Western and Eastern, sacramental and revivalistic, Arminian in emphasizing on free grace and radical in its demand for holiness.

John died on this date in 1791 in his house next to the City Road Chapel and is buried there. In his life he had preached more than 40,000 times, published about 500 books, sermons, tracts, and pamphlets, and covered more than 250,000 miles on horseback. At his death, in 1791, there were 79,000 Methodists in England and 40,000 in North America.

C. F. Guthrie

Isaiah 49:1-6
Psalm 98 (*UMH* 818)
Romans 12:9-20
Luke 9:2-6

O God, who plucked as a brand from the burning your servant John Wesley that he might kindle the flame of love in our hearts and illuminate our minds: Grant us such a warming of our hearts that we, being set afire by holy love, may spread its flame to the uttermost parts of the earth, through Jesus Christ our Lord. Amen.

[J. E. Rattenbury, alt. CFG]

Almighty God, who raised up your servant John Wesley to proclaim anew the gift of redemption and the life of holiness: Be with us his children, and revive your work among us; that inspired by the same faith and upheld by the same grace in Word and Sacrament, we and all your people may be made one in the unity of your Church on earth, even as in heaven we are made one in you; through Jesus Christ our Lord, who lives and reigns with you and the Holy Spirit, one God, in glory everlasting. Amen.

[Methodist Sacramental Fellowship, alt. TJC]

March 5
William McKendree (1835)
See Common of Pastors and Bishops

McKendree, the first American-born Methodist bishop, was born July 6, 1757 on a small farm near Richmond, Virginia. Reared Anglican, his family joined the Methodists when he was eighteen. Young McKendree commanded a regiment in the Revolutionary War and was present at the surrender of Cornwallis at Yorktown. After the war he experienced a conversion to God and a call to the ordained ministry which he entered in 1788. He served circuits in Virginia and the Carolinas until 1800 when Bishop Asbury sent him to organize circuits and conferences in the west. He skillfully superintended his large district, which extended from Ohio to Illinois through Kentucky to Tennessee and Mississippi. The record of his work in the west plus a memorable sermon before the General Conference of the church in 1808 led to his election as bishop a few days later.

McKendree gladly shared episcopal leadership with Francis Asbury, the man who was his bishop, mentor, and friend from the time he began riding a circuit, but he also made his own significant contributions. He initiated the bishop's cabinet and the episcopal address to General Conferences. Under his direction General Conferences began using standing committees to prepare its legislation. He vigorously promoted Sunday schools and helped organize the church's Missionary Society in 1819.

The press of business, however, did not crowd out this bishop's devotional life. For the whole of his ministry McKendree read five chapters out of the Bible daily (on his knees!), pausing on every fifth verse for prayer. He also continued to fast on Fridays:

Diary, Friday September 24, 1790: Having to ride fifteen miles and preach, I had some temptations to breakfast, but resisted them; and though I suffered on account of abstinence, yet the cross vanished, and I suffered less than usual on my fast days. Praise and power, honor and glory to God![58]

McKendree was a devout soul, an able administrator and an outstanding episcopal leader who greatly influenced the development of the Methodist Church in the U.S. He died at age seventy-eight in Sumner County, Tennessee on March 5, 1835. He was buried nearby, but his body was later reinterred on the campus of Vanderbilt University in Nashville.

K. E. Rowe

March 7
Perpetua and her Companions (c. 203)
See Common of Martyrs

Vibia Perpetua was the daughter of a prominent family in Thuburbo, North Africa. She and Felicitas, her friend and servant, were martyred at Carthage during the early Roman persecutions. Their witness, *The Martyrdom of Perpetua and Felicitas* is a famous account of spiritual leadership. If Perpetua was the author, it is one of the earliest examples of Christian women's literature.

Shortly after her arrest, Perpetua's father visits her in prison and begs her to renounce her faith for the sake of her infant son. She has been charged with treason for refusing to make sacrifices and burn incense in honor of the emperor. Her punishment will be public death in the arena.

When we were still with the imperial official, my father wanted to break down my resolution by his words and persisted in trying to fell me, out of his love for me. "Father," I said, "Do you see this vase laying here, for example, or this little pitcher, or whatever it is?" And he said, "I see it." And I said to him "Now can it be called by any other name than what is is?" And he replied, "No." "Just so, I cannot be said to be anything else than what I am, a Christian."

Perpetua's writings are filled with her prophetic dreams as well as loving details of her child. Her friend and servant Felicitas gives birth in the prison. Imprisoned, yet strangely free, the two women strengthen each other as they prepare to witness in blood.

The day of their triumph dawned, and they cheerfully came forth from the prison to the amphitheater, as if to Heaven, with faces composed; if perchance they trembled it was not from fear but from joy. Perpetua was following with a bright face and with calm gait, as the wife of Christ, as the women pleasing to God, by the power of her gaze casting down everyone's stares. Also Felicitas came forth, rejoicing that she had safely borne her child, so that she could fight the beast, going from blood to blood, from the midwife to the gladiator, about to wash after childbirth in a second baptism.[59]

H. M. Elkins

March 9
Gregory of Nyssa (c. 394)
See Common of Pastors and Bishops, Teachers

When he used his influence to have his younger brother Gregory named bishop of the small, provincial town of Nyssa, Basil of Caesarea said that he would rather have his brother bring distinction to the place, rather than the other way around. By the end of Gregory's career, Basil had gotten his wish.

Gregory's most signal contribution lies in his powerful and insightful vision of the ascent of the soul to God. Standing firmly within the Eastern Christian tradition, the language Gregory employed to describe the mystery of salvation was in many ways dissimilar to that which most North American Christians are accustomed to hearing. While we more often use the language of guilt, atonement, and new birth, Gregory was more prone to speak of the loss and restoration of the divine image in us, and of participation in the divine perfection. He took seriously the gospel injunction, "Be perfect, therefore, as your heavenly Father is perfect" (Mt 5:48). Because he also took human finitude and sinfulness seriously, he knew that our perfection comes not from ourselves, but from our desire and ability to share in and imitate God's perfection. Yet how is that possible? Can we become, like God, unchangeable, timeless, and eternal? Of course not! Change is part of our very nature, the one predictable element in life's sad, involuntary journey. But Gregory knew that our penchant for change is what makes growth possible, specifically growth in love. The one human capacity which most approaches God's perfection is simply the ability to love. Unlike almost every other human reality, love is not diminished as it is shared. It is the one thing about us which, like God, cannot be limited:

Changing in everything for the better, let [us] exchange "Glory for glory".... For this is truly perfection: never to stop growing toward what is better and never placing any limit on perfection.[60]

For Gregory the perfection, the completeness which makes us most like God is that growth in grace for which we neither expect, nor look for, an end; the striving to love as God loves is end enough of itself.

R. A. Ratcliff

March 10
Harriet Ross Tubman (1913)
See Common of Leaders, Prophets

Abolitionist, spy, Underground Railroad conductor, nurse, war hero, and activist, Harriet Tubman was born in Maryland in 1821 as the daughter of slaves. At 13, she intervened to help a runaway slave; the injury she received as punishment caused her blackouts the rest of her life.[61]

In 1827, John Russwurm and the Reverend Mr. Samuel Cornish began to publish Freedom's Journal, the first Black newspaper in the U.S.[62] As a result, more and more slaves were taking the risk of fleeing and going North. Tubman herself escaped to Philadelphia in 1849. She found work at a hotel, and began earning money that would support her bringing slaves North. During the next ten years, she made nineteen trips and freed 300 slaves, earning her the nickname, "Moses." She helped John Brown plan the raid on Harper's Ferry in October 1859.

In 1862, she agreed to serve the Union Army, and worked as a spy, scout, and nurse. In 1863, she led a gunboat expedition along the Combahee River during which nearly 800 slaves were brought to safety. Later, she was also active in the fight for women's suffrage. The Harriet Tubman Home for Indigent and Aged Negroes was started in 1896.

As a member of the African Methodist Episcopal Zion Church, Tubman was grounded in her faith. The actions she took, she said, were revealed to her by God through divine dreams and omens.[63] When once she needed money for some elderly people, she asked the Lord where she might find help. Directed by God to a man in New York, the man told her the Lord was mistaken in directing her there. Tubman remained in that office until she left, hours later, with triple the amount she had asked for. Tubman chose to work persistently for justice. She once said, "I think there's many a slaveholder'll get to Heaven. They don't know no better. They acts up to the light they have."[64]

We can celebrate her as a woman who made it her life's business to live up to the light she had.

T. M. Eugene

March 11
Thomas Ware (1842)
See Common of Preachers

Thomas Ware was an early Methodist circuitrider. His memoirs, *Sketches in the Life and Travels of Rev. Thomas Ware* (1839), reveal a faithful soul engaged in the difficult work of a traveling preacher. They also give us unique insights into the formation of the Methodist Episcopal Church.

Ware was born in Greenwich, New Jersey on December 19, 1758. Trained as a Calvinist and although he had a strong religious bent, he did not fully appreciate the deeper aspects of religion until his entrance into the Revolutionary War as a soldier. He was convinced that the cause was just, but was fearful of defeat and possible death:

'But there is a hereafter,' was suggested to my mind. True, thought I, but I will do the best I can, and trust in God. And so it was that as a soldier in the army I was more devout than when at home; and I prayed until a confidence sprang up within me, that I should return to my home and friends in safety, or not be cut off without time to make my peace with God.

Ware's military service was cut short when he contracted "swamp fever," and was discharged. He soon joined the Methodists and was sent by Asbury to the Dover circuit in 1783.

In December of 1784, he was an observer at the Christmas Conference and the formation of the Methodist Episcopal Church, and much of what we know of that gathering comes from his fond memories fifty years after the event.

As a circuitrider, Ware's method of visitation was novel. He would get on his horse and let the beast take its own course. When he arrived at a home he would advise the people there that he had come to preach. Usually he was heard, but on occasion, was asked to leave.

His ministerial career took him to appointments in Delaware, Maryland, North Carolina, Long Island, and the Holston mountains. He served four years as book agent, but returned to the pastorate in 1816 and continued to serve in the ministry until 1825, including a time as presiding elder and missionary to Jamaica.

In his memoirs he tells the story of meeting up with a minister from another denomination, who, seeing that he was always traveling, asked if he were a missionary. Ware writes, "I replied that I was a Methodist, and we were all missionaries."[65]

J. B. Weakley

March 12
Gregory the Great (604)
See Common of Pastors and Bishops, Teachers

Gregory was pope from 590-604, and is remembered as one of the most influential administrators and pastors in the history of the western church.

Born into a wealthy and powerful Italian family c. 540, Gregory rose quickly in the Roman civil service at the time when the Empire was crumbling in Western Europe due to the barbarian invasions. He decided to turn his back on his earlier life, however, when in 575 he transformed his family estate into a monastery and devoted himself to the life of contemplation. His respite from the world was short lived, however, for in 579 the pope made Gregory his envoy to the Byzantine Emperor in Constantinople. Upon his return to Rome he himself became pope.

Gregory's great work *Pastoral Care* deals with the qualifications and duties of one who would exercise pastoral rule over God's flock. It is a fascinating window into the heart of a person who had known both the quiet of the monastery and the noisome bustle of the papal court, and whose eyes were open to the satisfactions and temptations of either place. Gregory can, for example, warn against those who would seek pastoral office for the glory and recognition it brings, while in the next breath denouncing those who have been gifted by God with great skill at preaching, teaching, and leadership, yet who retire from the world, hiding their light under a bushel.

Indeed, it is the ideas of *balance* and *accommodation* that shine throughout the work. Commenting on the different subjects of one's pastoral care, he asks

> What else are the minds of attentive hearers but . . . the taut strings of a harp, which the skillful harpist plays with a variety of strokes . . . ? Hence, too, every teacher, in order to edify all in the one virtue of charity, must touch the hearts of his hearers by using one and the same doctrine, but not by giving to all one and the same exhortation.[66]

Those for whom we would care have each their own graces, gifts, needs, and problems. Gregory, the recluse who became pope, had learned the patience of serving God in the very different circumstances of his own life. He taught us the similar patience of caring response to the differing circumstances of those to whom we are called to minister.

R. A. Ratcliff

March 16
Lucy Rider Meyer (1922)
See Common of Teachers

Rider Meyer founded the Methodist Deaconess Movement in America, and the Chicago Training School for Mission and Social Service. As a church leader, social worker, writer, and educator, she was remarkable for her numerous accomplishments and her breadth of education. Graduating from Oberlin College, Lucy Rider married Josiah Shelly Meyer in 1885. She received her M.D. in 1887 from the Woman's Medical College of Northwestern University. Her son was born the same year. She also studied at the University of Chicago Divinity School.

Rider Meyer wrote about the development of the office of deaconess from its origins in the New Testament and the early Church to its recent reemergence in Europe. She argued that the time had come for this ministry, uniquely performed by women, to be supported and recognized by the Methodist Church in America:

> And the fact that there is a strong movement in the church at the present time toward reestablishing woman in the office which she held with honor and profit at the first, is a strong illustration, not only of the true emancipation of women in the nineteenth century, but also of the full though informal recognition of her true place, and the value of her work, in the early church.[67]

Rider Meyer wanted deaconesses to receive adequate training in theology, social work, and nursing. She founded the Chicago Training School with its two year course of study to train deaconesses. These women received subsistence stipends while engaging in full-time ministry of nursing care, education, and other assistance to the urban poor. In 1888 the General Conference of the Methodist Church officially recognized deaconess work. Rider Meyer eventually became embroiled in a divisive controversy over who should govern the work of deaconesses in the church and opposed efforts to place deaconesses under the oversight of the Woman's Home Missionary Society. In spite of such struggles, she maintained her convictions concerning the importance of the work of deaconesses in the contemporary church, and her own role in preparing women for this Christian ministry. One of her students, Isabelle Horton, recalls these words of Lucy Rider Meyer: "The deaconess movement puts the mother into the church. It supplies the feminine element so greatly needed in the Protestant Church, and thus is rooted deep in the very heart of humanity's needs."[68]

J. A. Mercer

March 17
Patrick (c. 461)
See Common of Pastors and Bishops, Evangelists

Born during the final years of Roman Britain (c. 390), Patrick enjoyed an upbringing of social privilege. This ended violently. At sixteen, Patrick was seized by Irish raiders on a plundering spree along the west coast of England. He was sold and put to work as a shepherd-slave on Ireland's Atlantic coast. Here, the orphan found his God: "the Lord opened the understanding of my unbelieving heart. [He] protected me . . . and strengthened me as a father comforts his son." A two-hundred mile trek and a Gaul-bound voyage with a cargo of Irish wolfhounds completed his escape, some six years later. He returned to the ease of home and eventually became a priest. A dream commanded his return to Ireland.

Around 432, Patrick was made bishop in circumstances controversial enough to ensure that his departure from Britain was permanent. He became both evangelist and exile. Though his was not the first mission to Ireland, it was the decisive initiative. Addressing his preaching to the Irish chiefs and their families, Patrick succeeded, with their support, in organizing churches and building religious houses over much of Ulster and Connaught. With political craft and a strong sense of episcopal status, he established his see at Armagh, near the royal center of the kings of Ulster.

Patrick's missionary fervor mixes a Romano-British urge to civilize with Christian apocalypticism. The Irish are the people of "the utmost parts of the world." Their evangelization, therefore, completes Jesus' commission to take the gospel "to the end of the world," and their conversion, Patrick claims, fulfills Isaiah's vision of the Spirit's coming in "the last days." Toward the end of his life, Patrick wrote the autobiographical *Confession*. It discloses a man of small scholarship but great evangelistic passion and a moving identification with the Irish people. Such sympathy is an example for all mission. In Ireland, "the outcast" and former slave found home if not rest. Patrick ends his book by referring all achievement to God: he begs that "whosoever deigns to look at . . . this writing which Patrick, a sinner, unlearned, has composed in Ireland" shall conclude that "if I did or showed forth anything however small according to God's good pleasure . . . it was the gift of God."[69]

A. P. R. Gregory

March 18
Cyril of Jerusalem (387)
See Common of Pastors and Bishops, Teachers

Little is known about Cyril's life prior to his becoming the bishop of Jerusalem c. 349. We do know that he had been chosen by his predecessor Maximus. Included in the stories about his life is a legend that a luminous appearance in the heavens, called the "Apparition of the Cross," marked the beginning of his episcopate.

Cyril's time as bishop of Jerusalem was dominated by conflict on two fronts. On the one hand, he was in conflict with Arian theologians contending for acceptance and power within the church. This conflict led to Cyril's deposition, expulsion, and reinstatement three times, in 357, 360, and 367. On the other hand he was in conflict with the orthodox language of Nicea. He rejected as a "man-made term" its claim for the *homoousios* of Christ and God as the means for describing the relationship of human and divine in the person of Christ. Nevertheless, in order to prove his orthodoxy at the Council of Constantinople in 381, be cleared of all heresy charges and reinstated, Cyril recited the creed traditionally in use at Jerusalem which, like the Nicene Creed, contained the *homoousios*.

Cyril is remembered today by a collection of pre-baptismal catechetical lectures delivered early in his episcopacy to those who were moving through the final stages of preparation for baptism at the Easter Vigil. These lectures provide a systematic exposition of the Jerusalem creed, moving back and forth between the scriptural basis for the claims of the creed and its implications for the Christian's post-baptismal life. The following statement from the first lecture provides a window into Cyril's understanding of the cooperative nature of the Christian life:

> While it rests with [God] to plant and water, it is your part to bring forth fruit. It rests with God to bestow grace, but with you to accept and cherish it. Do not despise the grace because it is freely given, but rather cherish it with reverence once you have received it.[70]

E. B. Anderson

March 19
Joseph, Mary's Husband
See Common of Saints

Joseph is revered as the faithful husband of Mary and caring stepfather of Jesus. In the Gospels he appears mostly in the birth narratives in Matthew and Luke. Matthew traces the lineage of Joseph back to David. He probably owned property in Bethlehem, so he and Mary went there for the census.

Betrothal in biblical times was more binding than present day engagement practices. The fact of Mary's pregnancy was viewed as the equivalent of adultery. Joseph was distressed by this, but did not wish to disgrace Mary. He thought to handle it quietly by ending the betrothal but was reassured in a dream that Mary indeed had conceived by the Holy Spirit. Further dreams directed him to protect his family's welfare by fleeing from Herod and later returning to Galilee to avoid Herod's successor.

Some apocryphal stories refer to Joseph as being an old man when he became betrothed to Mary, a tradition probably connected with claims of Mary's perpetual virginity. If Joseph were a widower marrying again in later life, those referred to as brothers and sisters of Jesus might be from Joseph's first marriage.

Another tradition is told that Mary was consecrated to the temple with other virgins until marrying age. As was the custom, young men would offer the gift of a branch on the altar. It was said that Joseph's branch burst into bloom and a dove from heaven perched on it as a confirmation to Mary that she indeed was to marry.

The story of Jesus talking with the temple elders (Lk 2:41f) shows Joseph's respect for the tradition of keeping the Passover and his concern for his son. Joseph, as a craftsman or carpenter, shared his trade with Jesus who is also identified as a carpenter (Mk 6:3). Since there is little other mention of Joseph in the New Testament, and as Jesus arranges for the care of his mother at his crucifixion, Joseph may have died before the ministry of Jesus.

Joseph is often depicted holding a lily and a staff. When remembering him, we can think of his caring and loving parenting, his integrity as a husband, and his courage to follow visions.

S. Webb Phillips

March 22
Jonathan Edwards (1758)
See Common of Preachers, Teachers

Unfairly known by many solely for his famous sermon, "Sinners in the Hands of an Angry God," Jonathan Edwards was a preacher, philosopher-teacher, and perhaps the most truly original American theological mind. Born in East Windsor, Connecticut in 1703, he was swept into the first Great Awakening in New England in the 1730's, reflecting deeply out of his Calvinist heritage on the matter of conversion and the Christian life in his remarkable *Treatise on the Religious Affections* (1746).

Edwards was "Valley-born and Valley-bred, a product of that wild frontier where massacre was a constant threat," and educated at newly founded Yale. He assumed leadership of the Presbyterian parish of Northampton, Massachusetts when his grandfather and the church's pastor, Solomon Stoddard, died in 1729. His preaching on justification by faith and the 1737 publication of *A Faithful Narrative of the Surprising Work of God* added fuel to the revival fire being stirred up by George Whitefield. Edwards was dismissed from his pastorate in 1750 when, in an attempt to revive the parish by raising the standards for admission to Communion, the congregation rebelled and voted him out. For the next six years he was pastor of a Native-American mission in Stockbridge. He was appointed president of Princeton University, but died shortly into his tenure.

Throughout his ministry the depth of his insistence on the sovereignty of God and the beauty of Christ brought many to repentance and others to disputation. His writings reveal a vigorous embrace of human history, filled with ambiguities, but an even more profound grasp of the abiding sovereignty of God in whose gracious yet judging hands the world rests. "It is certain with me," he observed, "that the world exists anew every moment," but that we, "every moment see the same proof of a God as we should have seen if we had seen God create the world at first."[71]

We recall this day how, through a tangled and difficult ministry, Jonathan Edwards, the soul of New England soil, still centuries later, urges us toward the beauty of God in all things.

D. E. Saliers

March 23
Martin and Henry Boehm (1812 and 1875)
See Common of Pastors and Bishops

Martin Boehm, born in a German Mennonite home in 1725, was chosen by lot in 1756 to be a preacher. However, as his son Henry reports:

> For some time he preached without a knowledge of sins forgiven; but in 1761 he found redemption in the blood of the Lamb, and then he became a flame of fire, and preached with the Holy Ghost sent down from heaven. His success was wonderful and the seals to his ministry were numerous.

The following year he was chosen a Mennonite bishop, again by lot. Influenced by George Whitefield, he joined with other evangelical ministers in "great meetings." One of these was held in 1767 at Isaac Long's barn in Lancaster County, Pennsylvania. On Pentecost Sunday, Boehm preached there to an overflow crowd, among whom was a Reformed pastor, Philip William Otterbein, who rushed forward and embraced Boehm, exclaiming: "Wir sind Brüder" (we are brethren).

Otterbein and Boehm began to work together in ministering with the German-speaking peoples of Pennsylvania and Maryland. When Boehm was excommunicated from the Mennonites for (among other things) "associations with outsiders," he turned his farm over to his son and began preaching full-time. In 1789, he met with others at Otterbein's parsonage in Baltimore to plan their ongoing work and in 1800 the Church of the United Brethren in Christ was established with Otterbein and Boehm (then 75) elected the first bishops. Boehm was also a part of the Methodist class which met at his home and he also joined the Methodist Episcopal Church. He died on this date in 1812. Asbury, who arrived a few days later, preached a memorial sermon for his deceased friend.

Martin's son Henry began to itinerate as a preacher of the Methodist Episcopal Church at the age of 25 and was a traveling companion of Asbury. At Asbury's request he oversaw the translation of the 1805 Discipline into German and was later appointed presiding elder and held pastorates in Pennsylvania and New Jersey. A living link with the birth of both American Methodism and the United Brethren, Henry preached at the age of one hundred that,

> I rejoice that the enjoyment of the favor of God, the love of God, is something that does not get old. It is ever new, it is ever precious . . . may thy name, O Lord, be glorified here in the salvation of hundreds of precious souls. Amen.[72]

D. W. Vogel

March 24
Ida Bell Wells-Barnett (1931)
See Common of Prophets

Wells-Barnett was an active participant in the various movements for social changes of her day. Her greatest contributions were her untiring work in the anti-lynching movement and her vocation as a journalist and social justice advocate. She negotiated societal conventions surrounding domesticity and took time away from the sociopolitical world to raise her children, returning to her work as quickly as time and circumstance allowed.

Wells created a standard for herself, her people, and United States society. She forged a deep and abiding spirituality rooted in the Black Church of the South. She had a strong sense of Christian duty that came from a God who offers salvation illustrated by her words to twelve Black men jailed unjustly in Elaine, Arkansas:

> I have been listening to you for nearly two hours. You have talked and sung and prayed about dying, and forgiving your enemies, and of feeling sure that you are going to be received in the New Jerusalem because your God knows that you are innocent of the offense for which you expect to be electrocuted. But why don't you pray to live and ask to be freed? The God you serve is the God of Paul and Silas who opened their prison gates, and if you have all the faith you say you have, you ought to believe that he will open your prison doors too.[73]

Wells-Barnett never slowed her pace. Only a year before her death on March 25, 1931, she was a candidate for the state senate. In March of that year, she recorded in her diary that she spent time "reviewing [her] campaign and urging women voters to do their Christian duty and vote for race women on Primary Day April 8th." Wells yoked Christian duty and womanhood with justice, moral agency, and vocation. True womanhood meant virtue and right action both in the private and public realms. Wells did not believe that woman's moral influence had any limits. A woman must never content herself with her own salvation. She was responsible for her race as well. Her obituary in the *Chicago Defender* captured her essence, ". . . elegant, striking, and always well groomed, . . . regal though somewhat intolerant and impulsive."

E. M. Townes

The Annunciation

From earliest times in the Christian witness Mary has occupied a special place of honor as the bearer of the Incarnate One. In the mystery of God's way with us she becomes what millions of Christians call *theotokos*, "Mother of God." On this day we join that company to call to mind her obedience and consent to the divine self-communication. We are invited, by meditating upon the Lukan account (1:26-38), to ponder her whole-hearted, wonder-filled, act of vulnerability to God. Mary herself, in the face of the angel's words, realized she could not understand. Neither can we pretend to do so.

Under the figure of an angel's "evangel," the Holy Spirit of God overshadows this Jewish girl, and human history is turned about. Her active receptivity to the seed of God's Word participates in that Word's becoming flesh. The moment of acknowledging herself to be the chosen one of a chosen people was a fresh conception of God. Thus we celebrate a day in which the Word who is Son of Mary empowers Mary the virgin to be a mother to the Word. We rightly honor both Mother and Son, both the Lady of Sorrows, Wisdom, and Joy, and the Christ whom she was to bear. Mary's tremulous question, "How can these things be?" we ask now in this time and place.

Although keeping this feast on this day accords with Anglican, Roman, and Eastern practice, some United Methodists may wish to celebrate the Annunciation on December 18 — the date for it set by the ancient Spanish (Mozarabic) calendar. This has the advantage of keeping it out of Lent and placing it nearer the celebration of Christmas, a practice implied by its placement in *The United Methodist Book of Worship*.

D. E. Saliers

Isaiah 7:10-14
Psalm 45 or Psalm 40 (*UMH* 774)
Hebrews 10:4-10
Luke 1:26-38

Almighty God, who sent the angel Gabriel to the virgin Mary and through her obedience and faith brought forth your Son: Grant that we too may remain receptive to your visitation and believe the word you speak to us, through Jesus Christ our Lord, who lives and reigns with you and the Holy Spirit, one God, now and forever. Amen.

[DTB]

God of vision and dream,
  our world and experience are not porous to your strange stirrings.
By your Holy Spirit, make our hearts and minds penetrable like Mary's,
  and conceive Christ in our imaginations, hopes and habits. Amen.

[DTB]

See *The United Methodist Book of Worship,* 256.

March 26
Richard Allen (1831)
See Common of Pastors and Bishops, Leaders

Founding bishop of the African Methodist Episcopal Church, Allen was born in 1760 in Philadelphia, the slave of a Quaker master. Allen later passed into the hands of a Methodist farmer and converted to Methodism when seventeen: "All of a sudden my dungeon shook, my chains flew off and, glory to God, I cried . . . enough for me — the Savior died!" he later remembered.[74] He purchased his freedom and began to travel as a lay preacher, returning to Philadelphia in 1786 where he joined St. George's Methodist Church's growing black membership. When racism reared its ugly head, he sought to establish a black Methodist congregation that would be free of the discrimination experienced in St. George's.

Allen was convinced that Methodism best suited the religious needs of African Americans. The theme of hope sounds from the very first lines in his *Collection of Hymns and Spiritual Songs*, published in 1801 for the growing family of black Methodist congregations: "The voice of Free Grace cries escape to the mountain, for Adam's lost race Christ hath open'd a fountain."[75]

Bethel Church was dedicated in 1794, but Allen was not ordained by Bishop Asbury until 1799 and then only as a special local deacon, with no conference ties. Allen eventually led African Methodists into a separate denomination in 1816 after many years of struggle against white control and the failure to ordain black preachers.

In addition to serving as bishop, Allen took an active part in promoting the welfare of blacks in Philadelphia. He worked as a shoemaker, teamster, and labor contractor, opened his home to fugitive slaves, and assisted fellow citizens during a yellow fever epidemic. He opposed the colonization movement which proposed to send free blacks back to Africa and hosted the first national convention of black religious and political leaders in Bethel Church in 1830. He died in Philadelphia on this date in 1831 in Philadelphia and is buried in the undercroft of Mother Bethel A.M.E. Church.[76]

K. E. Rowe

Charles Wesley

Born in 1707, Charles was the youngest son of Samuel and Susanna Wesley. Together with John his brother and George Whitefield he formed the Oxford Holy Club, with its emphasis on Bible study, sacramental spirituality, and social outreach. Ordained into the priesthood, he joined John in a missionary journey to Georgia. There he prepared the first hymnal published in America, the *Charleston Hymnal of 1737*. Unhappy, however, he soon left that work and made his way back to England. Influenced by the Moravians, he continued to struggle with his inner spirituality. He received the assurance of salvation he was seeking on Pentecost Sunday, May 21, 1738, though he writes in his journal, "I knew not how or when." Two days later he began to write a hymn. Three days later his brother John had his Aldersgate experience.

As the movement developed, Charles traveled, preached, pastored, and — most important for the whole church — wrote. He was already an able poet, but his newfound spiritual conviction provided the motivation for the outpouring of over six thousand hymn texts using at least forty-five different poetic meters. His texts are so filled with scriptural allusions that scholars are still identifying them.

He married in 1749, settled in Bristol in 1756 and ministered there until 1771 when he and his family moved to London. His covenant with his wife, his family, and the churches he pastored were important to him. In this, he is a more adequate model than his brother. He remained a faithful priest of the Church of England until his death in 1788.

The influence of his hymn texts on the people called Methodists as well as the wider church is extensive. He helps us celebrate the church year: "Come thou long expected Jesus," "Hark the herald angels sing," "Christ whose glory fills the sky," "O Love Divine, what hast thou done?", "Christ the Lord is risen today," "Hail the day that sees him rise," and "See how great a flame aspires." Our spirituality is molded by phrases from Charles' hymns: "O for a thousand tongues to sing," "Jesus, lover of my soul," "Love divine, all loves excelling," and "A charge to keep I have." He placed his artistic genius in the service of God:

> If well I know the tuneful art
> To captivate a human heart,
>   The glory, Lord, be thine.
> A servant of thy blessed will
> I here devote my utmost skill
>   To sound the praise divine.
> (*Redemption Hymns,* 1747)

D. W. Vogel

Genesis 32:22-32
Psalm 96 (*UMH* 815)
Colossians 3:12-17
Matthew 26:26-30

Almighty and passionate God, the source of all seers and poets who give expression to the deep mystery of faith, you inspired Charles Wesley to pour out his love for you in his vocation as poet, pastor, and preacher: Grant, that continually encouraged by his hymns and example, we too may rise up to be faithful followers of Jesus Christ our Lord, who lives and reigns with you and the Holy Spirit, one God, now and forever. Amen.

[DTB and CFG]

Anointing Spirit whose grace is ever fresh in the songs and hymns of the church, pour out your dreams and visions upon us in worship and devotion that we may do justice and act with compassion for the poor and oppressed through Christ, our Lord. Amen.

[DTB]

March 31
John Donne (1631)
See Common of Musicians, Saints

Donne was born into a wealthy Roman Catholic family in Protestant England in 1572. The imprisonment and death of his younger brother drove John to investigate the debates which rent the Church: "Show me, dear Christ, thy spouse, so bright and clear" was his earnest prayer.[77] Eventually accepting Anglicanism, Donne embarked on a promising career in government service. After an illegal marriage with Ann More (the niece of Lord Ellesmere) brought his political career to a standstill, Donne strove to gain new patrons, dedicating religious and commemorative poetry to nobles and religious tracts to the king, who several times urged him to accept ordination. Donne wrestled with his vocation for forty-two years before finally abandoning secular in favor of ecclesiastical ambition. His ordination in 1615 was a coming home: "I date my life from my Ministry; for I received mercy, as I received the Ministry."[78]

During his time as Dean of St. Paul's Cathedral in London, Donne wrote his *Sermons*, several *Divine Poems*, and, towards the end of his life, the *Devotions*. He brought the passion of his youth into his relationship with God and God's Church. His mastery of poetic metaphor brings life to his sermons as he explores the believer's relationship to Christ as one of profoundest love and kindness: "All the Virgins shall see my uncleanness, and all the martyrs see my tergiversations, and all the Confessors shall see my double-dealings, . . . and say to one another, 'Will this Lamb have anything to do with this soul?' And yet there and then this Lamb will marry me, and marry me . . . forever."[79] Donne sought to ravish rather than simply persuade his congregation.

Donne reflected upon his life of wandering and searching through the lens of God's love, a love which would not desert him in death: "Enable me by thy grace to look forward to mine end, and to look backward too, to the considerations of thy mercies afforded me from the beginning." Donne encourages those whose lives are marked by searching and yearning, seeking, yet not easily finding, to consider God's favor and love at work in the journey as well as at its destination. Donne defends the sanctity of creation, human love, and of each individual human life: his conviction that "every man's death diminishes me"[80] speaks powerfully to a generation in which issues of life, death, and violence figure so prominently.

D. A. deSilva

March 31
Francis Asbury (1816)
See Common of Pastors and Bishops

Founding bishop of the Methodist Episcopal Church in the U.S., Asbury was born at Hamstead, England, the only surviving child of Elizabeth and Joseph Asbury, a farmer. The family moved to Great Barr where young Asbury received his education and was apprenticed to a blacksmith. As a young man he gave up attending his parish church for another whose Rector was an evangelical. In addition he sometimes walked three miles to a Methodist Chapel where he heard Methodist leaders, including John Wesley, preach.

At sixteen Asbury experienced conversion. At eighteen he began to lead Methodist meetings and to preach. At twenty-one he gave up his job and became one of John Wesley's traveling preachers. At twenty-six he volunteered to go to North America and wrote in his journal: "Whither am I going? To the New World. What to do? To gain honour? No, if I know my own heart. To get money? No. I am going to live to God, and to bring others to do so."[81]

For the next forty-five years he lived to God and brought many others to do so in his adopted country. Alone among the British preachers Asbury remained in the colonies during the Revolutionary War, but was forced into hiding in Delaware because of colonial draft laws. After the war in 1784 he helped organize the Methodist Episcopal Church in Baltimore. Elected and ordained deacon, elder, and bishop at the Christmas Conference, he began ordaining other preachers for the new church. In the years that followed he led the preachers in a superb strategy of missionary expansion up and down the thirteen original colonies and out to the mountains and beyond. He summed up the Methodist message in a journal entry for September 27, 1807: "We live by faith in a prayer-hearing, soul-converting, soul-sanctifying, soul-restoring, soul-comforting God."

Asbury died March 31, 1816 at age seventy-one in Virginia and is buried in Mount Olivet Cemetery in Baltimore. He was the primitive bishop, an itinerant monk, and a holy man. He travelled until he died; he preached and prayed with the people until they could barely hear his voice; he spent himself in a way demanded of no one else. At the end he was the very spirit of Methodism.

K. E. Rowe

April 4 (*alt. date January 15*)
Martin Luther King, Jr. (1968)
See Common of Martyrs, Leaders, Prophets

Martin Luther King, Jr., "a drum major for the Lord," was the spiritual leader of the modern Civil Rights movement who championed nonviolent resistance in the struggle to end racial segregation, intolerance, poverty, and violence in mid-twentieth century America.

Born January 15, 1929, in Atlanta, Georgia, King graduated from high school at age 16, received a B.A. from Morehouse College, attended Crozer Theological Seminary, and earned a Ph.D. from Boston University. In 1954, he accepted an offer to pastor Dexter Avenue Baptist Church in Montgomery Alabama, where despite threats to his life and the bombing of his home, he led the famous bus boycott against segregation. King was soon after elected president of the Southern Christian Leadership Council which spearheaded massive nonviolent protest marches against segregation in the South.

In August 1963 King delivered his famous "I Have a Dream" speech before over 250,000 marchers gathered at the Lincoln Memorial in Washington, D. C. His "dream" of an America where justice and racial harmony prevail captured the imagination of the nation. King's ideals were rooted in faith.

Jesus . . . said, 'Love your enemies.' We should be happy he did not say, "Like your enemies" . . . "Like" is a sentimental and affectionate word. How can we be affectionate toward a person whose avowed aim is to crush our very being and place innumerable stumbling blocks in our path? How can we like a persons who is threatening our children and bombing our homes? It is impossible. But Jesus recognized that *love* is greater than *like*. When Jesus bids us to love our enemies, he is speaking neither of *eros* or *filia*; he is speaking of *agape*, understanding and creative, redemptive goodwill for all.[82]

After being awarded the Nobel Peace Prize in 1964, King launched a drive to secure voting rights for African Americans in the South. In 1966 he went North to challenge segregated housing and job discrimination. In his final campaign in 1968, he helped organize The Poor Peoples Campaign against poverty. King was killed on this date in 1968 by a sniper in Memphis, Tennessee, where he had gone to help the organizers of a sanitation workers strike.

A. M. Israel

April 5
George Miller, John Walter, and John Dreisbach
(1816, 1819, and 1871)
See Common of Pastors and Bishops, Saints

George Miller (1774-1816) and John Walter (1781-1819) were coworkers with Jacob Albright in founding the *Evangelische Gemeinschaft* (Evangelical Association) in Pennsylvania. Walter was converted through Albright's preaching and became his first assistant in 1802. He published the first hymnbook of the denomination in 1810 with fifty-six hymns including a number he had written. Tuberculosis forced him to stop itinerating in 1813, and he died at his home five years later.

It was also in 1802 that Albright asked for a night's lodging and was invited to preach in the Miller home. Later, while at work in his own mill, George Miller made a complete surrender to God and began to preach under the direction of Albright and Walter. He was ordained elder at the first conference of the emerging church in 1807, but ill health kept him from accepting any definite appointment after 1809. At the urging of his church, he wrote the original draft of seventy-five pages for the first Discipline of the church, as well as a book of rules for conference business, and a biography of Jacob Albright. He died on this day in 1816.

John Dreisbach (1789-1871) was a charter member of the class established in November, 1806 by Jacob Albright and his coworkers. His license to preach, granted in 1807, bears Albright's signature. A probationer only 18 years old, he was left alone on his first field by Albright's death and the illness of his senior colleague, George Miller. He was elected the first presiding elder in 1814 and presided over most conference sessions of Albright's followers until his health broke in 1821. He dedicated the first church building and established the first printing concern of the Evangelical Association.

On April 17, 1816 (soon after the death of George Miller and the day before setting the tombstone for his deceased wife's grave), John Dreisbach wrote in his journal:

> O Lord, give my soul grace for renewed, sincere and true fruitfulness in thy service, so that at the close of my day I may have a portion with those already triumphant, who now are beholding and praising their Redeemer, exalted far beyond all earth's trials and sufferings.[83]

D. W. Vogel

April 9
William Law (1761)
See Common of Teachers

Born in 1686 in Northamptonshire, Law was elected a fellow of Emmanuel College, Cambridge in 1711, ordained shortly after, and appeared to have a bright future in the Church. This changed, however, when he refused to take an oath of allegiance to King George I in 1714. Becoming a Non-Juror cost him the position at Cambridge and stalled his ecclesiastical career. By 1727 he was tutoring Edward Gibbon (the father of the author of *The Rise and Fall of the Roman Empire*) and living in the Gibbon home. From 1740 he lived at his birthplace from where he supervised schools and homes for the poor and followed a strict rule of prayer and service.

Denied ecclesiastical advancement, Law turned to devotional writing. *A Practical Treatise upon Christian Perfection* (1726) addressed the common misconception that perfection required a monastic lifestyle. Stressing the inner disposition of the Christian, he held that the pursuit of perfection required the formation of religious societies for fellowship, exhortation, and spiritual examination.

His more well known book, *A Serious Call to a Devout and Holy Life* (1728), is a call to live the Christian life in its fullness: "Who is . . . humble, or meek, or devout, or just, or faithful? Is it . . . [one] who has several times done acts of humility, meekness, devotion, justice, or fidelity? No. It is. . .[one] who lives in the habitual exercise of these virtues.[84]

This call for holy living for ordinary Christians had a profound influence upon the young John Wesley and George Whitefield and so helped spark the great revivals of the eighteenth century in both England and America. Wesley himself writes of Law's books that, "These convinced me more than ever of the absolute impossibility of being *half a Christian*, and I determined, through his grace (the absolute necessity of which I was deeply sensible of) to be *all-devoted* to God: to give him *all* my soul, my body and my substance."[85]

A mystic in an age when rationalism was highly prized, Law's work continues to influence those seeking to understand the relationship between Christian doctrine and Christian living.

G. L. Hayes

April 9
Dietrich Bonhoeffer (1945)
See Common of Martyrs

A martyr of the Confessing Church of Germany, Bonhoeffer's father was a successful university professor in psychiatry and his mother a teacher. Dietrich had seven siblings, among them a twin sister. He was drawn first to theology as an academic discipline, studying at Berlin University with the famous historian, Adolf von Harnack, and influenced by the writings of Karl Barth. After stunning dissertations, he was accepted as a lecturer in theology at the University of Berlin at only 24. He spent a year at New York's Union Theological Seminary, where the advocates of the "social gospel" made a lasting impression. Not long after his return to Germany, he had a "great liberation" of discovering Bible and prayer "for the first time."[86] From then on, the theologian lived and wrote as a committed member of the Church, as evidenced by writings on the Christian life, notably, *The Cost of Discipleship*.

Bonhoeffer helped organize Christian resistance to the Nazi programs of anti-Semitism and the takeover of the German churches. Through radio addresses, sermons, ecumenical involvement, and the founding of an alternative seminary at Finkenwalde, Bonhoeffer was instrumental in the formation of the small but vigorous "Confessing Church." He sought restoration of a true, witnessing community rooted in a "life together" with Christ as its center. He wrote of such a fellowship, "let [one] who cannot be alone beware of community," and "let [one] who is not in community beware of being alone."[87] Although the planned book remained unfinished, he also wrote on a new ethic for a "world come of age."

After the Nazis closed Finkenwalde and all but snuffed out the Confessing Church, Bonhoeffer became convinced that strong measures were required. He joined plans to kill Hitler. After months of preparation, Bonhoeffer was arrested with other conspirators, including his older brother. From a military prison, he wrote the famous *Letters and Papers from Prison* which foresaw the need for a "religionless Christianity." After the failure of the *coup* in 1944, he knew his fate was sealed. Some months before his death at the hands of the Nazis, he prayed:

> Wondrous the works which thou has done by me,
> changing my cup from gall to sweet delight.
>
> Grant me to witness through the veil of death
> my people at their high triumphant feast.
>
> I fail, and sink in thine eternity,
> but see my people marching forward, free.[88]

L. A. Goleman

April 11
Garfield Bromley Oxnam (1963)
See Common of Pastors and Bishops

Garfield Bromley Oxnam was born on August 14, 1891 in Sonora, California. He was the second of four surviving children of Thomas Henry Oxnam and Mary Ann "Mamie" (Jobe) Oxnam, both Methodists. His father was a native of Cornwall, England, a miner who worked in England, Scotland, and South Africa before immigrating to the United States. Though he would not live to see it come true, Oxnam's father dreamed his son would preach in Wesley Chapel and become a bishop in the church.

After studying both business and liberal arts, Oxnam received a degree in Sacred Theology from Boston University in 1915 and was ordained in the Methodist Episcopal Church in 1916. The eleven years he spent as a local church pastor were marked by a passion for the social gospel and an emphasis on numerous programs to serve the needs of the community. Oxnam then served one year as a professor at Boston University and eight years as the president of DePauw University where he made many lasting, positive contributions. He and his wife, Ruth endeared themselves to the students. In contrast and unfortunately, Oxnam's authoritarian leadership style alienated him from most of the faculty members.

In 1936 at the age of 44, Oxnam became the youngest bishop of the Methodist Episcopal Church. He served in the episcopacy for twenty four years in the Omaha, Boston, New York and Washington, D.C. areas. He worked closely with district superintendents and went to painstaking lengths to visit each pastor and church in his jurisdiction. He published innumerable articles and books and delivered thousands of speeches around the world. Perhaps most notably, he became known as one of the foremost leaders in the Federal, National, and World Councils of Churches. He made many significant contributions, especially with regards to organizational and financial matters. He worked closely with other Protestant leaders and engaged in lively conversations with Catholic and Jewish leaders as well.

Oxnam spoke of a vision of God's people uniting together to bring about peace and justice around the world. He often prayed, "Grant us the wisdom to discover the concrete means whereby the ethical ideals of religion may be translated into the realities of world law and order, economic justice, and racial brotherhood."[89]

Oxnam retired in 1960, struggling with Parkinson's disease. He died in White Plains, New York in 1963.

J. C. McGhee

April 18
Francis Burns (1863)
See Common of Pastors and Bishops

Burns was the first African American to serve as bishop in the Methodist Episcopal (M.E.) Church. The adversities that he overcame, including the racism of nineteenth century America, make this distinction even more remarkable.

When he was only four, his impoverished parents were forced to give the small boy to a New York farmer. He attended public schools, but most of his youth carried the status of indentured servant. His teen-age conversion and membership in the M.E. Church led to a calling to preach, but he was bound to his master until the age of 21. His intelligence, character, and integrity of faith were evident as he waited for liberty and prepared for the ministry. Two years after he received his freedom, he sailed to Liberia as a missionary teacher. A year later, still suffering from malaria, he was admitted into the Liberian Methodist clergy and appointed to supervise the church and seminary in the capital city of Monrovia. In the 20 years that followed, he served as presiding elder of the Conference, editor of both Africa's Luminary and the Conference Journal, Conference secretary, and seminary professor.

Burns' life in Liberia was punctuated by hardship. He was dogged by illness, suffered from petty persecutions by local Methodist leaders, and his beloved Liberian missionary effort was neglected by its American benefactor, the M.E. Church, threatening its collapse. Reflecting on the crises in Liberia, Burns revealed his profound spirituality:

> I cannot help looking up to the 'Father of Lights' for wisdom in such an emergency. . . . With a firm reliance on Him who saveth not by many or few, I believe we are, after all, perfectly safe. This reliance I hope we shall not forget.[90]

In 1856, the M.E. General Conference voted to provide a bishop for the struggling Liberian effort with the unspoken condition that Francis Burns would fill the role. Burns' episcopacy stabilized the church there. In a sweet and holy irony, he served the first Holy Communion in many former strongholds of Liberian slave traders. Francis Burns led as he lived — with the quiet courage of Christ. As Methodism's first African American bishop, he opened new routes for the Gospel, not only in Liberia, but the United States as well.

T. Gildemeister

April 19
Philip Melanchthon (1560)
See Common of Teachers

Melanchthon was born on February 16, 1497 in Bretten, Germany to Georg Schwartzert and his wife, Barbara Reuter, who was the niece of Johann Reuchlin (1455-1522) the German humanist. His famous uncle early recognized his gifts and while Philip was in preparatory school changed his surname (which means "black earth") to Melanchthon, its Greek equivalent. Studies at Heidelberg and Tübingen universities earned Melanchthon B.A. and M.A. degrees, respectively. The latter was granted when he was seventeen and lecturing on Aristotle. In 1518 Melanchthon joined Wittenberg University as a professor of Greek. A dedicated humanist and admirer of Erasmus, under Luther's influence he became committed to the theology and cause of the Reformation.

Strongly advocating biblical authority, he also regarded Paul's epistle to the Romans as the key to the New Testament. His major works were the *Loci communes* (commonplaces) (1521), the *Augsburg Confession* (1530), and *The Apology of the Augsburg Confession* (1531). Melanchthon was the leading Lutheran theologian at the Diet of Augsburg, where on June 25, 1530 the confession he authored was read to Emperor Charles V and the German princes.

Melanchthon became known as "the Preceptor of Germany." As many as five hundred students often attended his lectures in theology.[91] Advocating educational reform he helped to found or reorganize twelve of Germany's best universities. In 1520 Melanchthon married Katharine Krapp, a faithful and supportive wife and mother to their four children.

Although he was Luther's hand-picked successor, Melanchthon's life was often difficult. Some Lutheran theologians accused him of being too desirous of reunion with Rome and of blurring the Lutheran and Calvinist sacramental differences. He lamented "the rage of the theologians." Still, he enunciated Luther's *sola gratia* doctrine. He wrote,

Faith is believing that all the words of God, including the promise of grace, are true; it is a heartfelt trust in the Son of God. It is light and trust which God produces in us, to bring comfort, life, and joy in God. Through this faith our hearts conclude that our sins are forgiven and that we are pleasing to God *for the sake of Christ*, who gives us his merit and clothes us with his righteousness.[92]

K. J. Stein

April 21
Anselm (1109)
See Common of Pastors and Bishops, Teachers

Anselm, archbishop of Canterbury and theologian, once prayed, "Always, Lord, let me go on with humility to better things and never grow slack."[93] An answered prayer, it appears, for Anselm was a saint of prodigious energy: administrative, political, and theological. In 1063, Anselm, only four years a monk, was appointed prior of the new abbey at Bec in Normandy. He was elected abbot in 1078. His administrative duties included occasional visits to England where the abbey had land and where Lanfranc, abbot of Bec when Anselm first arrived, was now archbishop of Canterbury. On Lanfranc's death, England's second Norman king, William Rufus, kept the see vacant in order to appropriate its revenues. Severe illness, however, had Rufus fearing the displeasure of God and, in 1093, he nominated Anselm as archbishop. So began a taxing political career. Jealous of their power and eager for money, Rufus and his successor, Henry I, pressured the Church. Anselm's resistance cost him arduous journeys to Rome and two extended periods of exile. Reconciliation with Henry in 1107 allowed a final return to Canterbury. During his last two years, Anselm worked to enforce clerical celibacy and struggled to maintain the primacy of Canterbury over the see of York.

Anselm's theological writings include treatises on free will, the existence and attributes of God, the incarnation and atonement, evil, and logic. He also wrote a superbly crafted series of prayers and meditations. Anselm urged that the labor of reason is a necessary labor of faith. Intellectual reflection — careful, critical, demanding — is part of what we owe to God. Critical examination, however, is not freewheeling skepticism. Reasoning arises from believing: "I do not seek to understand so that I may believe, but I believe so that I may understand."[94] "Faith seeking understanding," attempts to grasp, as much as a finite mind can, the logic of what we affirm about God and God's ways with us.

To understand the claim that God's ways are "reasonable" we must also remember Anselm's emphasis upon beauty. For him, human sin violates "the order and beauty of the universe."[95] In *Cur Deus Homo*, therefore, he argues that the incarnation and crucifixion is the most beauteous response to sin. God acts here in the only way consonant with the beauty of the created order. To "understand" the atonement is to recognize that this redemption is "fitting."

A. P. R. Gregory

April 24
Samuel Wesley (1735)
See Common of Saints, Pastors and Bishops

Samuel Wesley, the father of John and Charles Wesley, was rector of the parish of Epworth. Although his father was a nonconformist minister, Samuel returned to the Church of England and, after graduating from Exeter College, Oxford, was ordained a priest in 1689. He married Susanna Annesley while a curate in a London parish. With high church leanings, Samuel celebrated a monthly rather than quarterly Eucharist, urged the public rather than the private baptism of children, and encouraged the use of contemporary hymns rather than the "Old Version" Psalter. He achieved some fame for his prose and poetic writings, including a major work on the book of Job. He died on April 25, 1732.

Samuel's years at Epworth were frustrating and difficult. After preaching there in 1742 while standing upon his father's tombstone, John Wesley wrote in his journal, "Nearly forty years did my father labour here; but he saw little fruit of his labour. . . . But now the fruit appeared." He later wrote, "If those in Paradise know what passes on earth, I doubt not by my father is rejoicing and praising God; who has, in his own manner and time, accomplished what he had so often attempted in vain."[96]

After John Wesley's rescue from the parsonage fire in 1709, Samuel reportedly cried out, "Let us give thanks to God! He has given me all my eight children: Let the house go; I am rich enough." The day after the fire, he discovered in the garden a leaf from his Polyglot Bible on which he read the Latin text of the verse, "Go, sell all that thou hast; and take up thy cross, and follow me."[97] He also found a partially burned manuscript of the hymn, "Behold the Savior of Mankind," a meditation on the suffering of Christ which he had recently written. Two of the original six stanzas constitute a prayer:

> Though far unequal our low praise
>   To thy vast sufferings prove,
> O Lamb of God, thus all our days,
>   Thus will we grieve and love.
>
> Thy loss our ruin did repair;
>   Death by thy death is slain;
> Thou wilt at length exalt us where
>   Thou dost in glory reign.[98]

B. W. Coe

Mark

The unnamed writer of the second gospel is traditionally associated with the John Mark mentioned in Acts as a missionary companion of Paul and Barnabas (Mark's cousin) and with the Mark that appears in 1 Peter 5:13. Papias, a second century bishop, says that Mark was the "interpreter" of Peter's teaching of Jesus. This tradition, along with Mark's dependence on Peter, has been both defended and denied, depending on critical evaluation of the Papias tradition and on evidence internal to the gospel itself. Mark is the earliest of the four gospels and thus our Evangelist was the first to fashion the gospel genre as we know it. Although Eusebius says he went to Alexandria, we do not have reliable information about where or when he died. His supposed remains were translated to Venice in the ninth century of which city he became the patron saint. The Evangelist is usually pictured as the winged lion of Ezekiel, recalling the majesty of Jesus, the Lion of Judah.

The breathless story Mark tells reveals the mighty works of Jesus and the mystery that his proclamation of God's Kingdom sometimes bears fruit and other times does not (4:10-12). His disciples, although hapless and thickheaded, must serve and suffer with him (8:31-38; 9:30-37; 10:32-45). But Jesus' march toward death in Jerusalem is really God's hidden way toward victory: human authority is destroyed (11:27-33; 12:24-27; 14:60-62), the temple loses its power to save (15:38), and Jesus, a convicted criminal, is authenticated as God's own Son (15:39). As Son of Man he will rise again (8:31; 9:9, 31; 10:34). In Mark's startling climax at 16:7, a young man in white speaks from the empty tomb to the three women who had come to anoint Jesus' body: "But go, tell his disciples and Peter that he is going ahead of you to Galilee: there you will see him, just as he told you." It is this word of promise that extends God's mercy to the disciples who have misunderstood, betrayed, denied, and deserted Jesus and undoubtedly sustained the embattled community for which Mark writes. But the response to this message is far from the excited triumph related in the other gospels; the women fled the tomb, "for terror and amazement had seized them, and they said nothing to anyone, for they were afraid."

I. W. Batdorf

Isaiah 52:7-10
Psalm 2 (*UMH* 739)
Ephesians 4:7—8, 11-16
Mark 1:1-15

Holy God, who inspired your servant Mark to set down in his gospel the saving work of Jesus of Nazareth, we pray that you will always give your Church faithful interpreters of the good news of Jesus Christ, the Son of God, who lives and reigns with you and the Holy Spirit, one God, now and forever. Amen.

[CFG]

Son of God, Lord Jesus Christ, once for all crucified:
We thank you for Mark and his gospel to believers under pressure and persecution.
   Walk with us on the road to the cross,
      employ us in your ministry of healing and announcing
      God's reign,
         and keep us faithful under fire. Amen.

[DTB]

April 27
Peter Boehler (1775)
See Common of Saints

Peter Boehler, a Moravian leader, is most known to United Methodists for the influence he had upon John and Charles Wesley in the days immediately preceding the Aldersgate experience. We are most accustomed to hearing the account from their perspective, particularly Boehler's words to an uncertain Wesley to, "Preach faith till you have it; and then, because you have it, you will preach faith."[99] But Boehler also recalls the Wesleys in his autobiography:

> I had the opportunity to talk extensively with both Wesleys, to press the gospel on them, and also beseech them to proclaim it in accordance with the opportunity God has given them in Oxford and elsewhere. They then disclosed to me the doubts which they had of the truth of the doctrine of free grace and of the merit of Jesus by which poor sinners received forgiveness and freedom from sins. But the Savior granted me grace to convince them from the scripture, and there was nothing left for them but to see such people who had experienced this. . . . When that was done [interviews with those who had the experience of salvation] he took me alone to his room and began to weep bitterly over himself, that he had not yet experienced any of this, etc., admitted that he was poor in spirit and because of his confusion he did not know what to do. From that time on he was like a child toward me. He had indeed prepared several sermons. Now when he came into the chancel for the first time after this occurrence, he is reported to have preached of the crucified Savior with such energy that the several thousand listeners were completely amazed.[100]

Four things stand out in Boehler's mentoring activity. (1) He took advantage of the opportunity at hand. (2) He acknowledged that any success he had was through grace given by Christ. (3) He did not fear to work with others, i. e., he was not jealous of the influence of others. (4) He was not possessive of the relationship in which Wesley "was like a child toward" him, but was willing to let it go into God's care after he had done what opportunity afforded; he did not even go to hear Wesley preach!

K. K. McCabe

April 29
Catherine of Siena (1380)
See Common of Teachers

Catherine was an Italian mystic and teacher. The youngest of the twenty-five children of the Sienese Benincasa family, at six she dedicated her life to serve God through her chastity. Her parents tried to get her to marry, but showing her resolution to devote herself to a life of prayer and service she cut off her hair. She was eventually accepted into the Dominican Tertiaries although it was normally comprised of widows. After three years spent in prayer and asceticism she went out to serve the poor and sick in her own city and beyond.

In one of her many visions, Jesus told her, ". . . love of me and love of neighbor are one and the same thing: Since love of neighbor has its source in me, the more the soul loves me, the more she loves her neighbors." She reached out to prisoners and became skilled at mediating disputes and helping individuals reconcile differences. Her work of compassion was one piece of her connection with the spiritual and political life of her day. In her later years she became highly involved in ecclesiastical politics, trying to mediate the conflict between Florence and the Papal Government, and later, between Urban VI and the rival pope at Avignon.

Although she could not write, she dictated some four hundred letters and her *Dialogue,* a collection of insights gained in prayer and meditative visions. In the conclusion of the *Dialogue* is included this prayer:

O abyss! O eternal Godhead! O deep sea! What more could you have given me than the gift of your very self?

You are a fire always burning but never consuming; you are a fire consuming in your heat all the soul's selfish love; you are a fire lifting all chill and giving light. In your light you have made me know your truth: You are that light beyond all light who gives the mind's eye supernatural light in such fullness and perfection that you bring clarity even to the light of faith. In that faith I see my soul has life, and in that light receives you who are light.[101]

She receive the sign of the stigmata, though tradition says she felt its pain without the visible marks on her hands. Catherine's themes are God's providence, the role of Christ as redeemer and mediator, and the reform of the Church.

S. Webb Phillips

April 29
Laura Askew Haygood (1900)
See Common of Evangelists, Teachers

Laura Haygood, missionary of the Methodist Episcopal Church, South, was called by one of her contemporaries a "remarkable combination of intellectual and spiritual strength, she was the true exponent of the true teacher — a consecrated follower in the steps of the *Great Teacher*." Indeed, Haygood's life exemplified discipleship in her dedicated work as both an educator and missionary.

In Atlanta, Haygood was well known for her efforts at the Trinity Church Home Mission. Haygood organized a non-profit endeavor to teach jobless women a trade and provide work for them. A visitor commented to Haygood one day that simply giving them money directly would be less trouble. Her response was, "Quite true, but in giving them work we increase instead of diminish their self-respect. . . ." A testament to her character, her students gave bundles of clothes for the poor as a birthday gift.

But Haygood's great calling and lasting legacy would be in the mission field. Appointed to China in 1884, she wrote, "I have come to feel that if the work of God in China needs women, there is no woman in all the world under more obligation to go than I. As far as that decision rests with me, I am ready." In Shanghai she designed the model and spearheaded the fund-raising effort for the Mctyeire Home and School. Opening day has been described as "not only one of the crowning days of Miss Haygood's life, but a day of momentous import for the life of hundreds of Chinese girls and for the history of female education in China." The Home was for missionaries to become trained and acclimated to Chinese culture and language. The School, a secondary school for Chinese girls, had a creative curriculum combining Chinese classics, Western subjects and Christian teaching. Haygood remained there until her death in 1900. The Communists expropriated Mctyeire, but the Laura Haygood Memorial Home and School duplicated her model in Soochow.

Haygood battled poor health most of her life. For years at time, she would not be able to work as she wished. Her final words to the Women's Board back home were, "He has fulfilled to the uttermost to me all His promises to those who leave home and friends for His sake and the gospel's; not one of all His promises for good has failed me."[102]

S. K. Doyal

May 1
Color: Red

Philip and
James the Less

Today's apostles are not major actors on the biblical stage. The synoptic gospels only mention them in the list of the Twelve (Mt 10:3; Mk 3:18; Lk 6:14,15).

The Gospel of John mentions Philip on four occasions. He is called by Jesus and brings Nathaniel to Jesus (1:43-51); it is Philip whom Jesus asks where to buy bread for the multitude (6:5-7); it is to Philip that some Greeks apply to see Jesus (12:20-22); and it is Philip who makes the request at the Last Supper for Jesus to "show us the Father" (14:8). In all these incidents Philip functions in some way to introduce us to Jesus. First, it is as "him about whom Moses in the law and also the prophets wrote, Jesus son of Joseph from Nazareth." Philip reminds us that the witness of the Hebrew scriptures leads us to a particular person, that the Christian revelation is one set in history. There can be no gospel abstracted from human thought or aspiration; it has to do with the son of a person with a proper name from a town we can find on the map. Second, Philip, by pointing out the impossibility of providing sufficient bread for the multitude, sets the stage for our introduction to Jesus as the bread of life. Third, through Philip the point is made that the good news reaches beyond racial divisions and that to serve Christ is to live in his presence. Finally, Philip's request to see the Father provides the most profound introduction to Jesus of all: "Whoever has seen me has seen the Father."

Of James the son of Alphaeus we know nothing beyond the record of his membership among the Twelve. He has been confused with that James who headed the Jerusalem church. The appellation "the Less" refers either to his height or age in comparison to James the brother of John and is not intended as a comment on his relative contribution to the apostolic college! For Christians who live when "high profiles" are important and candidates for the episcopal college must keep their resumes updated, it is salutary to spend a day with a saint who has to share it with somebody else and whose deeds and faith are known in heaven alone.

K. K. McCabe

Isaiah 30:18-21
Psalm 119:33-40 (*UMH* 842)
2 Corinthians 4:1-6
John 14:6-14

Self-revealing God, you have made yourself known to us and so given us life: Help us like Philip and James to introduce others to your gospel that all your people may know and have life in you through Jesus Christ, who lives and reigns with you and the Holy Spirit, one God, now and forever. Amen.

[CFG]

Our Teacher,
  it seems that we have walked with you a long way
  not to know you better than we do.
Impatiently we ask, like Philip, to be satisfied with a heavenly vision,
  but your answer of sharpening our hunger for you
  is wiser.
Way, Truth, and Life, we know more of God as we know more of you.

[CFG]

May 2
Athanasius (373)
See Common of Teachers, Pastors and Bishops

Athanasius (born c. 295), Bishop of Alexandria, had a long career in ecclesiastical service. He attended the council at Nicea in 325 as an advisor to Bishop Alexander and became bishop of Alexandria himself three years later. Much of his energy was spent as an ardent opponent of Arius and his followers. He defended the theology of Nicea and refuted the Arians in several treatises, but the polemic finds its way into other works as well. Conflicts with the Arians and disputes over Athanasius' episcopal authority led to his being exiled from Alexandria five times during his forty-five years as bishop.

Athanasius was a writer and a leader at a time when the church was seeking clearer articulation of theological ideas. The apologetic character of his theology emerges from his works as he sought both to defend and to define the faith in relation to non-Christians. In memorable words he helped to shape trinitarian doctrine, especially with his discussion of the incarnation: "So the eternal Son of God, being joined together by a likeness with all, naturally clothed all with immortality by the promise of the resurrection."[103]

This defender of theological formulae often described the divine in images which show surprising sensitivity and simplicity of expression. He described how God is present in the Son, ". . . just as the sun is in its rays, and the thought is in the word, and the streams are in the river."[104] His life was touched by the monks of the Egyptian desert with whom he had much contact. At the beginning of the *Life of Antony*, which Athanasius wrote during one of the periods of exile, he tells us that he saw Antony often. In the *Life* we see the bishop's respect for discipline and reverence for the contemplative life.

In his strident zeal in defending true doctrine and his patient tenacity throughout a long life of service to the church, Athanasius can be for us a model of perseverance. His words, while harsh and unrelenting in matters of doctrine, nevertheless also offer hope. Athanasius suggested that since humanity had become like a portrait that has grown faint and stained, Christ came to show again the one whose likeness was shown in the painting, remaking us anew in the image of God.[105]

A. Berry Wylie

May 3
Thomas Coke (1814)
See Common of Evangelists, Pastors and Bishops

Thomas Coke was born in Wales in 1747 and educated at Oxford where he received B.A., M.A., and Doctor of Civil Law degrees. An ordained Anglican priest, he was forced by disgruntled parishioners to leave his parish because of his Methodist sympathies. From 1777 through 1784 he served as John Wesley's secretary, confident, and legal advisor.

The always ambitious Coke wrote to Wesley pleading for his personal backing and the authority to ordain others for America, saying, "I may want all the influence, in America, which you can throw into my scale."[106] Wesley then appointed Coke as the first superintendent of the Methodists in America. On December 24, 1784 in Baltimore, "Dr. Coke" (as he was called in America) convened the Christmas Conference, a gathering of Methodist preachers who officially organized the Methodist Episcopal Church in America. He and Asbury became its first bishops. Coke was consistently and adamantly opposed to slavery, and in 1785 he and Asbury visited George Washington to present an antislavery petition. They met with Washington again in 1789 to congratulate him upon his election to the presidency.

But the courtly and well-educated Coke was not always enthusiastically received as a leader among American Methodists. His ties with British Methodism and mission work meant that he was more frequently abroad than in America. In 1786 he became caught up in a conflict over Wesley's authority in America. The 1808 General Conference ended Coke's official relationship with American Methodism by declaring that he was a resident of Europe and rescinding his authority as superintendent.

Coke continued in his missionary work. Crossing the Atlantic eighteen times, he was involved in Methodist expansion in England, Ireland, the United States, Nova Scotia, and the West Indies and gave away his personal fortune in support of these missionary endeavors. He died while traveling to Ceylon and was buried in the Indian Ocean.

Coke once prayed for God to give Methodist preachers a deep spirit of prayer:

Glory be given to thee, thou has already bestowed much of it upon them: O! preserve it, increase it, inflame it, till their very life be one constant sacrifice to thee: till, by being daily stamped with brighter and brighter characters of thyself, they continually bring down, like thy servant Moses, a bright shining from the Mount.[107]

B. W. Coe

May 4
Monica (387)
See Common of Saints

The mother of Augustine, the great theologian of the fourth and fifth centuries, Monica was a strong, tenacious woman of faith. Born to Christian parents in North Africa, she was raised with a strict religious education to become a woman of profound piety and prayer. The hardships she overcame in her life were numerous. After a drinking problem in her youth, she was confronted and was able to stop. She married an unbeliever who had a hot temper and was unfaithful to her, but through persistence she convinced him to be baptized one year before his death. She took care of a difficult mother-in-law in her own home and finally won her over through her loyalty and compassion. She raised three children, the most promising of which spurned her and her religion until his adult conversion. Monica stood by her beliefs to the point of refusing to allow her talented son to live with her during his period of Manichean beliefs.

Monica was known for her constant piety and prayer. She prayed resolutely for the conversion of her son and made offerings at the altar twice daily on his behalf. She adhered to traditional North African practices that some Romans considered superstitious including meals at the tombs of the dead, Sabbath fasts, and ecstatic visions. One vision included a visit by a radiant youth who consoled her with the sight of her son at her side. When she related the dream to Augustine he scoffed that if she gave up the faith, they would be together. She replied firmly, "No, for it was not told me that 'where he is, there shall you be,' but 'where you are, there shall he be.'"[108] The dream haunted Augustine until his conversion years later.

Following her son to Rome and Milan, she joined his household and gained the favor of Ambrose, the influential bishop and theologian. After Augustine's baptism and training, they agreed to return home to North Africa. En route she fell ill and died at age 55. Her resolution and faith persisted to the end; a few days before her death she said, "What I can still do here, and why I am here, I do not know . . . One thing there was, for which I desired to linger a little while in this life, that I might see you a Catholic Christian before I died. God has granted this to me in more than abundance, for I see you his servant."[109]

L. A. Goleman

May 5
Olof Gustav Hedström (1877)
See Common of Evangelists

Hedström was an innovative pastor who ministered to the needs of Swedish immigrants to the United States during the nineteenth century. He served as pastor of the Bethel Society, a unique Methodist enterprise whose 'building' was a ship floating in New York Harbor.

Olof Hedström was born in Kalmer, Sweden in 1803. He immigrated to the United States unwittingly when, at age 22, he had attempted to travel to South America as a sailor in search of adventure. He made New York, but his ship's crew was disbanded there. Not having the money to go further, he found employment in a clothing establishment as a foreman and married an American woman.

He converted to Methodism in 1835 and joined the New York Conference on trial, serving in English congregations for ten years. Hedström's ministry attracted Methodist lay person, Peter Bergner, who was planning to develop a ministry to Scandinavian immigrants to the United States. Bergner and other Swedish Methodists acquired a two-masted ship named the *Henry Leeds*, renamed the vessel the *John Wesley*, and began the Bethel Society. The ship, bound to a pier, became a chapel for the society's work.

Hedström became pastor of the society in 1845 and served in that capacity until his death on May 5, 1877. His ministry consisted of boarding every ship from Sweden, Denmark, and Norway that entered New York harbor and ministering to the sailors and immigrants. He also visited the sick in nearby hospitals and boarding houses. Soon, Immanuel Church, the first Swedish Methodist congregation, was founded in Brooklyn.

This beginning in New York coupled with the work of Hedström's brother Jonas in the West, had a profound impact. Methodist work among the Swedish grew by 1924 to four annual conferences and two missionary conferences, including some 128 preachers, 217 churches, and 20,000 church members. This does not include the number of Swedish citizens that returned to Sweden and helped to establish Methodism in their native land.

J. B. Weakley

May 8
Julian of Norwich (1417)
See Common of Saints

Julian lived as an anchoress in a cell of the parish Church of St. Julian in Norwich, England. Little is known of her life other than what she tells us in her writings and what Margery Kempe reports of meeting with her.

Julian's remarkable work, *Showings* (or *Revelations of Divine Love*), is the first book known to have been authored by a woman in English. She wrote the "Short Text" directly after sixteen visions visited upon her on May 13, 1373. The "Long Text," written twenty years later, consists of Julian's reflections on the meanings of the revelations.

Living at a time of multiple disasters in the world (bubonic plague, frequent famine, and The Hundred Years' War), Julian saw vivid images of Christ's passion, convincing her how much Christ loved her. She then wrote of God as "Creator . . . protector . . . lover."

Julian offers us solid experiential reflections concerning what sin is, who God is, and how to live in the tension between our sin and God's "courteous" mercy. Sin, for Julian, hinders us from living as true images of God. Yet "God . . . will do it . . . and my sin will not impede the operation of his goodness." Again and again, Julian expresses the actions of God:

> God rejoices that he is our Father, and . . . that he is our Mother, and . . . that he is our true spouse, and that our soul is his beloved wife. And Christ rejoices that he is our brother, and Jesus rejoices that he is our saviour. These are five great joys . . . in which he wants us to rejoice, praising him, thanking him, loving him, endlessly blessing him. . . .

She develops the quality of motherhood in the second person of the Trinity, especially in Jesus' taking our flesh, bearing our wounds in his passion, and feeding us in the eucharist. She offers hope, grounded in the endless love of God who will let none of God's children perish. She recommends three kinds of knowledge: "that we know our Lord God . . . that we know ourselves . . . that we know humbly that our self is opposed to our sin and to our weakness." Her strong affirmation towards the end of the Long Text inspires us:

> What, do you wish to know your Lord's meaning in this thing? Know it well, love was his meaning. Who reveals it to you? Love. What did he reveal to you? Love. Why does he reveal it to you? For love. Remain in this, and you will know more of the same.[110]

B. B. Troxell
For All The Saints/119

May 9
Gregory of Nazianzus (389)
See Common of Pastors and Bishops, Teachers

Gregory of Nazianzus, Bishop of Constantinople, was a man of letters and ascetic piety who reluctantly accepted the calls to ecclesial leadership which periodically interrupted his solitary prayer and study. Born in 329 to a leading family of Nazianzus in the Byzantine province of Cappadocia, Gregory eventually studied at all the great academic centers of the Eastern Mediterranean. In Athens he became close friends with Basil of Caesarea. Having finished his studies in 359, Gregory joined Basil in Pontus to pursue a life of ascetic practice and scholarship. Within a few years, however, Gregory's father, long the Bishop of Nazianzus, insisted upon his accepting the office of presbyter there. In 372 Basil, by then Metropolitan of Caesarea, appointed Gregory bishop of the obscure and ugly town of Sasima in an effort to establish as many orthodox bishops as possible over against the Eastern domination by Arianism under the Emperor Valens. Gregory accepted the episcopacy under protest but never set foot in Sasima and, sadly, never forgave Basil. He retired to solitude in Seleucia.

In 379 Gregory's third and final call to church leadership became the occasion for his writing a series of sermons, called *Theological Orations,* that are the principal reason for his being honored as not only a saint but also "the Theologian," a title otherwise given only to John the Evangelist. Appointed bishop to the beleaguered orthodox congregation in Constantinople, Gregory delivered his five great orations on the Trinity to confirm and encourage their adherence to the tradition of Nicaea. Abounding in theological insights that strike a balance between illuminating images and apophatic reserve, the orations have among their highlights the only explicit statement to that date of the Holy Spirit's divinity: "What then? Is the Spirit God? Most certainly."[111] Such work, along with that of Gregory's fellow Cappadocians Basil and Gregory of Nyssa, was crucial to the decrees issued by the Eastern bishops convened in Constantinople under the orthodox Emperor Theodosius in 381.

The First Council of Constantinople was, however, marred by ecclesial politics that led Gregory to resign his see, partially in disgust but also with a sense that his work was finished. He returned to his preferred life of mystical prayer and writing near Nazianzus, augmenting the corpus of his letters, poems, and sermons until his death in 389.

B. T. Morrill

May 16
William Nast (1889)
See Common of Leaders, Evangelists

Widely regarded as the "Patriarch of German Methodism,"[112] Johann Wilhelm Nast was born in Stuttgart in 1807. He was confirmed a Lutheran at fourteen and was engaged in studies to become a pastor and theologian but he was dismayed by the liberal theology he found at the University of Tübingen. Deep in doubt, he decided to quit his studies and move to America. There he landed a job as a tutor and became involved with his female employer, but his conscience was troubled about their liaison and their relationship ended bitterly.

Nast's search for peace from his religious melancholia took many turns, but after attending a number of Methodist camp meetings he had a conversion experience in 1835 in Gambier, Ohio. The Methodists, who wanted to begin missionary work among the growing German population of Cincinnati, quickly ordained Nast and appointed him to that work. Unable to stir up much interest at first, he overcame his shyness and went from door to door handing out tracts. When he did preach he was met with derision: the German-language newspapers ridiculed him and once while he was preaching his coattails were quietly snipped off. After a year of hard work he had only gathered a class of twelve.

Despite the difficult beginnings, Nast persevered and the movement grew rapidly through the 1840s and gained new leaders. He traveled extensively to dedicate the numerous German Methodist churches being built in cities like Louisville, St. Louis, Cleveland, Dayton, and Chicago. He pushed the formation of German Methodist Conferences and became a presiding elder. Upon returning from a trip to Germany in 1844, he brought back a report that spurred the General Conference to send missionaries, and so helped pioneer Methodism there. He was a sincere, if not stunning, preacher and a learned scholar. His books included a monumental *Commentary on the New Testament.*

But his major influence was wielded through a weekly newspaper *Der Christliche Apologete,* which he founded in 1838 and edited for fifty years. This paper held the widely spread German Methodist community together, keeping it informed on religious and political developments in America and Germany, but often reflecting Nast's anti-Roman Catholic bias.

It is difficult to appreciate now the importance of Nast's work, for within a century of its beginning German Methodism had declined from slowing immigration and the Americanization of subsequent generations. Yet at the turn of the century there were some 63,000 German Methodists who had six colleges, two seminaries, four orphanages, and four hospitals.

C. F. Guthrie

May 17
Harry Hosier (1806)
See Common of Preachers

Harry Hosier, "Black Harry," was born a slave (possibly in North Carolina) and later manumitted; nothing is known of his early life. Reportedly the first African-American Methodist to be licensed to preach, Hosier traveled as a servant and an itinerant preacher with many of the main figures of early American Methodism: Francis Asbury, Thomas Coke, Richard Whatcoat, and Freeborn Garrettson. He is believed to have attended the 1784 Christmas Conference at Lovely Lane Chapel in Baltimore.

Though illiterate and without formal oratorical training, Hosier was able, by persuasive preaching, to garner the attention of audiences without distinction of color.

When he was questioned as to his preaching abilities, complete command of voice, aptness in language, and free delivery, as to Scriptural and doctrinal truth, his reply was a description of the Elocution of Faith: "I sing by faith, pray by faith, preach by faith, and do everything by faith; without faith in the Lord Jesus I can do nothing."[113]

He was a popular preacher, often a more desired speaker than his distinguished traveling companions, and was the first Methodist preacher, black or white, to be commented upon in a New York City newspaper (the *New York Packet*).

Success and fame took a toll, however, and Hosier succumbed for a short time to the power of strong drink. Yet at the end of his life, his backsliding behind him, Hosier died a "happy death" as a faithful disciple of Jesus Christ.

Harry Hosier lived and died as a member of the Methodist Episcopal Church, though many African Americans of his age, in the face of injustice, left that body to form other denominations. His ministry was to all who stood in need of hearing the saving word of the Gospel, regardless of race, thereby serving as a reminder of the truth that in Christ there is neither slave nor free (Gal 3:28).

K. B. Westerfield Tucker

May 18
Jacob Albright (1808)
See Common of Leaders, Pastors and Bishops

Founder of the Evangelical Association, Albright was born near Pottstown, Pennsylvania, the child of German immigrants, and was baptized and confirmed as a Lutheran. He married and settled on a farm in Lancaster County, where in addition to farming he conducted a successful tile and brick factory and became known as "the honest tile maker."

The sudden death of several of his children and the sermon preached at their funeral brought on a severe inward struggle. He turned to a neighbor, a follower of the United Brethren, who gave him counsel and led him through prayer to experience the peace of God. In the home of another neighbor he was led into the fellowship of a Methodist class and found the disciplined spiritual formation that he needed. Through this class he was eventually licensed as a Methodist exhorter (lay speaker).

He felt the call to preach but was deeply conscious of his lack of theological education. After a long struggle he started preaching in barns, log cabins, and schoolhouses to the many German-speaking people of Pennsylvania, Maryland, and Virginia and organized those who responded into classes.

In 1803 a council from his classes ordained him, and in 1807 they gathered into "The Newly Formed Methodist Conference" and elected him their bishop. This conference, however, was not accepted by the Methodists, partly because they used the German language, which the Methodists believed would not long continue in this country, and also because Albright's absences while preaching had caused his membership in his Lancaster County Methodist class to lapse. Worn out by his labors and by a tubercular condition, he died at the home of a friend on May 18, 1808. After his death his followers completed the organization of the denomination that they named the Evangelical Association.

By reaching out in the face of shattering tragedy and accepting spiritual help from friends and from a supportive small group, he became a teacher and example to many others. By persistently following God's call to minister among German Americans in the face of self-doubt and ecclesiastical rejection, even at the cost of broken health and early death, he left behind a community of faith that is today an important part of The United Methodist Church.

H. L. Hickman

May 18
Mary McLeod Bethune (1955)
See Common of Leaders

One of the most influential African American leaders of the twentieth century, Mary McLeod Bethune was born in Mayesville, South Carolina in 1875 to freed slaves who had helped organize an African-American Methodist church. Mary attended this church as a child but was enrolled in a new Presbyterian school in 1884 and became a member of the sponsoring congregation at twelve.

She won a scholarship to attend Scotia Seminary in North Carolina and in 1894 became the first Black to go to the Moody Bible Institute, thinking she would become a missionary. There she had a "mighty baptism of the Holy Spirit" that marked her deeply. When she applied for Presbyterian missions work she was told there were no openings for Blacks. She went instead to work as a teacher in Augusta, Georgia and then in Sumter, South Carolina, where she met and married Albertus Bethune.

Moving to Florida, she organized the Daytona Normal and Industrial Institute for Negro Girls in 1904, managing to keep the doors open by bakesales and door-to-door solicitation for twenty years before finances forced her to seek denominational sponsorship. She received an offer from the Methodist Episcopal Church and promptly joined the denomination in 1924. She was elected a delegate to the 1928 General Conference, and was reelected every four years until her death, becoming a national leader in the Church. In 1936 she angrily opposed the plan of union between the northern and southern Methodist churches that placed Blacks in a separate Central Jurisdiction.

With the merging of her college with Cookman Institute, she became president of Bethune-Cookman College, the first four-year college to be founded by a Black woman. After struggling with the college trustees for control of the school and feeling frustrated in fulfilling her primary mission to black women through the college, she founded the National Council of Negro Women (NCNW). She was also appointed to a high level post in the National Youth Administration and was an advisor to Presidents Hoover, Franklin, and Truman. In the last years of her life she experienced continuing conflict over leadership of the college and disappointment that Methodism was not sufficiently radical in Christian practice. She wrote that the voice of the Church "has not been heard, clearly. A strong, unequivocal acceptance of the truth that there is no second-class citizenship in God's world has been lacking. The church has trailed social advance. Many times the words of the great old hymns have been sung off key."[114]

C. F. Guthrie

May 24
William Edwin Robert Sangster (1960)
See Common of Preachers

William Sangster identified himself simply as a "traveling preacher."[115] From beginnings on rough back streets of London, Sangster served Westminster's Central Hall for sixteen years and became the "central voice of Methodism." A prolific author, President of the Methodist Conference in 1950 and later the General Secretary of the Home Mission Department. He was a driven man who was often quoted as saying "I just cannot do enough."

As a child, Sangster (b. 1900) had a self-described "puritan streak" which served to estrange him from many people. Extremely demanding of himself in both his studies and his conduct, Sangster preached his first sermon at the age of sixteen. A nonsmoker and nondrinker, he was often the object of ridicule among his fellow soldiers while in the army. One evening while praying by his bunk, someone slapped Sangster with a bayonet. Young Will promptly rose and knocked the man off his feet with a single punch, an episode for which Sangster had difficulty forgiving himself.

Early in his ministry Sangster suffered a personal crisis, nearly resigning the ministry because he felt unworthy. On a retreat he listed his faults and wondered "Is God not exposing me to the folly and futility of *my way*?" He concluded this private list with the words: "Pray. Pray. Pray. The secret is in prayer. Strive after holiness like an athlete prepares for a race. The secret is in prayer. The secret is in prayer."[116]

With renewed faith and zeal, Sangster returned to his ministry. His "perfectionism" may have led him to a greater appreciation of the concept of Christian Perfection in true Wesleyan tradition. He strove to reflect a life in perfect love to God and man. He said, "Not happiness first and holiness if possible, but holiness first and bliss as a consequence."[117] He saw his churches through World War II air raids singing hymns in bomb shelters. His books include *Methodism Can Be Born Again (1938), Methodism's Unfinished Task* (1947), *The Path to Perfection* (1943), books on preaching, and several sermon collections. After a retirement of nine months when he could neither travel nor preach, W. E. Sangster died on May 24, 1960.

S. K. Doyal

May 25
The Venerable Bede (736)
See Common of Saints, Teachers

The Venerable Bede (b. 672 or 673), known as the 'Father of English History', is most famous as the author of *The Ecclesiastical History of the English People*. Presented at the age of seven to the newly-founded Benedictine monastery of Wearmouth in Northumberland, he spent the rest of his life as a monk there and at the sister house of Jarrow, where he died.

He describes his lifestyle and priorities thus: ". . . applying myself entirely to the study of the Scriptures . . . amid the observance of the discipline of the Rule and the daily task of singing in church, it has always been my delight to learn or to teach or to write."[118] Bede early acquired a reputation for scholarship and holiness. His substantial writings included fifteen commentaries on Scripture, lives of the saints, and definitive works on chronology; his scholarship was dedicated to God's glory. As a historian (the first in the post-classical world to weave multiple oral and written sources into a structured narrative, to quote documents and to give exact dates and places) he described the establishment of Christianity in England. On his death bed, his pupils, who held him in great affection, helped him with his last work, an English translation of John's Gospel.

Although fully canonized in 1899 as a saint and doctor of the Church, he is traditionally given the title, 'Venerable,' a recognition of sanctity that was accorded to him by the church very shortly after his death. His pupil Cuthbert's account of his death illustrates the profound faith which formed the context of his whole life. Confined to bed with increasing breathlessness, he took his leave of his friends on the eve of Ascension Day. He asked to be laid on the floor near his accustomed place of prayer, and repeated the Ascension antiphon 'O King of glory,': "And when he came to that word, 'do not forsake us,' he burst into tears, and wept much." He said "I have lived long; my merciful Judge well foresaw my life for me; the time of my dissolution draws night; for I desire to die and to be with Christ."[119]

M. P. Jones

May 27
John Calvin (1564)
See Common of Leaders, Teachers

Calvin was born a Frenchman into a confusing age of ecclesiastical conflict and Reform, Renaissance learning, and widespread cultural crisis. He studied Latin, Theology, and Law at the University of Paris before pursuing a Renaissance Humanist education in Classics. As a Humanist, Calvin joined the Reformers in seeking to recover the "true knowledge of God and of ourselves" that the medieval Church had distorted and lost. Drinking deeply from the clear springs of Scripture and guided by Reformation teachings, he found the true and saving knowledge of God in the Bible's assurance of God's free forgiveness of sin. His endless gratitude toward God's goodness and mercy inspired Calvin's theology of "piety," the selfless and total reliance on God:

> We are not our own: let not our reason nor our will, therefore, sway our plans and deeds. We are not our own: let us therefore not set it as our goal to seek what is expedient for us according to the flesh. We are not our own: in so far as we can, let us therefore forget ourselves and all that is ours.
> Conversely, we are God's: let us therefore live for him and die for him. We are God's: let his wisdom and will therefore rule all our actions. We are God's: let all the parts of our life accordingly strive toward him as our only lawful goal.[120]

Liberated from the sinful concern with self, Calvin devoted his prodigious abilities as a scholar and orator to proclaiming the saving knowledge of God and to applying it to the vast array of human affairs. Fleeing religious persecution in Paris, Calvin lived in permanent exile in Switzerland where he converted to Protestantism in 1533. He quickly became a leader of the second-generation of Reformers, solidifying the Protestant reforms while spreading and deepening their roots. The remarkable religious, social, and political transformations that he instituted as leader of the city of Geneva became a model for other European cities. Afraid that he would be superstitiously venerated and his teachings obscured, Calvin asked to be buried in an unmarked grave. He got his wish. His teachings spread across Europe, inspiring many of the progressive religious, social, political, and scientific movements that gave birth to the modern Western world.

S. D. Olson

The Visitation

Mary's first act after learning that she was to bear the Messiah was to hurry to the home of her cousin Elizabeth (Lk 1:39-56). She knew Elizabeth also was bearing a miracle child. Elizabeth, who was far beyond childbearing years, had been pregnant for six months. The angel had told Mary so (v. 36); she must see for herself. She rushed to the hill country and stayed for three months until the child John (the Baptist) was born.

When Mary arrived to embrace Elizabeth, the fetus leaped in Elisabeth's womb (v. 41): instant recognition and confirmation of the angel's message, women's experience validating the experience of women.

Some scholars think that the Magnificat (vv. 47-55) was originally the song of Elizabeth; in fact one manuscript has her name, not Mary's, in v. 46. It is a song of reversal. The eternal God has taken notice of a humble maiden, who will now be called blessed by future generations. God has elevated a woman and scattered to the winds those who are important in their own minds. God has brought down the dominant and lifted the lowly. God has fed the hungry with rich food and sent the rich away empty. The patriarchal pyramid has been upended.

For three months the two women — cousins, sisters — share their secret. God is at work in the wombs of the earth, making all things new.

The celebration of the Visitation entered the Christian calendar in the thirteenth century. It was originally commemorated on July 2 until the Roman Catholic Church revised its calendar in 1969.

N. A. Hardesty

1 Samuel 2:1-10
Psalm 113 (*UMH* 834)
Romans 12:9-16b
Luke 1:39-57

Ever-living God, you have made us one people through new birth in Christ:
With Mary and Elizabeth prompt us and your whole Church to always delight
in common worship and to rejoice greatly in our common destiny in Christ,
who lives and reigns with you and the Holy Spirit, one God, now and forever.
Amen.

[DTB]

God of leaping babies and singing women,
    we laugh at the surprise of your approach and the tickle of your mystery.
Like Elizabeth filled with the Holy Spirit,
    cause us to rejoice in the belief of others and
    to always exult in the coming of the Messiah.

[DTB]

See *The United Methodist Book of Worship*, 257

June 1
Justin (c. 167)
See Common of Martyrs, Teachers

Justin, Apologist and Martyr, was from a family of Greek origin in Samaria. His parents provided him the means to study philosophy which in Late Antiquity was the pursuit of knowledge and virtue as an entire way of life. Having moved through the Stoic, Aristotelian, and Pythagorean "schools" Justin, by then in his early thirties, was deeply engaged in Platonism when he encountered an old man who told him about the Hebrew prophets' teachings and their fulfillment in Jesus Christ. Justin converted to Christianity, embracing it as the true philosophy and adopting for himself the conventional role and garments of a teacher. For the remaining thirty years of his life he lectured, debated, and wrote about the Christian faith. Based in Ephesus since the early days of his studies, he moved to Rome in 151, where he wrote the two *Apologies* and *Dialogue with Trypho*, the only works to have survived him intact.

The "Apologist" Justin defended Christians in Rome against the accusations of atheism, immorality, and treason, which occasioned sporadic waves of persecution against them. Moreover, he made an original and momentous contribution to the history of Christian thought by identifying the Platonic concept of the *Logos* with the Word of God who became incarnate in Jesus Christ. Justin's *First Apology* also provides the earliest descriptions of baptismal and eucharistic liturgies in Rome, as well as reflection upon their meaning and significance. Concerning the Eucharist he wrote:

> For not as common bread and common drink do we receive these; but in like manner as Jesus Christ our Saviour, having been made flesh by the Word of God, had both flesh and blood for our salvation, so likewise have we been taught that the food which is blessed by the prayer of His word, and from which our blood and flesh by transmutation are nourished, is the flesh and blood of that Jesus who was made flesh.[121]

Refusing to sacrifice to the gods before a Roman prefect, Justin was decapitated in 165. His life and death remain a witness to the Christian faith as a complete way of life, a participation and fellowship of mind, heart, and body in Christ Jesus, the very Word of God.

B. T. Morrill

June 2
The Martyrs of Lyons (177)
See Common of Martyrs

In Book Five of his *Ecclesiastical History*, the fourth-century historian Eusebius of Caesarea quotes extensively from the text of a letter written in the year 177 from Christians in the cities of Vienne and Lyons in Gaul to their Christian sisters and brothers in Asia Minor. Portions of Gaul were populated by natives of Asia Minor (Irenaeus was such a person), and the two Christian communities maintained ties of fellowship. The letter describes the outbreak of persecution of Christians in Lyons.

Noteworthy in Eusebius' account is mention of some of the charges brought against the Christians: atheism, Oedipal intercourse, and cannibalism. In the eyes of many of their Roman neighbors, Christians were atheists because they denied the existence of the traditional Roman pantheon which (so the Romans believed) sustained Roman society and the world itself. The other accusations stemmed from Roman misunderstanding of Christian worship practices: eating one's children, engaging in intercourse with one's mother, and eating one's fellow human beings can be seen as Roman misinterpretation of Christian language of eating Christ in the eucharist, and perhaps the Christian practice of exchanging the kiss of peace during worship. The Romans probably also thought that any group so antisocial as to not worship the gods probably also engaged in a variety of repulsive practices.

Popular sentiment rose so strongly against the Christians in Lyons that they were subject to increasing acts of violence and murder, first by mobs and then by organized public spectacle. The letter mentions some of those martyred by name: Sanctus, Blandina, Ponticus, Biblis, Alexander, Attalus, Maturus, and their bishop Pothinus, more than ninety years old. The letter reports the tortures inflicted upon Blandina, and the martyrs' significance for faith:

> ... but Blandina was hung on a stake and offered as a prey to the wild beasts that were let in. She seemed to be hanging in the shape of a cross, and by her continuous prayer gave great zeal to the combatants, while they looked on during the contest, and with their outward eyes saw in the form of their sister him who was crucified for them, to persuade those who believe on him that all who suffer for the glory of Christ have for ever fellowship with the living God.[122]

G. S. Sperry-White

June 5
Boniface (754)
See Common of Evangelists, Martyrs

Boniface, known as Wynfrith until admission into monastic life, was born at Crediton in southwest England in the late 7th century. Although his intellect and leadership insured a settled career in the Church, he chose instead the hazardous life of the missionary, preaching in the pagan outposts of 8th century Germany.

His first venture was an unqualified failure. Unvanquished, Boniface patiently garnered the support of Rome and local monarchs — both vital to his future success. Yet he maintained his piety and integrity, boldly confronting his benefactors' moral conduct and abuses of power. Indeed, Christ's teaching to be wise as serpents and innocent as doves distinguished the life of this holy man.

His second missionary endeavor won him the distinction as "the Apostle to Germany," but it was not without obstacles. Heresy, egregious behavior, and evangelical reticence characterized the Christian communities established in southern Germany. Further, the Hessian tribes were hospitable but committed to their own gods. In a daring act, Boniface interrupted a pagan ceremony and felled the Sacred Oak of Thor, the principle idol of the region. Thousands were drawn to this intrepid missionary for baptism, and Boniface gained the leverage to reform the Church throughout central Europe.

Boniface could be as nurturing as he was resolute, as his letter to the abbess Bugga demonstrates:

> I am sending you a brotherly letter of comfort and exhortation. Remember that word of Truth: "Possess your souls in patience." . . . In that hope, beloved sister, rejoice and be glad always, for you shall not be put to shame. Scorn earthly trials with your whole soul, for all soldiers of Christ, men and women, have despised temporal troubles and tempests and have held the frailties of this world as naught.[123]

At the age of 75, Boniface resigned as Archbishop of Mainz to carry Christ's message a third and final time to the German people. In the early morning on this date in 754, Boniface was martyred by the people for whose salvation he longed.

Boniface gracefully finessed the world of popes and kings, but never for personal gain. In his friendships and ministry, his singular priority was to increase God's love. Less than a year after his death, Boniface was canonized and given the unusual distinction of having both the date of his birth and martyrdom recognized by the Church.

T. Gildemeister

June 7
Chief Seattle (1866)
See Common of Leaders, Saints

Seattle was a Duwamish Indian of the Puget Sound area (now Washington State). A warrior in his youth, he converted to Christianity and became a peace-seeker under the influence of Catholic missionaries in the 1830s. As more whites moved into the Northwest, conflict between them and the Native Americans increased. In 1855, Washington Governor Isaac Stevens called for a council meeting to persuade the various tribes to move onto reservations. Seattle was the first signer of the Port Elliott Treaty accepting movement to the Port Madison Reservation. While some Anglo historians emphasize Seattle's role as a friend to white people during periods of intense conflict in the Northwest, Seattle's own words reflect an ironic pragmatism about the fate of his people under the oppression of white occupation of Native American lands. In an 1854 speech to Governor Stevens, Seattle said,

> The White Chief says that Big Chief at Washington sends us greeting of friendship and goodwill. That is kind of him for we know he has little need of our friendship in return. His people are many. They are like the grass that covers vast prairies. My people are few. They resemble the scattering trees of a storm-swept plain . . . I will not dwell on, nor mourn over, our untimely decay. . . . It matters little where we pass the remnant of our days. They will not be many . . . . Your time of decay may be distant, but it will surely come, for even the White Man whose God walked and talked with him as friend with friend, cannot be exempt from the common destiny. We may be brothers after all. . . .[124]

Seattle's spirituality resounds with a keen awareness of the interconnections of all creatures and peoples with one another. In a letter to U.S. President Franklin Pierce, Seattle wrote these prayerful and prophetic words:

> The Indian prefers the soft sound of the wind darting over the face of the pond . . . the air is precious to the red man. For all things share the same breath — the beasts, the trees, the man. . . . What is [humankind] without the beasts? If all the beasts were gone, [people] would die from great loneliness of spirit, for whatever happens to the beasts also happens to [people]. All things are connected. Whatever befalls the earth befalls the sons of the earth.[125]

J. A. Mercer

June 9
Columba and Aidan (597 and 651)
See Common of Evangelists, Saints

Known as the "Apostle of Caledonia," Columba was an Irish, Celtic missionary of the sixth century to the land known today as Scotland. The son of an Ulster chieftain, Columba was educated in Christianity and the poetry and song of Irish bards. He had a voice so loud and melodious that "those who stood at a distance of more than a mile . . . could distinguish every syllable in the verses that he sang."[126] Inducted as a monk by the famous Finnian, Columba founded a monastery and school that became the center for evangelizing the Picts and teaching the Scots in northern Caledonia. He won over King Barde of the Picts through his charisma and miracles, including a prayer that threw open the bolts and doors of the royal castle. He consecrated the new king of the Scots and was sought back in Ireland for disputes over the social status of the bards and over the service of women in the military. He was a gifted manuscript scribe of the Psalms and gospels and a talented hymn writer. Although legends exaggerate his missionary scope, Columba and the monks of Iona did give birth to numerous churches in the Celtic part of Scotland. Iona continues to this day as an ecumenical school and retreat of the Church of Scotland.

A hymn from the period, the *Altus Prosator*, usually attributed to Columba, tells of the glory of the saints after the fires of judgment:

Zeal of the Lord, consuming fire,
Shall whelm the foes, amazed and dumb,
Whose stony hearts will not receive
That Christ hath from the Father come:
But we shall soar our Lord to meet,
And so with Him shall ever be,
To reap the due rewards amidst
The glories of Eternity.[127]

Aidan was the monk of Iona in the seventh century who became the "missionary to the English." He was summoned to the Northumbrian land of what is now northern England by King Oswald, who gave him the island of Lindesfarne for his outpost. There, he established a school for English youths and launched a missionary campaign throughout the region. He bought freedom for numerous slaves and trained many of them to become clerics in the church. Aidan lived his entire life in poverty and ascetic detachment, and his reputation for gentleness, peace, and humility grew. He advised lay people to take up monastic practices of ongoing prayer, study, and care for the sick and poor.

L. A. Goleman

June 11
Color: Red

Barnabas

Originally named Joseph, Barnabas was a native of the island of Cyprus and a Jew of the tribe of Levi who, along with Paul, came to be one of the chief supporters of the missionary work to the Gentiles. He is first mentioned in Acts as an example of the New Testament church's communal ethic: he sold a field he owned and contributed the proceeds to the support of the Jerusalem community. For such generosity (or perhaps for his preaching ministry), the apostles gave him the name Barnabas which means, "son of encouragement" (Acts 4:36-37), a name whose suitability would be proven many times.

It was Barnabas who first introduced Paul to the apostolic company while they were still afraid of him and distrusted the sincerity of his conversion (Acts 9:26-27). He introduced Paul to the Christian community at Antioch and shared the "co-pastorate" with him for a year before becoming his missionary companion (Acts 11:22-26). He and Paul argued at the Council of Jerusalem against the requirement that Gentile converts become circumcised, and supported the ministry of John Mark by taking him back to Cyprus with him when Paul rejected the young man for not demonstrating sufficient perseverance and endurance in the missionary effort (Acts 15:37-39). Luke's report that, "he was a good man, full of the Holy Spirit and of faith" (Acts 11:24), attests to the high esteem in which Barnabas was held by the community. Charles Wesley meditates on this description of Barnabas as follows:

> Faith and the Holy Ghost bestowed
> on man, can make the evil good:
> And such who formed them by his grace,
> God only knows his saints to praise:
> And saints all other praise disown
> But that which comes from God alone.[128]

Barnabas is traditionally considered the founder of the church in Cyprus and was said to have been stoned to death there in the city of Salamis in the year 61 A. D., though this is a late tradition.

K. K. McCabe

Isaiah 42:5-12
Psalm 112 (*UMH* 833)
Acts 11:19-30, 13:1-3
Matthew 10:7-16

God of Grace, who showers down righteousness and causes salvation to spring up upon the earth: Help us, like Barnabas, to deal generously and justly with others so that we might be like him, full of the Spirit and of faith in Jesus Christ, our Lord, who lives and reigns with you and the Holy Spirit, one God, now and forever. Amen.

[CFG]

You who alone are God,
you ask that we who are followers of your son be like sheep
  among the wolves of this world.
So that we, like Barnabas, may be strong for others,
Also make us wise like serpents, but as innocent as doves,
  that those who suffer may be encouraged
  and those who are poor may be comforted with good things
  in the powerful name of Christ. Amen.

[CFG]

June 14
Basil the Great (379)
See Common of Teachers, Pastors and Bishops

Basil was born into an aristocratic family in the Roman province of Cappadocia. His family was Christian, largely because of the conversion of his grandmother Macrina. He was educated in Constantinople and Athens and returned home to take up the profession of a teacher of rhetoric. His sister Macrina (see July 19) persuaded Basil to abandon his work in order to pursue a life of asceticism. After a variety of experiments in solitary and communal ascetic living (including visits to Christian ascetics in Syria and Egypt), Basil began to form small communities of ascetics who strove to live what they believed was the authentic life of discipleship. His communities were an urban phenomenon and remained closely associated with the urban churches of Cappadocia. In Basil's *Ascetic Discourse, Longer Rules*, and *Shorter Rules*, he applies the precepts of the New Testament writings to these communities. Basil never refers to his ascetics as monks in these writings. He simply calls them Christians.

Basil's work as a theologian, bishop, ascetic, and author of liturgical texts earned him the title, "the Great." His treatise *On the Holy Spirit* helped lay the groundwork for the formal definition of the equal divinity of the Spirit at the Council of Constantinople in 381, and with other Cappadocian theologians he helped shape the doctrine of the Trinity in eastern Christian circles. A theological disciple of Origen, he managed to perpetuate the teaching of the Alexandrian while avoiding Origen's more speculative views.

Basil's vision of the disciplined Christian life challenges us today to take seriously the demands of the Gospel. His writing on the Holy Spirit calls us to recognize the work of the Spirit in the life of discipleship:

> Through the Holy Spirit comes our restoration to paradise, our ascension into the kingdom of heaven, our return to the adoption of sons, our liberty to call God our Father, our being made partakers of the grace of Christ, our being called children of light, our sharing in eternal glory, and, in a word, our being brought into a state of all "fullness of blessing" (Rom 15:29), both in this world and in the world to come, of all the good gifts that are in store for us, by promise whereof, through faith, beholding the reflection of their grace as though they were already present, we await the full enjoyment. If such is the earnest, what the perfection? If such the first fruits, what the complete fulfillment?[129]

G. S. Sperry-White

June 15
Evelyn Underhill (1941)
See Common of Teachers

Writer, teacher, "artist of the infinite life,"[130] Evelyn Underhill was attuned to the spiritual yearning of her age and becomes a wise guide to us today.

Underhill's two central works among over four hundred writings, *Mysticism* (1911) and *Worship* (1936), are thoroughly researched expressions of life in God. Steeped in the Christian mystics early on, Underhill later came to know personally the mystic way of "the passionate longing of the soul for God . . . loved, sought and adored in Himself for Himself alone."[131]

In the ecumenical volume, *Worship*, Underhill integrated diverse historical and institutional dimensions of faith in the One who is to be adored. She had a strong incarnational bent, evident not only in this book, but in her appreciation of the natural world, her cats and flowers, and the beauty in great art.

After years of wrestling with whether to become a Roman Catholic (to which Church she was deeply drawn), with the help of von Hügel and other spiritual guides, Underhill committed herself within the Church of England, where she had been baptized as a child. She offered retreats for both clergy and laity, and kept up a remarkable correspondence with spiritual directees. A handwritten letter about 1929 to the then Archbishop of Canterbury, Cosmo Gordon Lang, suggests that the bishops assembled at Lambeth "call the clergy . . . to a greater interiority and cultivation of the personal life of prayer."[132]

She was a devoted friend to many and worked regularly among the poor, while she and her husband lived in financial security. Early in the second World War, Underhill became a pacifist, which she saw as an authentic following of the will of God.

In the various struggles of her soul, Evelyn Underhill maintained a healthy balance between the inner and outer journeys. After her death, this prayer was offered in the Chapel at Pleshey where she had offered many retreats:

O God, who by the lives of those who love Thee dost refashion the souls of [all], We give Thee thanks for the ministry of Thy servant Evelyn; In whose life and words Thy love and majesty were made known to us, whose loving spirit set our spirits on fire, who learnt from Thee the Shepherd's care for His sheep; Grant that some measure of the Spirit which she received from Thee may fall on us who loved her. We ask it for the sake of Jesus Christ our Lord. Amen.[133]

B. B. Troxell

June 18
Matthew Simpson (1884)
See Common of Pastors and Bishops

For twenty years preceding and following the Civil War, through the offices of itinerant preacher, college professor, president of Indiana Asbury University (DePauw), Western Christian Advocate editor, Methodist Episcopal Church Bishop, and advisor and associate of four U.S. Presidential administrations, Matthew Simpson was arguably the best known and most loved man in American Methodism.

Born June 21, 1811 in Cadiz, Ohio, Simpson's home was often a night stopover for traveling Methodist ministers. According to town stories, one particular traveling preacher, Francis Asbury, performed the infant Matthew's baptism.

Simpson's mother and uncle taught him that he was a Child of Providence. What they meant, never revealing to Simpson until he had discerned his vocational call, was that as a newborn infant he had been consecrated to God in the hope of someday becoming a Christian minister. When consulting his mother for advice on entering the ordained ministry, she responded, "My son, I have been looking for this hour since the very hour you were born."

His overpowering oratorical eloquence contrasted the simplicity of his manner and the coarseness of his attire, as well as his tall, stooped, ungainly appearance. The voice, and the aura which surrounded him could lift human souls to the heavens until they could endure no more. His impassioned conviction in the unquestionable truth of Christianity could draw a tear from the most hardened heart and bring the strongest man to the point of weeping like a child.

Simpson, always mindful of preserving his beloved Methodist Episcopal Church, provided an amicable plan of separation as a response to Southern Church's threats of a potentially volatile cessation from the church over the issue of slavery's inherent right to go anywhere in the church in the form of slave-holding bishops. He also earned the distinction of proposing the formation of what would become the Church's Pacific Conference.

As Western Advocate editor, Simpson advanced the Church's voice in national public policy, believing, uncharacteristically for period, that the religious press had the inherent right to pursue an independent course, distinct from various political associations, and that Christian responsibility must do battle with right, and right was inextricably bound up with public affairs. He was a trusted friend of Abraham Lincoln and conducted his funeral service.

Elected to the Episcopacy in 1852, he served until his death in 1884.

M. B. McGhee

June 21
Thomas Bowman Stephenson (1912)
See Common of Pastors and Bishops

Stephenson, a British Methodist preacher, was born December 22, 1839. He entered the ministry of the Wesleyan Methodist Church in 1860. The young preacher's mustache, a worldly adornment at the time, raised more than a few eyebrows and communicated something of his rather progressive disposition. Stephenson drew crowds with his powerful baritone voice and was the first Methodist to rent a theater for evangelistic purposes. He became a leading advocate for admitting laymen to Conference — a privilege long guarded by the ordained. His two most important innovations were the founding of a children's home and the training of Methodist deaconesses.

Stephenson lived in the England of Charles Dickens and Lord Shaftesbury. Here many children were exploited in factories and mines, used as chimney-sweeps, and abandoned to the streets. While riding his circuits, Stephenson had witnessed the sufferings of countless boys and girls. At thirty he set about forming a home for children. In 1869 The Children's Home opened with the object of rescuing "children who, through the death or vice or extreme poverty of their parents, are in danger of falling into criminal ways." Instead of gathering children into huge dormitories as orphanages typically did, Stephenson formed "families" of eight to ten children under a married couple's guardianship. Each family lived in a separate house, maintaining its own intimate relations and interests. All families were united by common school, worship, and principal. In 1871 the Wesleyan Conference officially recognized the Home. Principal Stephenson retired in 1890, having established extensions of his Children's Home in England and Canada.

In running the Children's Home, Stephenson was assisted by many laywomen. Indeed, he grew particularly concerned with women and ministry, an issue that few of his ordained colleagues wished to consider. In 1890 he published his book, *Sisterhoods*, in which he outlined the history and described the duties of a deaconess. In the early Church, deaconesses had ecclesiastical status, received episcopal benediction, and were considered part of the official ministry, reported Stephenson. Their duties ranged from assisting in the baptism of women and children to tending the sick and hungry. Stephenson was deeply convinced that the Methodist Church worldwide needed deaconesses. Hence, in 1890, he organized the Wesley Deaconess Institute, which became a college in 1902. A lifelong visionary, Stephenson closed his eyes to this world on this date in 1912.

T. J. Bell

June 22
Alban (c. 304)
See Common of Martyrs

Alban is honored as the first martyr of Britain. Nothing is known of his life, and it is not even certain in which period of persecution he died. The account of his martyrdom is given by Bede in his *Ecclesiastical History of the English People*, based on a lesser-known fifth-century 'Passion of Alban.' According to these accounts, Alban, a citizen of Roman Verulamium (near present-day St. Alban's in Hertfordshire) gave shelter to a Christian priest fleeing from persecution, and was so impressed by his continual prayer that he began to seek instruction and became a Christian. When soldiers came to search for the priest, Alban gave himself up instead and was eventually executed by beheading.

Alban typifies the convert who finds a new identity in the new faith community. When asked about his family he replied "What does it concern you . . . of what stock I am? If you desire to hear the truth of my religion, be it known to you, that I am now a Christian, and bound by Christian duties." He remained steadfast in his loyalty to the faith which he had so newly entered.

His story extends, however, beyond his death. By 429 a shrine was in existence at which, according to Bede writing in c.730 "there ceases not to this day the cure of sick persons, and the frequent working of wonders."[134] His place of execution is described in some detail as a smooth and beautiful hill, covered in wild flowers, and separated from the town of Verulamium by a rapid river. This description fits extraordinarily well with the site of the existing twelfth-century abbey church of St. Alban's, which is now the cathedral of a diocese. Associated Roman-British Christian burials testify to the site's ancient sanctity which persists to this day. So Alban speaks across the centuries not only of the martyr's steadfastness, but also of the continuity of the faith and the importance of sacred and numinous places in bearing that continuity.[135]

M. P. Jones

The Nativity of John the Baptist

The feast of the nativity of John the Baptist is an irregularity in the liturgical calendar because we commemorate John's birth day rather than the day of his death (the only other exceptions being Christ and Mary). Six months in advance of the birth of Jesus, we remember the birth of the baby that leapt in the womb of Elizabeth at the approach of the newly pregnant Mary.

We honor the story of John's nativity because of its importance in the opening of the Gospel of Luke. There John's birth to Elizabeth and Zechariah is portrayed not only as God's blessing to a childless, elderly couple but also as the start of God's plan of salvation through Christ. John's role in God's saving economy is also highlighted in the prophecy of the Spirit-filled Zechariah:

> And you, child, will be called the prophet of the Most High; for you will go before the Lord to prepare his ways, to give knowledge of salvation to his people by the forgiveness of their sins. By the tender mercy of our God, the dawn from on high will break upon us. (Lk 1:76-78)

John's birth is thus the sign that the sun of righteousness stands ready on the horizon, its healing light even now burning through the darkness of sin. The Orthodox sing in joy about John's birth:

> On this day the herald of grace more dazzling than the dawn announces the Sun of glory and proclaims that his radiance will enlighten the entire world.

> By your birth, O forerunner, the godless night has been driven away from the earth. From one end to the other the rays of divine grace shine forth because you announce the Sun which never sets.[136]

L. Ruth

Isaiah 40:1-11
Psalm 85 (*UMH* 806)
Acts 13:13-26
Luke 1:57-80

Most High God, you sent John the Baptist as a prophet and as a witness to the Light: Evermore prepare in us hearts ready to bear the fruit of repentance and to welcome the fire of the Holy Spirit, through Christ our Lord. Amen.

[DTB]

God of crooked ways made straight,
 cause us to always rejoice in the approach of Jesus.
 Like John the baptizer, work in us such humility and joy,
 that when Jesus calls we never hinder his increase as Lord of all.
 When we fret in the prisons of delay and martyrdom,
 send us news of Messiah Jesus so we hold on in faith to the end. Amen.

[DTB]

June 28
Irenaeus (c. 202)
See Common of Teachers

Irenaeus was truly a "lover of peace," according to the words of a letter with which his fellow Christians in Gaul sent him to Eleutherius, Bishop of Rome, in 177. At the time a presbyter in the city of Lyons, Irenaeus was, like many Christians there, concerned about the strained relations between Eleutherius and the Montanist party in their native land. Unlike many of those Christians in Lyons, however, Irenaeus was spared martyrdom in a fierce persecution that arose there while he was away on his diplomatic mission. With the city's bishop among those who had died for the faith, Irenaeus assumed the episcopacy upon returning from Rome. A decade later Irenaeus successfully brought peace between Rome and another group of Asiatic Christians, the Quatrodecimans.

Within his own diocese Irenaeus worked to stem the tide of numerous Gnostic movements into which Gaulish Christians were fragmenting. His *Against Heresies*, one of only complete two works to have survived him, is characterized by fair and moderate treatment of various Gnostic positions and a desire to convert their adherents. His effort to bring unity among Christians through peaceful persuasion was an ethical practice consistent with his belief in the God who redeemed humanity from Satan's grasp:

> By reason of the fact that the apostate power, by making us his own pupils, oppressed us unjustly and alienated us in a way contrary to nature (for by nature we belong to almighty God), the Logos of God, powerful in every way and unfailing in justice, acted justly even in opposing that same apostate power. He redeemed his own from it, not by violence (which is the way that power got control of us to begin with: it snatched insatiably at what did not belong to it) but by persuasion, for that is the proper way for a God who persuades and does not compel in order to get what he wants.[137]

Irenaeus countered Gnostic claims that this world is fundamentally evil and that secretive salvific knowledge is available only for an elect few by appealing to scriptural accounts of creation and redemption and by highlighting the public quality and constancy of the tradition passed in unbroken succession from the Apostles. This appeal to scripture and tradition became the standard theological method in the early centuries.

B. T. Morrill

June 28
Peter Jones, or *Kahkewaquonaby* (1856)
See Common of Preachers

Peter Jones spent his life poised between two worlds. His mother, *Tuhbenahneequay*, was an Ojibwa Indian and the daughter of a chief. His father, Augustus Jones, was a white land surveyor and a farmer. Until he was fourteen years old, *Kahkewaquonaby* (Sacred Feathers) lived with his mother and her people near Lake Ontario, Canada. In 1816, he moved into his father's household, took the name Peter Jones, and began schooling to learn English and the ways of a white man.

Though Jones was baptized when he was eighteen, he later acknowledged he had done so from a sense of duty to his father and the Great Spirit. Christianity did not appeal to him because of the immorality of many white people who called themselves Christians. Yet, by the time he was twenty-one, Jones had experienced the spiritual crisis that led to his conversion. Increasingly overwhelmed by a sense of personal sin, he attended a Methodist camp meeting where he had a vision of Christ. He later wrote,

Every thing now appeared in a new light, and all the works of God seemed to unite with me in uttering the praises of the Lord. The people, the trees of the woods, the gentle winds, the warbling notes of the birds, and the approaching sun, all declared the power and goodness of the Great Spirit.[138]

Jones was now ready to begin his life work of bringing Christianity to the Canadian Indians. Energized by an intense belief in a living God of grace, Jones preached in his native tongue, then translated his sermons into English for curious whites. He completed an Ojibwa translation of the Bible, as well as an Ojibwa hymnal that remains in use more than 150 years later. He ultimately traveled to America and Great Britain to raise money for missionary work. All the while, he worked tirelessly to secure land titles for Canadian Indians, to provide them with an adequate educational system, and to gain for them the right of self-government.

Jones faced many obstacles. Racism, church factionalism, and tribal distrust repeatedly tested him. The continuing oppression of Indians disheartened him. Through faith, however, he served as a living bridge between races, cultures, and doctrines. Today marks the eve of his death on June 29, 1856.

S. H. Hill

Peter and Paul

Peter and Paul, "twin pillars" of the Church, were martyrs for the sake of Gospel. According to tradition, Peter was executed by upside-down crucifixion (the method used to kill slaves), Paul by beheading. During the persecution of Valerian in the third century, the church at Rome appointed this single day to commemorate their martyrdoms under Nero. Some argue that this was the date when in 258 the relics of both Peter and Paul were translated to the catacombs.

In a sermon for this feast day,[139] Augustine wrote:

The passion of the most blessed apostles Peter and Paul has made this day holy for us. "The sound of them has gone out through all the earth, and their words to the end of the world."

In Peter, strength is especially commended to the Church, for he followed the Lord going to his passion; yet a certain weakness is also observed, for when he was questioned by a servant girl, he three times denied the Lord. The lover suddenly became a denier. But then what? "The Lord looked at him," and "he went out," that is, to confess, and "he wept bitterly," who had known what it is to love.

After his Resurrection, the Lord instructed this same Peter to feed his sheep. Three times the Lord asked, "Do you love me?" And three times his confession triumphed in love, where three times his conceit had triumphed in fear.

Paul comes out of Saul, the lamb out of the wolf. First enemy, then apostle; first persecutor, then preacher. Our Lord Jesus Christ said, "I will show him what he must suffer for my name." And then he occupied him in his service. He exercised him in chains, in stripes, in prisons, in shipwrecks. He put him through suffering, and he brought him to this day.

One day of suffering for two apostles. But these two were one. Though they suffered on different days, they were one. Peter went ahead; Paul followed. Let us then celebrate their feast day which has been consecrated for us by their blood. Let us love their faith, their life, their labors, their sufferings, their confessions, their preaching.

Peter and Paul are remembered separately elsewhere in the calendar: the Confession of Peter on January 18 and the Conversion of Paul on January 25.

K. B. Westerfield Tucker

Ezekiel 34:11-16
Psalm 87:1-2, 4-6; or 126 (*UMH* 847)
2 Timothy 4:1-8
John 21:15-19

Almighty and everlasting God, who has adorned the sacred body of your
Church by the confessions of your servants Peter and Paul: Grant us, we
pray, that both by their doctrines and their pious example we may follow
after what is pleasing in your sight, through Jesus Christ our Lord, who
with you and the Holy Spirit lives and reigns, one God for ever and ever.
Amen.

[Leonine Sacramentary; alt. TJC]

Pursuing, shepherding, and converting God,
Your risen Son appeared to both Peter and Paul
  undoing their past,
  claiming them for the work of your Church,
  spilling them out as witnesses to a deeper love.
Undo and claim us,
  that we too may finish the race you set before us in Christ Jesus. Amen.

[CFG]

July 2
Anna Howard Shaw (1919)
See Common of Preachers

> ... influenced by lofty motives, stimulated by the wail of humanity
> and the glory of God, woman may go forth and enter into any field
> of usefulness that opens up before her.[140]

Anna Howard Shaw's words to the 1888 International Council of Women summarize her own life.

Though born in England, Anna Howard grew up on the Michigan frontier. Her father returned to Massachusetts with his older sons, leaving an overwhelmed wife, three daughters, and a small son to cope. She found strength at an early age.

She also heard a call to preach. The forest trees were her first congregation. Knowing she must be educated, she read voraciously, attended school whenever possible, and became a teacher. Learning of her call, the Methodists agreed to test her skills. In 1870 she preached 36 times. In 1871 the Conference gave her a license though her family and community opposed the idea.

When Mary Livermore came to lecture in Big Rapids, Anna Howard went to shake her hand. Another woman urged Livermore not to encourage her and noted that she was sickly anyway. Mrs. Livermore agreed she appeared ill, but said, "But it is better that she should die doing the thing she wants to do than that she should die because she can't do it."

At age 26 Anna entered Albion College, supporting herself by lecturing on temperance. Two years later she became a divinity student at Boston University. Ineligible for the aid given male students, she almost died of starvation until rescued by members of the Woman's Foreign Missionary Society.

While pastoring two small churches on Cape Cod, she applied for ordination in the Methodist Episcopal Church. Not only was she denied ordination by the General Conference of 1880, her preaching license (and those of all other women) was revoked. She turned to the Methodist Protestant Church and was the first woman it ordained.

The local pastorate did not offer Shaw a wide enough field of usefulness so she went back to medical school at Boston University, receiving her M.D. in 1886. She became a full-time lecturer for the Woman's Christian Temperance Union and an organizer for the Massachusetts Woman's Suffrage Association. In 1891 she became a national lecturer for the National American Woman's Suffrage Association. Serving as vice-president to Susan B. Anthony and Carrie Chapman Catt from 1892 to 1904, she became president of the association from 1904 to 1915. Her autobiography, *The Story of a Pioneer,* shows a life committed to helping women achieve their divine potential.[141]

N. A. Hardesty

July 4
Jashwant Rao Chitambar (1940)
See Common of Pastors and Bishops

Chitambar became an outstanding leader of Methodism in North India as educator, evangelist, first bishop in the Methodist Church of India, and worldwide representative of Indian Methodism. Although his family was initially Hindu, his father converted to Christianity and became a Methodist Episcopal Church pastor in 1889. Chitambar recalled that, "My father was a Brahmin who bought a Bible to find errors in it, but he became convinced of the truth of Christianity and was baptized."

Rather than rejecting his Hindu and Muslim brothers and sisters, Chitambar worked with them for the bettering of India. One of his closest associates wrote: "He yielded to none in his love for the Motherland, and he improved every occasion that came to him to serve her. Wherever he went he aroused the Indian Christian community to take its due share in the political uplift and edification of the country. India was ever on his heart. Of her he dreamed, for her he wrought, for her he lived, and, verily, he was a noble son of Mother India."

Chitambar was also tireless in his work for the Methodist community. He helped found the National Missionary Society of India in 1905, an evangelism organization which carried out work throughout India. He was named the first Indian principal of Lucknow College in 1922. He sought to build up Indian Methodism's spiritual life by translating numerous hymns such as, "At the Cross," and "Lovingly, Tenderly Jesus is Calling." He also translated the *Book of Discipline* in 1925. He was consecrated bishop on January 4, 1931.

Chitambar's faith was a simple and evangelical. His most oft-repeated prayer was,

Let the beauty of Jesus be seen in me,
All His wondrous compassion and purity:
O, Thou Spirit Divine, all my nature refine,
Till the beauty of Jesus be seen in me.

E. Stanley Jones wrote at Chitambar's death: "With the death of Bishop Chitambar there falls one of the first fruits of Indian leadership from the tree planted by Christian missions in India. He was the outstanding leader of the Methodist Church for a generation."[142]

C. G. Lindquist

July 5
Richard Whatcoat (1806)
See Common of Pastors and Bishops

The second elected American bishop and a deeply respected spiritual leader of early Methodism, Whatcoat was born in Gloucestershire in 1736. As a young man, Whatcoat began attending Methodist meetings and in 1758 he experienced the assurance of his salvation and soon became a class-leader and band-leader. "I felt a strong desire," he wrote, "for others to partake of the same happiness with myself." He was accepted as lay preacher at the 1769 Conference and spent the next fifteen years itinerating in circuits throughout England, Ireland, and Wales.

The need for more ordained missionaries in America was raised at the 1784 Conference. "At first," he writes, "it appeared to me as though I was not concerned in the matter; but soon my mind was drawn to meditate on the subject: the power of God came upon me." Wesley ordained him along with Thomas Vasey, and with Thomas Coke appointed to be a general superintendent, the three were sent to America. Whatcoat traveled widely with Asbury throughout the middle colonies and into the Kentucky and Tennessee wilderness. For a time he served as the presiding elder in Philadelphia and as pastor of the famous Johns' Street church. His preaching was plain, but spiritual and highly effective. Revivals often accompanied his pastoral work.

In 1786, Wesley directed that Whatcoat should be made a bishop, but the American conference refused, being concerned that Asbury might be recalled to England and resenting Wesley's continuing control. Four years later, however, Whatcoat was narrowly elected bishop after tying with Jesse Lee on the first ballot. Whatcoat's gentle demeanor proved a good foil to Asbury's authoritarian streak and they traveled and worked well together. But Whatcoat's advancing age and the hardships of long and constant travel were taking their toll. He died on this date after a lingering illness and was buried beneath the altar of Wesley Chapel in Dover, Delaware, where Asbury preached his funeral sermon. Asbury said of him, "A man so uniformily good I have not known in Europe or America."[143] Laban Clark wrote, "I think I may safely say that if I ever knew one who came up to St. James' descriptions of a perfect man, — one who bridled his tongue and kept in subjection his whole body, — that man was Bishop Whatcoat.[144]

C. F. Guthrie

July 6
John Hus (1415)
See Common of Prophets

O most kind Christ, draw us weaklings after thyself, for unless thou draw us, we cannot follow thee. Give us a courageous spirit that it may be ready; and if the flesh is weak, may thy grace go before, now as well as subsequently. For without thee we can do nothing, and particularly to go to a cruel death for Thy sake. Give us a valiant spirit, a fearless heart, the right faith, a firm hope, and perfect love, that we may offer our lives for thy sake with the greatest patience and joy. Amen.[145]

John Hus included this prayer in a letter from prison to a friend, dated June 23, 1415. It typifies the ardor by which he lived and died. Son of a poor Bohemian peasant family, he received a bachelors degree in 1393 and a masters degree in 1396 from Prague University. In 1400 he was ordained and the following year appointed preacher at Prague's Bethlehem Chapel. In 1402 he was made rector of Prague University.

A fiery preacher in his native Czech language, Hus sometimes drew congregations of three thousand people. He fulminated against corruption in the medieval church. Hus saw the Holy Scriptures essentially as "Christ's law" and urged priests, nobles, and common people to forsake worldliness and to live according to Christ's law.[146] While Hus in this respect differed from the subsequent Protestant Reformation, his opposition to clerical abuses and the sale of indulgences, as well as his translation of the Scriptures into the Czech language earned him the title of "pre-Reformer." Hus was partly influenced by the writings of John Wycliff (c.1325-1384).

Hus' refusal to stop preaching led to his excommunication in 1412. Summoned to the Council of Constance under imperial safe conduct, Hus was jailed and treated as a heretic. Refusing to recant heresies he did not hold, he died at the stake on July 6, 1415.

Bohemia thereupon rose up in rebellion. Never subjected by military force, Hus' followers after 1458 were known as the Unity of the Bohemian Brethren, which in the eighteenth century became the spiritual ancestor to the Moravian church.

K. J. Stein

July 11
Benedict of Nursia (c. 540)
See Common of Saints, Teachers

"Listen carefully . . . to the master's instructions, and attend to them with the ear of your heart," begins the Rule of St. Benedict. This patterned life became a way of ordering Christian communities of prayer and work for over fifteen centuries, breathing the gracious and supple spirit of Benedict into many different times, places, and cultures. Benedict writes that the Rule is best thought of as

> a school for the Lord's service. In drawing up its regulations, we hope to set down nothing harsh, nothing burdensome. The good of all concerned, however, may prompt us to a little strictness in order to amend faults and to safeguard love (Prologue, 45-47).[147]

Born toward the end of the fifth century in northern Italy, Benedict left all to follow Christ, soon finding a community gathering around him to seek a way of salvation rooted in common life, and grounded in the Christian virtues of poverty, humility, and obedience. He founded a monastery at Montecassino which, through war and tumult, still remains the mother-house for all Benedictines the world over.

He admonishes members of the monastic community that "the love of Christ must come before all else" (Chapter 4, vs. 21). In pondering this day the moderation and the communal wisdom of the Rule which bears his name, we may be drawn more deeply into such love. Far from sentimentality, such a love of Christ bears the work and stability of Christ's constancy. Far from an individualist feeling, such love bears accountability and responsibility within real social history. Countless women and men have, over the centuries, been living testimony of the grace of gentle discipline, prayer, and honest work for the common good which Benedict still brings forth for us today.

D. E. Saliers

July 19
Macrina the Younger (379)
See Common of Saints, Teachers

Macrina the Younger was a member of one of the most illustrious families of ancient Christianity, "a troop of saints," to use Robert Taft's phrase.[148] She was the oldest of the ten children of a wealthy land-owning family of Cappadocia in Asia Minor, and was named for her grandmother who may have been the first member of the family to embrace the Christian faith. Macrina's brothers included Basil the Great, Peter of Sebaste, and Gregory of Nyssa. Her story is recounted by Gregory in his *Life of Saint Macrina*.

Macrina was betrothed at twelve to a young lawyer, but he died before they were married. Although her beauty attracted many suitors, she convinced her father that it would be inappropriate for her to marry because her betrothed was "living in God because of the hope of the resurrection." Instead, she dedicated herself to caring for her mother and brothers and to a life of "philosophy," a life devoted to God in Christ by living the disciplines of simplicity, prayer, fasting, and service. When Basil returned from school "excessively puffed up," she persuaded him to abandon the fame he would enjoy as a classical rhetorician and also take up the life of philosophy.

Macrina's organization of her household into a kind of ascetic community influenced Basil's ideas concerning how to live as a Christian and modeled a way for women to have more authority than they typically had in Christian communities. Returning from a synod at Antioch and after an eight-year absence, Gregory found Macrina, now Superior of her monastic community, on her deathbed. Their conversation became the basis for Gregory's work, *On the Soul and Resurrection*. In this work, Macrina dominates the conversation and Gregory calls her his teacher, indicating the theological and religious sway she had over her family. Her last audible words before death were a prayer to God to "forgive me so that I may be refreshed and may be found before You once I have put off my body, having no fault in the form of my soul, but blameless and spotless may my soul be taken into Your hands as an offering before Your face."[149]

G. S. Sperry-White

July 20
Belle Harris Bennett (1922)
See Common of Prophets, Teachers

One of the foremost lay women in the Methodist Church, South, Belle Harris Bennett was born in 1852, the seventh of eight children. She was well educated, and because she was financially supported by her family she was able to work without salary, going wherever she saw a need.[150]

She was born in 1852, shortly after slavery's abolition in the North and at a time when women rarely spoke in public. The fifteenth amendment, permitting Black men to vote but not women of any race, was hotly debated in the late 1860's. The 1890s saw the explosion of the anti-lynching campaign.[151] It was in this period of monumental societal change that Bennett began her work. She took her religious life seriously, participating in prayer, Bible study, hymn singing, and devotions. A gifted organizer, her concern for the proper training of missionaries led her to raise money for what became in 1892 the Scarritt Bible and Training School, a women's missionary school in Kansas City, Missouri (it moved to Nashville in 1924). Her later missionary work included the foundation of new mission fields and a women's college in Rio de Janeiro. Her leadership and interest in the needs of cities and the education of women spurred the founding of almost 50 homes for young working women.

Although initially discouraged by her church, she often preached against race prejudice. She also convinced the Women's Board of Home Missions to build an industrial department and dormitories (both for women) at the Paine Institute for Negroes in Augusta, Georgia. Bennett was a strong advocate for women's lay rights in the Southern Methodist General Conference, and was elected Kentucky's first woman delegate to the General Conference of 1922.[152] She served as the president of the Woman's Missionary Council from 1910 until her death from cancer in 1922.

Bennett's ministry tended to the Reign of God on earth in very practical ways. After learning of a woman whose attendance at school was endangered because she was pregnant, Bennett immediately wrote the institution's president suggesting the school start a child care program. She well embodied a sentence from a letter she wrote in 1918: "It takes a heart life — *a lived experience* — to interpret the Word of God."[153]

T. M. Eugene

Mary Magdalene

Although the figure of Mary Magdalene has a rich history in the art and literature of the church, historical knowledge of her is scant. She first appears in the Gospels of Mark and Matthew observing the crucifixion of Jesus "from far off" with other women who had ministered to Jesus (Mk 15:40, Mt 27:56). The absence of Jesus' disciples at the cross makes the women's presence all the more significant. In the Gospel of Luke, Mary Magdalene is described as one from whom Jesus had cast out seven demons (Lk 8:2). According to Luke, she then accompanied Jesus, along with the disciples and several other women, as he traveled throughout the cities and villages.

Mary's intimate relationship with Jesus is emphasized most strongly in John's Gospel. While all four gospels portray Mary's presence at the tomb, indicating the importance of this tradition to the early church, John describes with detailed poignancy a private scene of revelation between Jesus and Mary (Jn 20:1-18). In John's account, Mary is instructed by Jesus to give word of his ascension to the disciples. Mary's subsequent announcement of her Easter experience to the disciples earned her the title *Apostola Apostolorum* (apostle to the apostles). This aspect of Mary has long inspired devotion among women — over the years various noble women have commissioned illuminations in which Mary is depicted speaking before a group of eleven disciples.[154] In recent years, Mary's role as first witness to the resurrection has provided an important model for women leaders in the church.

Noticeably absent from the New Testament accounts of Mary Magdalene is any description of her as a repentant prostitute. This well known image appears later, as the romantic myth surrounding Mary's identity developed within the church. Most likely it grew out of an association with the "sinner" of Luke 7:36-50 who anoints Jesus' feet with her tears. For the medieval church, in particular, Mary embodied sexuality, sin, and womankind, repentant and redeemed through Christ. More recently, based on the New Testament witness, this identification of Mary as a prostitute has been challenged. Her memory might be better served through meditation on her words, "I have seen the Lord!" (Jn 20:18).

C. C. Grant

Zephaniah 3:14-20
Psalm 42 (*UMH* 777)
2 Corinthians 5:14-18
John 20:11-18

Holy God, whose risen Son called Mary by name to be a witness of his resurrection: Call us also by name that we may know you and bear witness, and grant that those who remain in grief and confusion may hear her words of new life in Jesus Christ, our Lord, who lives and reigns with you and the Holy Spirit, one God, now and forever. Amen.

[CFG]

Teacher!
  Lost and weeping I went looking for you,
  It was not you I saw at first, but someone else,
  Then you called me by name.
  Let me cling to you!
  No. Send me to tell what I have seen and heard,
      for the old has passed and everything become new,
      through your rising. Amen.

[CFG]

July 24
Thomas à Kempis (1471)
See Common of Pastors and Bishops

Born at Kempen in Germany, Thomas Hemerken went at age twelve to the Netherlands to study under the Brothers of the Common Life, an association desiring to imitate the lives of the early Christians. Founded by Geert Groote, they stressed the spiritual life, education, and meditation and were a part of a reform movement called the "Devotio moderna" (New Devotion). The Brothers soon organized an Augustinian monastery near Zwolle to establish a more stable organization. Thomas was among the first to enter the monastery and was ordained priest in 1413.

During the period after his ordination he authored his famous *Imitation of Christ,* a work that has been called the "best loved religious book of the world, with the exception of the Bible."[155] Its purpose is to teach the Christian the way of perfection by following the example of Christ:

> Jesus has many who love his kingdom in heaven, but few who bear his cross. He has many who desire comfort, but few who desire suffering. . . . Many love Jesus as long as no hardship touches them. . . . They who love Jesus for his own sake, and not for the sake of comfort for themselves, bless him in every trial and anguish of heart.

As in baptism we imitate the death of Christ, in imitation of his life we can hope to walk in newness of life. Thomas hears the voice of Jesus say, "if you would be exalted in heaven, humble yourself here on earth; and if you would reign with me, bear the cross with me, for, truly, only the servants of the cross will find the life of blessedness and of everlasting life." Written when the intellectual and religious foundations of Europe were crumbling, the book calls for examination of interior life.

Thomas does not, however, lapse into religious individualism; participation in the Eucharist is integral to the life of faith: "Oh, the grace of this Sacrament is marvelously and secretly hidden, and only the faithful people of God know it."[156] He would remind the reader that an examined life, nurtured by the reception of the Body and Blood of Christ, is necessary for those seeking to be faithful during times of drastic change.

Thomas wrote many other but lesser known devotional works and two biographies, including one on Groote. He died on the feast day of James the Elder (July 25), but his commemoration is moved forward to this day.

G. L. Hayes

James the Elder

The James commemorated today is not to be confused with James the brother of the Lord (October 23). The person we remember today was a fisherman, the brother of John and a son of Zebedee. This James is the only apostle whose death the New Testament records: "About that time King Herod laid violent hands upon some who belonged to the church. He had James, the brother of John, killed with the sword" (Acts 12:2). Thus his death probably occurred around the year 42 C.E. The date of his feast probably is connected with the translation of his relics.

Jesus gave the name Boanerges to James and John; Mark records that the name means "Sons of Thunder" (Mk 3:17). Along with Peter and John, James is portrayed as one of the inner circle of Jesus' disciples: only they are present at the rising to life of Jarius' daughter (Mk 5:21ff), and at the transfiguration (Mk 9:2-8). At the same time, Mark portrays James and John as radically misunderstanding the nature of discipleship: they ask Jesus to place them at his right and left hand when he comes into his kingdom (Mk 10:35-45).

The fourth-century historian Eusebius of Caesarea records in his *Ecclesiastical History* a tradition concerning James' martyrdom taken from a lost work of Clement of Alexandria. In this story, James' prosecutor is converted and willingly martyred alongside him:

> he who brought him to the court was so moved at seeing him testify as to confess that he also was himself a Christian. "So they were both led away together," he says, "and on the way he asked for forgiveness for himself from James. And James looked at him for a moment and said, 'Peace be to you,' and kissed him. So both were beheaded at the same time."[157]

G. S. Sperry-White

Jeremiah 45:1-5
Psalm 7:1-10 (alt. Psalm 39 *UMH* 773)
Acts 11:27-12:3
Mark 10:35-45

Holy God, whose servant James was the first among the apostles to be
martyred, so clarify our own witness before the world's authorities that,
like James, our life and death in you may testify to the source of all true
power, through Jesus Christ, who lives and reigns with you and the Holy
Spirit, one God, now and forever. Amen.

[CFG]

Servant Son,
in the strange wisdom of your kingdom
  the great ones are least of all,
  rulers are to be servants,
  and those who long most to be near you are the first to learn the cost.
Before we casually claim our ability to partake of your cup and your
baptism,
  give us holy pause
and teach us care in what we ask in your strong name. Amen.

[CFG]

July 26
Charles Albert Tindley (1933)
See Common of Preachers, Musicians

Born to slaves in Delaware in 1851, Charles would find bits of newspaper, and while others were asleep secretly study his A B Cs by candlelight. One Sunday he went barefoot to church and intended to hide in the gallery, but when children "who could read the Bible" were invited to come to the front pew, he went forward and read to the congregation's astonishment. After working in the field all day, he would run fourteen miles to a teacher who later offered to give him lessons.

Charles and his bride Daisy Henry moved to Philadelphia and stayed with a family who invited them to attend the John Wesley Methodist Episcopal Church. He was a hod carrier by day and attended school or church meetings at night. As the unpaid sexton at the church, he had access to the books there, reading whatever his pastor or presiding elder recommended. Despite his lack of formal education, he received high marks from a rigorous ministerial examining committee and was admitted into the Delaware Conference as a probationer.

As he pastored, he mastered both Hebrew and Greek and read widely. After serving as a presiding elder, he was appointed pastor of the church which he had served as sexton. Soon he was preaching to capacity crowds, many of whom held domestic and menial jobs and knew Tindley could understand their life and work. He would often illustrate his point with a song. Sometimes both the tune and the words were unfamiliar, and he would explain that it was one he had just written and "line it out" until the congregation knew it. When large numbers of African Americans came from the south to take jobs during the first world war, Tindley led efforts to provide them with housing; their ranks swelled the membership of the church.

His dream of building a "cathedral" was realized, but it was left unfinished and with a burden of debt the denomination had promised to assume but did not. Although he was nominated for the episcopacy three times, his humble origins and race were used cruelly against him. Yet his influence as a "prince of preachers" and the writer of gospel songs is far-reaching (See *UMH* 373, 512, 522, 524, 525, and 846). His prayer: "when the storms of life are raging, stand by me" came from deep personal experience.[158]

D. W. Vogel

July 28
Johann Sebastian Bach and
George Frederick Handel (1750 and 1759)
See Common of Musicians

J. S. Bach was born in 1685 and died on this date in 1750. As a young organist in Muhlhausen he served with a pastor who was deeply influenced by the pietism of Spener. Bach's profound and simple faith, his deep religious experience, and his personal devotion to Jesus Christ are evident in his letters and his music, especially his treatment of German hymnody. Contemporary worshippers are unable to think of the texts of "O Sacred Head Now Wounded" or "Jesus, Joy of our Desiring" apart from his harmonizations. He composed nearly three hundred church cantatas, as well as passions, oratorios, and motets, and a great deal of sacred organ music including preludes for many Lutheran chorales. His devotional interpretation of hymn texts through music has been called, "the greatest of all contributions to the praise of God through the hymn." He consistently inscribed his compositions "*soli Deo gloria*" — "to the glory of God alone." A few days before he died, he composed a prelude on a chorale whose text in English is:

> Before thy throne, my God, I stand
> Myself, my all are in thy hand; . . .
> Grant that my end may worthy be,
> And that I wake thy face to see,
> Thyself for evermore to know!
> Amen, Amen, God grant it so![159]

Like Bach, George Frederick Handel grew up in a German Protestant environment. He traveled widely and became well known for providing secular and sacred music for the middle classes as well as the elite. He composed music for three denominations: Roman Catholic, Lutheran, and Anglican, often writing music for specific occasions. Most of his impact for us comes from his work while in England and Ireland. His settings of the texts in *Messiah* are moving and unforgettable. Listen for the music through which we know these texts:

> Comfort, comfort ye my people . . . And the glory, the glory of the Lord shall be revealed . . . For unto us a child is born . . . Surely, he has born our griefs and carried our sorrows . . . Blessing and honor, glory and power be unto him that sitteth upon the throne and unto the Lamb . . . And he shall reign forever and ever, King of kings and Lord of lords! Hallelujah! Hallelujah! Hallelujah!

D. W. Vogel

July 29
Mary and Martha of Bethany
See Common of Saints

The New Testament stories of Mary and Martha witness to the importance of these sisters in the memory of the Church. The women appear briefly in the Gospel of Luke (10:38-42) and more extensively in the Gospel of John (11:1-44; 12:1-8). From these two Gospels come two very different depictions of the sisters.

Luke's portrayal of the women, the worried activity of Martha contrasted with the quiet reflectiveness of Mary, has traditionally received more attention. As a result, Martha has often been viewed in a negative light, on the wrong side of the Reformation's opposition to "works." Mary, on the other hand, has been praised as the contemplative, faithful follower of Jesus. Instead of stressing this polarity, one might consider Jesus' rebuke of Martha a liberating statement, one that frees women from their traditional duties. Similarly, Jesus' encouragement of Mary demonstrates an acceptance of women as students and disciples.

In John's Gospel, both women appear positively as faithful disciples of Jesus. Martha is depicted as a bold and forthright woman, who does not hesitate to confront Jesus with her sorrow. At the same time, she shows trust in Jesus as one who can bestow God's gifts (11:21-22). Moreover, Martha offers a full confession of Jesus as the Messiah, "Yes, Lord, I believe that you are the Messiah, the Son of God, the one coming into the world" (11:27). The significance of this confession is made stronger by its echo at the conclusion of the Gospel (20:31).

Mary also shows a willingness to confront Jesus and lay her grief before him. Indeed, he is moved to tears by her sorrow. In John 12, it is Mary who anoints the feet of Jesus with expensive oil. Her action is interpreted by Jesus as a preparation for his death and burial. Thus, Mary's extravagant act of love for Jesus points the way to Jesus' ultimate act of love for humankind. Similarly, the anointing of his feet rather than his head foreshadows the footwashing that serves as a lesson of discipleship in chapter 13.

The initiative of Martha and Mary in sending for Jesus, their bold faith, the grief they bring to him, their willingness to engage Jesus in conversations about life, death, and faith, and their deep love for Jesus are all marks of discipleship in the Gospel of John.[160]

C. C. Grant

July 30
Susanna Wesley (1742)
See Common of Saints

The mother of John and Charles, Susanna Wesley played a critical role in the initial and ongoing shape of the Methodist movement. Born in 1669, Susanna was the youngest daughter and the twenty-fifth child of the distinguished Puritan minister, Dr. Samuel Annesley. At thirteen, she broke with her nonconformist upbringing and united with the Church of England. Marrying an Anglican priest, Samuel Wesley, Susanna herself gave birth to nineteen children, but only ten of them survived infancy. Her methodical organization of this large household provided the example for John Wesley's disciplined approach to life and the systematic structuring of the Methodist societies.

When Susanna died on this date in 1742, John included in his journal entry a lengthy letter she had written to John in 1732 detailing the methods she employed in raising her children.[161] Susanna provided a primary education for them at home and insisted that, "no girl be taught to work till she can read very well." Instruction in reading began on a child's fifth birthday, and they were taught the alphabet in one day. The household was disrupted by the parsonage fire of 1709 and the children disbursed among several families. Upon being reunited, Susanna instituted for the family a system of daily psalm-singing, Bible reading, and prayers, partly to counter the bad habits the children had picked up in the other households.

Susanna was a highly educated woman who knew Latin and Greek and argued theology with her husband and sons. During Samuel's absences, she would hold 'family devotions' at which up to two hundred parishioners would attend. John Wesley wrote that she, like her father, grandfather, and three sons, had been a "preacher of righteousness."

After Samuel died she had a conversion experience while receiving the sacrament and became more supportive of the Methodist movement. Her defense of the lay preaching of Thomas Maxfield overcame John's reluctance at this unusual ministry, and thus opened the door to one of Methodism's most effective tools.

The esteem John had for his mother is revealed in his comment that, "From the time I was six or seven years old, if any one spoke to me concerning marrying, I used to say, I thought I never should, 'Because I should never find such a woman as my father had.'"[162] For a prayer attributed to Susanna, see *The United Methodist Book of Worship* (528).

B. W. Coe

August 7
John Mason Neale (1866)
See Common of Musicians, Saints

An Anglican priest, author, hymn writer, and translator, was born in 1818. Imbued with the High Church ideals of the Oxford Tractarians, Neale was one of the founders of the Cambridge Camden Society, a society for the study of ecclesiastical art. Through its publication, "The Ecclesiologist," the society attempted to stimulate interest in church architecture, especially medieval Gothic architecture, and traditional Catholic worship. The society's work contributed to the liturgical and ceremonial revival in the Church of England in the late nineteenth century.

Although ordained, his Anglo-Catholic ideals prevented many bishops from offering him a parish and ill health prevented his taking a parish when it was offered to him. For twenty years Neale held the wardenship of Sackville College, a foundation for the shelter and maintenance of some thirty poor and elderly people. While at Sackville, he divided his time between the care of his wards and his literary and patristic work. Using the college chapel to implement many of his architectural ideals, he was eventually censured by the bishop of the diocese. His work within the college eventually led to the establishment of the Sisterhood of St. Margaret for the care of the sick and the education of girls. While his liturgical work provoked riots, the sisterhood gained the esteem of the community.

As a writer, Neale produced a commentary on the psalms, in effect a compilation from patristic and medieval authors, and a history of the eastern church. He also produced a number of children's books written to present Christian teaching "in a simple and attractive form."[163] Although the work of the Sisterhood remains significant, Neale is remembered today primarily for his contributions to the hymnody of the church. While his original contributions have not always survived, his translations of Greek and Latin hymns remain in the ecumenical core of many contemporary hymnals. They include, "Of the Father's Love Begotten," "Good Christian Friends, Rejoice," "All Glory, Laud and Honor," "Come, Ye Faithful, Raise the Strain," and "Christ is Made the Sure Foundation." One text which holds together his literary and pastoral work is his translation of the eighth century Greek hymn, "Art Thou Weary, Art Thou Languid":

Art thou weary, art thou languid, art thou sore distressed?
"Come to me," saith One, "and, coming, be at rest."[164]

E. B. Anderson

August 8
Dominic (1221)
See Common of Preachers

Dominic is best known for founding the mendicant order that bears his name, the Dominicans. This Order of Friars Preachers or "Blackfriars" distinguished itself through vows of poverty, and in preaching, teaching, and scholarship. Unlike many other religious orders, the Dominicans traveled into the world, living not by their manual labor but on the freewill gifts of others.

Dominic Guzman was born at Calaruega in Spain in 1170. Taking his formal education from his uncle, an archpriest, at 26 he was assigned to the cathedral at Osma where he became subprior of the community and worked closely with the bishop, Diego. Traveling with Diego in Toulouse, Dominic first encountered there a growing heretical element known as the Albigensians or Cathars. They held to dualistic notions of creation and divinity and their spiritual practices included an extreme asceticism designed to perfect their bodies.

In 1206, Bishop Diego was sent as a missionary to the Cathars and chose Dominic to accompany him. Diego's method of confronting the heretical members through conversation defied the church's more traditional use of coercive power. But a year after their arrival, Diego died. Then in 1208, Albigensian adherents murdered an official papal legate. In response, Pope Innocent III preached a crusade against the heretics that resulted in civil war. In the midst of this, Dominic assumed the leadership of Diego's mission and committed himself to furthering Diego's more peaceful methods of converting the Cathars through holy living and the preaching of pure doctrine. Establishing his headquarters in Toulouse, he also founded numerous centers for both men and women, particularly in university towns. Dominic spent the rest of his life preaching, traveling, and building the order. He died on August 6 at Bologna in 1221.

While his methods had uncertain results among the Albigensians, Dominic's centers of study provided the church an enduring intellectual life. Fittingly, Albert the Great and Thomas Aquinas were both friars. Dominicans also provided numerous missionaries to India, China, and the New World.

Dominic is portrayed in the church's symbols as a star, a lily, and a black and white dog with a torch in its mouth. The latter image comes from a play on Dominic's name. The Latin words, "Domini canus," mean, "Dog of the Lord."

J. S. Hudgins

August 10
Laurence (258)
See Common of Martyrs

According to early tradition, Laurence was one of the deacons of Rome martyred in the same persecution by Valerian which claimed Sixtus II, bishop of Rome, in 258. The remembrance of Lauence's martyrdom became popular very early in Rome's worship and beyond. In the early fourth century, Constantine built a church over Laurence's tomb. Every early liturgical calendar from Rome uniformly recognized his martyrdom. The numerous pictures of Laurence and the early dedications of churches to him further attest to his cult's popularity. His continuing importance was recently demonstrated in the revision of the Roman calendar in 1969. Here, Laurence remains as the only non-biblical person whose remembrance is included in the list of twenty-five saints' 'feasts.'

His popularity is largely a reflection of the stories surrounding his martyrdom. As recounted by Ambrose and other early patristic authors,[165] Laurence initially escaped capture when Sixtus II was arrested. Later, when Sixtus as being led to his beheading, Laurence, risking his own safety, went to meet his bishop and chide him for leaving him behind. Sixtus predicted to Laurence that he would soon meet his own martyrdom.

Subsequently he was arrested and also ordered to surrender all the treasures of the church. After some pleading, he gained permission for a few days to gather the church's riches. At the time designated for his return he invited the judge to come outdoors to see the treasures he had brought. When the judge stepped outside he was surprised to see that Laurence had not brought gold and silver but a multitude of poor people. "These," said Laurence, "are the treasures of the church." He was then led away to his martyrdom.

L. Ruth

August 11
Clare of Assisi (1253)
See Common of Saints

Clare of Assisi (b. 1194) was the third of five children born to Ortolana and Favarone di Offreduccio. She renounced her wealth and position for the religious life, and in 1212 she committed to following Francis in the pursuit of gospel perfection. After a short stay with some Benedictine nuns, she went to San Damiano, where she established a community of women known as the Poor Ladies and remained for 42 years.

In a simple, cloistered life at San Damiano, Clare practiced severe austerity in food and drink, fasting three days a week, and suffering from illness for many years. She and the other women wore poor garments in remembrance of the baby Jesus and his mother who wrapped him in swaddling clothes. Even in her role as abbess, a title which she took reluctantly, she displayed humility and kindness. She endeavored to set an example of virtue for the community, seeing it as her duty to console the ill and provide for them. Decisions were made with the advice of her sisters, and Clare's directions for the community emphasized a need for consent "to preserve the unity of mutual love and peace."

In Clare's conduct, in her counsel to others, and in her devotions, a remarkable commitment to poverty is pervasive. In a letter to princess Agnes of Prague, Clare writes of chosen poverty as an expression of Christ-like humility:

> O blessed poverty,
>   who bestows eternal riches on those who love and embrace her!
> O holy poverty,
>   God promises the kingdom of heaven
>   and, in fact, offers eternal glory and a blessed life
>   to those who possess and desire you!
> O God-centered poverty,
>   whom the Lord Jesus Christ
>   Who ruled and now rules heaven and earth,
>   Who spoke and things were made,
>   condescended to embrace before all else![166]

Although piously devoted to church authority and the sacraments, Clare was unyielding on the issue of poverty. She objected to a Rule given to her community that did not include the requirement of radical poverty, and she obtained a special privilege for the order to renounce all property. To protect the integrity of the Poor Ladies and the ideals of Francis, Clare wrote her own rule for her community, which received final approval in 1252, just two days before she died. She was canonized in 1255 and remains for us an example of extreme humility, grace, and devotion.

A. Berry Wylie

August 13
Florence Nightingale (1910)
See Common of Healers

Florence Nightingale, the "angel of mercy," was born in Florence, Italy on May 12, 1820. Reared as the elder daughter of affluent British parents, Florence received, along with her sister, an extensive classical education, primarily from her father. Taking an interest in nursing at an early age, her family found her interest repugnant and attempted for years to distract her from her determined course. She began at an early age a serious examination of the life of prayer, and a commitment to service soon followed.

A copious writer throughout her life, Florence recorded in her diary the following words as she prepared to pursue her calling to heal and reform: ". . . when each morning comes, I kneel down before the rising sun and only say, 'Behold the handmaid of the Lord — give me this day my work to do — no, not my work, but thine.'"[167]

In 1844 she began regular visits to hospitals throughout Europe. Although a Protestant, she was greatly influenced by her visits with the Catholic sisters of St. Vincent de Paul at Alexandria and by Pastor Fliedner's deaconesses at Kaiserswerth. Disgusted in general with the trifling concerns of her class, and in particular with the pressure within her family to conform, Florence found in the sufferings of the poor her life's meaning and purpose. She was thirty-three in 1853 when she took her first position as Superintendent of the Invalid Gentlewomen's Institution of Upper Harley Street in London.

But in October 1854, Nurse Nightingale discerned a new challenge: she offered to go to the Crimea to organize the nursing of the sick and wounded English soldiers. She found the main hospital, located in Scutari, in a terrible and unsanitary condition. The devotion, courage, and organizing skills of Nightingale soon improved conditions and considerably reduced the death rate. When she returned to England in 1856, weakened after a bout with the Crimean fever, she had gained a large following. The Nightingale School and Home for Nurses was founded in her honor at St. Thomas' Hospital in 1860. Mostly confined to her bed after the age of thirty-nine, Nightingale focused her energies on the restructuring of health care.

R. Brooks

August 14
John William Fletcher (1785)
See Common of Teachers, Pastors and Bishops

The French-Swiss born Jean Guillaume de la Flechère immigrated to England from Switzerland after distinguishing himself as a scholar and soldier. He came under the influence of Wesley, was ordained in the Church of England (1757), and, declining more noteworthy and prosperous livings, for twenty-five years served as the vicar of the small village of Madeley in Shropshire. Within that tiny area he found ample opportunity for extensive pastoral work, for a preaching ministry that produced results far beyond the village, for theological contemplation, for dispute and writing, and for the practice of piety that reflected a strong mystical bent. He worked zealously among the colliers and planted several Sunday-schools for boys and girls.

A vigorous supporter of Wesley and his methods, Fletcher used his keen talents as a theologian to defend Wesleyan Arminianism against Calvinism in his famous *Checks to Antinomianism*, one of the most widely read works among early American Methodists. So close was he to Wesley that Wesley chose him to succeed him as leader of the Methodist movement, an honor Fletcher declined.

The last four years of his life he was married to Mary Bosanquet who was well-known in the English society both for her preaching and charitable works (see September 9). In describing his death in her journal, she commented: "Often he had said, when hearing of happy deaths, "Well, let us get holy lives, and we will leave the rest to God."[168] Wesley attested to his holiness in his memorial sermon preached on the psalm text, "Mark the perfect man, and behold the upright; for the end of that man is peace." Wesley concludes his essay, "A Short Account of the Life and Death of the Rev. John Fletcher," writing, "So unblamable a man, in every respect, I have not found either in Europe or America. Nor do I expect to find another such on this side of eternity."[169]

In the conclusion of his *Essay on Truth*, Fletcher writes,

Visit the earth again, thou uncreated Sun of righteousness and truth; hasten thy second advent: Thy kingdom come! Shine without a cloud! Scatter the last remains of error's night! Kindle our minds into pure truth! our hearts into perfect love! our tongues into ardent praise! our lives into flaming obedience![170]

K. K. McCabe

August 14
Maximilian Kolbe (1941)
See Common of Martyrs, Pastors and Bishops

Known as the "Saint of Auschwitz," Kolbe is difficult to characterize. He received two doctorates at the Collegio in Rome where a professor called him a "rare natural genius"; but he was equally well-known for his humility and kindness, causing another professor to describe him as "a young saint." He was a mystic, ridiculed as an impractical dreamer; yet, in his Polish homeland, he established Niepokalanow (The City of Mary), a Franciscan foundation that utilized the most modern technology to publish newspapers that still reach millions of people world-wide. He was a missionary, profoundly committed to the orthodoxy of the Roman Catholic Church; but his compassionate acceptance of the Jewish prisoners at Auschwitz or the Buddhist and Shintoist people of Japan among which he worked as a missionary was never predicated on their response to the gospel.

The spirit of his life and his flourishing ministries becomes even more estimable when placed against the backdrop of both the constant physical pain he endured from tuberculosis and the political trauma caused by Hitler's 1939 invasion of Poland. For "Father Max," suffering was a gift that enabled his journey toward God. He writes, "God gives us this white ladder and wills that we use it, to scale the heights to come into his presence. This is only poetic imagery: the reality is incomparably more beautiful."[171]

In 1941, he was arrested by the Gestapo and sent to Auschwitz. Amid the squalor and horror, Kolbe became Christ for others — comforting the oppressed and confronting evil with love. To deter escape, the Auschwitz commandant routinely ordered a hideous death by starvation for ten of the escapee's friends. As this sentence was announced once again, one of the ten cried out for his family. Father Max volunteered to take his place. After two weeks, only this infirm, holy man remained alive. He was executed on August 14, 1941.

Kolbe practiced a "love without limits" — not only for his fellow prisoners, but for his tormentors as well. Canonized a martyr of the Church in 1981, he demonstrated to the Nazis and to the world that the true spirit of Christ will be invulnerable to hate and even to death.

T. Gildemeister

Mary

Mary, a young Jewish woman, was yet a virgin when she miraculously conceived a son by the power of the Holy Spirit. Before she gave birth to her son, Jesus, she was married to Joseph the carpenter. Together they raised Jesus in the town of Nazareth.

The angelic annunciation of Jesus' birth to Mary is recounted in the Gospel of Luke (1:26-38) and is remembered on March 25 (nine months before Christmas). According to Luke, Mary remained faithful throughout her life, keeping the Jewish law and observing the festivals in Jerusalem. In his Gospel, John includes Mary as one of the women at the Cross and records Jesus' last words to his mother.

According to apocryphal tradition, Mary herself was miraculously born to two aged parents, Joachim and Anna. To this day there stands a gate neat the Pool of Bethsada in Jerusalem (known in the Islamic tradition as *Bab Sitti Maryam*, "the Gate of the Lady Mary." It is said to be near the spot where Mary was born.

As Christianity grew and developed, so did Christian piety and doctrine concerning Mary. Through the writings of Justin, Irenaeus, and Tertullian, Mary became identified as the Second or New Eve. Belief in Mary's perpetual virginity grew, especially in the East. Perhaps nothing expresses the significance of Mary for the worshipping life of the Church than the fourth-century hymns of St. Ephrem the Syrian. The Mother of our Lord came to be celebrated as the exemplar of not only perfect faithfulness, humility and obedience, but also purity. Some scholars maintain that by the late fourth century "a commemoration of the ever-virgin Mary, Mother of God" was held at Antioch.[172] In Rome and Ephesus by the mid-fifth century, churches were built in veneration of Mary, the *Theotokos*, or "Mother of God," a doctrine officially upheld by the Council of Ephesus (431).

According to tradition, Mary died on the anniversary of Jesus' birth, Christmas Day. In Gaul, the celebration of her "heavenly birthday" was postponed to a separate feast day in the winter. However, in Syria and in the West, Mary's feast day was celebrated during the summer, in the middle of August.

M. F. Foskett

Isaiah 61:10-11
Psalm 34 (*UMH* 769)
Galatians 4:4-7
Luke 1:46-55

Redeeming God, whose daughter Mary trusted angelic voices, rejoiced with a song of praise, and wept at the foot of the cross: Give us such courage, faith, and hope as hers, that we, too, may praise you, trust you, and receive you through Jesus Christ our Lord, who lives and reigns with you and the Holy Spirit, one God, now and forever.

[EBA]

Receiving the Holy Spirit,
bearing the child of God,
pondering the mystery of Christ,
witnessing and following in the Way,
  So Mary witnessed to your saving grace;
  May we, O God, be as faithful and strong.

[EBA]

August 16
Charles Grandison Finney (1875)
See Common of Evangelists

Ordained Presbyterian, pastored as a Congregationalist, and teaching a Methodist theology, Charles G. Finney is quite likely the most influential figure in nineteenth-century American Christianity. He would be most surprised to be called a liturgical reformer but Finney has had more influence on North American worship than any other individual.

Converted on October 10, 1821, Finney began to preach revivals in upstate New York. In time, he reached the major urban areas of the east coast, spreading the revival techniques he had learned so well on the frontier. These "new measures," largely developed and employed by Methodists in the West became through Finney's influence a major force in Protestant worship across the country. Among other innovations, Finney encouraged women to pray in public in midweek prayer meetings. This was a major factor in encouraging women to become involved in social action reforms.

After a spectacular ministry in New York, Finney became professor and then president at Oberlin. Here women were first admitted as college students and Oberlin became a center of the crusades against slavery and for temperance. Finney's latter day writings were distinctly Arminian and foreshadowed much of the holiness movemennt. His most important contribution was in domesticating the frontier revival methods in American Christianity and this shifted much of the shape of worship in the Reformed, Puritan, and Methodist traditions and even impacted the Lutheran and Quaker traditions. Today the frontier tradition is the most prevalent in this country and is rapidly being exported overseas.

J. F. White

August 18
Francis John McConnell (1953)
See Common of Pastors and Bishops, Teachers

Bishop McConnell, one of American Methodism's great bishops, was also a great scholar. He became widely known through his many books and articles, most notably his biography of John Wesley (1939). A sentence he wrote about Wesley speaks well for McConnell's own piety: "He was one of those intensely vital beings who rejoice in the full expression and play of their energies. The so-called `integration' of Wesley's life was, so far as we can see, the absorption of his whole being in the task before him. He was contented and happy."[173]

McConnell influenced the church not only through his voluminous writings but also through his teaching. He was at various times visiting professor at Boston, Drew, Yale, and Garrett. He was a leader in the Sunday School movement, wrote widely for Sunday School publications and in 1916 was elected president of the Religious Education Association. He was a gifted and stimulating speaker much sought after for special events and programs.

Educated at Ohio Wesleyan University and at Boston University, McConnell joined the New England Conference in 1903. He later held a pastorate in Brooklyn, and was president of De Pauw University from 1909 to 1912. He was made bishop in 1923 and served the areas of Denver and Pittsburgh. Since the Denver episcopal area at that time included Mexico, McConnell labored to develop the Methodist Church there. In 1929 McConnell became president of the Methodist Federation for Social Action through which he became a national leader in the struggle for human rights.

While a student at Boston University, McConnell came under the influence of Borden Parker Bowne. Bowne's philosophy of religion known as 'Personalism' became a lifelong intellectual commitment for McConnell, who wrote a biography of Bowne (1929). His own autobiography was published in 1952.

In his time, McConnell was Methodism's preeminent intellectual leader. But in one of his most influential writings, *The Christlike God*, he explains that sanctity is not primarily a question of intelligence. There he writes, "If the kingdom of God were only for the acute intellect, able to muster intellectual mysteries, many would have to remain outside. They would not have the requisite understanding."[174]

R. A. Reed

August 20
Bernard of Clairvaux (1153)
See Common of Saints

The "Father of Western Mysticism," Bernard was born near Dijon, France to a gallant knight and a pious, Christian mother. He was too scrawny for military service, so his family designated him for a church vocation. Even in his youth, he was known for being a student of charm, wit, and learning. At 23, he entered the home monastery of the Cistercian monks, who later became a world influence under his inspiration. In 1115, he founded the monastery of Clairvaux, which became the mother house for an international order of over 340 houses during his lifetime. Bernard insisted on a more rigorous ascetic life than the Benedictines of Cluny, who were lax in his view, in following the Rule of St. Benedict. To this day, the Cistercians are known throughout the world for their life of silence, manual labor, poverty, and devotion.

Bernard exercised his influence throughout Europe. He arbitrated one of the papal schisms, helped found the Knights of Templar, and preached the Second Crusade even unto its failure.

The passion, rhetoric, and eloquence of his addresses survive in numerous sermons and treatises. Bernard's vision is of a practical mysticism which focuses on the believer's union with God in Christ while staying rooted in this world. In Medieval times, his writings served to increase devotion to Christ's humanity and to Mary, and during the Reformation, they informed numerous "worldly mysticism," including that of John Calvin. In one of his most famous treatises, "On Loving God," he admonishes us to love God "without measure." He prays,

> My God, my Helper, I shall love you in proportion to your gift and my capacity, less indeed than is just, but to do that is beyond me. Even though I cannot love you as much as I ought, still I cannot love you more than I am able. I shall be able to love you more only when you deign to give me more: and even then you can never find my love worthy.[175]

L. A. Goleman

August 20
William Booth and **Catherine Mumford Booth** (1912 and 1890)
See Common of Leaders

Even Salvation Army stationary says "William Booth, Founder." But William and Catherine Booth never did anything separately.

Catherine Mumford and William Booth, both born in 1829, met one another when, as an itinerant evangelists, Booth preached in her Wesleyan church. The only daughter in a family of five children, she learned to read by age three and had read the Bible through eight times by age twelve. Her father was a gifted lay preacher committed to the cause of temperance. By twelve, Catherine was also writing letters to temperance journals.

In a husband she wanted a Christian man who was her equal. She believed that married couples should find a "oneness of view and tastes, any idea of lordship or ownership being lost in love." William was her equal, but he required some convincing on the subject of equality in marriage. They were engaged in May 1852 and married June 16, 1855.

It was William who urged her to preach in his own pulpit. She confessed to parishioners that while they thought her a model preacher's wife, she had been too timid about using her gifts (even though she was pregnant three times in their first four and a half years of marriage!). When William fell ill shortly thereafter, she supplied the pulpit regularly.

The Booth's dream was to become evangelists, but the conference repeatedly denied William's request and reassigned him to small parishes. Finally in the 1861 annual conference he could take no more. He glanced up at Catherine, listening in the balcony. She nodded assent, and together they walked out of British Methodism.

Slowly their own mission began to evolve. William founded the East London Christian Mission in 1865, but he later remarked, "I have been trying all my life to stretch out my arms so as to reach with one hand the poor and at the same time keep the other in touch with the rich. But my arms are not long enough."[176] While William worked among the poor, Catherine kept in touch with the rich, urging them to assume their responsibilities toward the masses. Together their efforts became in 1878 the Salvation Army, one of the first Christian groups to grant men and women equal ministerial credentials and to encourage them to work side by side for the kingdom of God.

N. A. Hardesty

August 21
Georgia Harkness (1974)
See Common of Teachers

Harkness was a systematic theologian and a product of the Social Gospel of the 1920's and early 1930's. She was the first woman to teach in a mainline Protestant seminary in the United States. She combined her early training in philosophy with a spirituality nurtured by prayer, poetry, and worship which she shared with others through religious poetry, hymns, and devotional writings.

Born in 1891, Harkness was raised in upstate New York, experienced a conversion as a youth, went to college at Cornell on a scholarship, and vowed to be a missionary. Instead, she went on to graduate school at Boston University where she earned degrees in Religious Education and Arts and a Ph.D. in philosophy. She then went on to teach at Elmira College (1922-37) and Mount Holyoke College (1938).

Beginning in 1920, Harkness became a committed pacifist until her death and a Christian socialist who demanded economic justice for all people. She critiqued racism and opposed the merger of the Methodist and Evangelical United Brethren churches in 1968 until the segregated Central Jurisdiction of the Methodist Church was abolished. In the Middles East, she realized the need for American Christians to understand Jewish and Palestinian positions. She also supported the ordination of women and believed in the ministry of all people. Harkness was ordained to local deacon's and elder's orders, but never sought full Conference membership.

Harkness taught at Garrett Biblical Institute in Evanston, Illinois (1939-50) and the Pacific School of Religion in Berkeley, California (1950-61). The death of her father in 1937 and a personal spiritual struggle discussed in her book, *The Dark Night of the Soul* (1945), led her to a more Christocentric expression of faith and theology. She was a pastor's theologian as she wrote with an eye to both the church and to the academy. Her hymn, "Hope of the World," was the theme hymn for the 1954 World Council of Churches in Evanston and remains a favorite in *The United Methodist Hymnal* (178).

In spite of her many contributions and wide influence, in an interview shortly before her death, Harkness said, "I have not become a big name in theology. My talent, if I have one, lies in making theology understandable to people."[177]

E. M. Townes

Bartholomew

The New Testament fails to offer any information concerning Bartholomew other than listing him among the Twelve chosen by Jesus (Mark 3:18; Matt 10:3; Luke 6:14; Acts 1:13). Since the ninth century attempts have been made to identify Bartholomew with Nathanael. There are several reasons for this: Bartholomew is not mentioned in the Fourth Gospel and Nathanael is not mentioned in the Synoptics; in three of the lists of the Twelve Bartholomew is paired with Philip (not in Acts) and in John 1:43-51 Philip brings Nathanael to Jesus; and, finally, "Bartholomew" can be considered a patronymic instead of a proper name — thus the apostle might be Nathanael, Bar-Tholami (i.e., son of Tholami, or some such name). Such identification, however, is pure speculation and in the end cannot be supported.

Tradition stepped in to speak where the canon was silent. Legendary stories claims he made missionary journeys to India, Armenia, Phrygia, Lycaonia, Mesopotamia, and Persia. One such tradition is found in Eusebius' Ecclesiastical History, where the historian claims that Pantaenus (late 2nd c.) came to India from Alexandria and found there some who already knew Christ because, "Bartholomew, one of the apostles had preached to them and had left the writing of Matthew in Hebrew letters, which was preserved until the time mentioned" (i.e., Pantaenus's arrival).[178]

Similarly, there are several apocryphal writings attributed to this apostle: one example is the "Questions of Bartholomew," a Gnostic dialogue in which Bartholomew questions the resurrected Jesus, Mary, and Satan about such things as heaven and Hades.

Finally, tradition claims that the apostle was martyred. Stories conflict, however, concerning the manner of his death: in one version he is flayed alive and then beheaded, in another crucified, and in yet another bound in a sack and cast into the sea.

O. W. Allen

Deuteronomy 18:15-18
Psalm 91 (*UMH* 810)
1 Corinthians 4:9-15
Luke 22:24-30

God of the prophets, you raise up among your people those whom you would have speak for you. Continue to send us, we pray, faithful messengers like Bartholomew, that we might hear and take comfort in your saving Word, Jesus Christ, who lives and reigns with you and the Holy Spirit, one God, now and forever.

[CFG]

Like Bartholomew
We, innumerable and unknown fools for Christ,
  remain with you, listening, watching, suffering.
Refresh and strengthen us, Jesus,
  with food and drink from the table you host for us,
  now and in your eternal kingdom. Amen.

[CFG]

August 28
Abba Moses of Scete (c. 395)
See Common of Saints

Abba Moses is rare among the desert abbas and ammas in that the tradition records that he was a black man. The sayings and anecdotes attributed to him in the anonymous fifth-century collection known as the *Sayings of the Fathers* reveal a mixture of veneration with the memory of Moses' having suffered abuse from his superiors and fellow ascetics because of the color of his skin.

In spite of the abuse the tradition records him suffering, Moses became a revered figure in the ascetic communities of Scete, a barren region southwest of Alexandria. His wisdom exerted a wide influence in eastern Christian circles, and he is commemorated on this day in the Greek Orthodox calendar. Tradition states that he was martyred at his cell along with seven companions.

Moses had a reputation for being a reluctant teacher. One account states that he had an

inflexible rule never to give instruction in the spiritual life except to persons who sought it in faith and heartfelt contrition. For he was afraid that if he poured out the water of life indiscriminately to people who had no use for it or were hardly even thirsty, he would cast his pearls before swine and would be liable to the charge either of boasting about his prowess or of betraying his trust.[179]

Another anecdote from the *Sayings* captures his sense of humility:

In Scete a brother was once found guilty. They assembled the elders, and sent a message to Abba Moses telling him to come. But he would not come. Then the presbyter sent, saying: "Come, for a meeting of monks is waiting for you." Moses rose up and went. He took with him an old basket which he filled with sand and carried on his back. The people who went to meet him said: "What is this, father?" The old man said them: "My sins are chasing me, and I do not see them — have I come today to judge the sins of someone else?" They listened to him, and said nothing to the erring brother, but pardoned him.[180]

G. S. Sperry-White

August 28
Augustine of Hippo (430)
See Common of Teachers

Born in Tagaste, North Africa of a Christian mother, Monica, and a pagan father, Augustine's interest in philosophy led him through a pilgrimage of persuasions until in 387 he was baptized at the Easter vigil. His conversion was due to many influences, but predominantly his mother and the preaching of Ambrose, bishop of Milan. Augustine returned to Tagaste and established a monastic fellowship. On a visit to Hippo he was seized by admiring Christians who presented him to bishop Valerius for ordination. By 396 he was bishop of Hippo, where he served until his death in 430.

During his lifetime as leader, preacher, and teacher Augustine addressed three great controversies that disturbed the church. Against the dualistic religion of Manichaeism affirmed God as the sole creator. Against the Donatists he held that the church is one and is holy because of its nature and purpose, not because all in the church are holy. And against the Pelagians, Augustine argued that divine gifts imparted to human nature by God were lost in the fall, that sin was hereditary, and that grace was determinative in human destiny. His monumental work, *The City of God*, expressed confidence in God's sovereignty for a church sorely shaken by the fall of Rome to Alaric in 410. Here his theology takes on predestinarian tones and hence was very influential during the Reformation, especially upon Calvin.

He is still best known for his *Confessions* which is at once the narrative of a journey in faith, a manual of prayer, and a theology of piety. Its famous opening words have become fundamental to our understanding of the relation of God to humanity and of the nature and goal of prayer:

Our heart is restless until it rests in you. Lord, grant me to know and understand which is first, to call upon you or to praise you, and also which is first, to know you or to call upon you? But how does one who does not know you call upon you? For one who does not know you might call upon another instead of you. Or must you rather be called upon so that you may be known?[181]

R. A. Reed

August 29
Maggie Newton Van Cott (1914)
See Common of Preachers

Maggie Newton Van Cott is best known as the first American woman to be given a Methodist preaching license. For her it was a second career.

Margaret Ann Newton was born March 25, 1830, in New York City, the eldest of four children. Her father was a wealthy real estate broker. She was confirmed as an Episcopalian.

In 1848 she married Peter Van Cott, who owned a dry goods store. Shortly thereafter he bough a wholesale pharmaceutical business. They had two girls, one of whom died as an infant. When Peter became chronically ill in 1850, Maggie took over the business and skillfully managed it until after his death in 1866.

Given the stress of her life, Van Cott sought spiritual help. She experienced conversion during the "Businessmen's Revival" in the winter of 1857-58. She began attending prayer meetings at the Duane Street Methodist Church. She soon was leading Bible studies and prayer meetings. She also volunteered at the Five Points Mission, made famous by such women as Phoebe Palmer.

Her soul-winning success led a pastor to ask her in 1868 to preach a revival in his church. "You must preach!" he begged. The statement triggered a memory for Maggie, the memory of a dream she had had a few weeks previously.

In her dream she had heard a voice say, "You must preach." When she rose in the pulpit in her dream and looked out expecting to see a church full of people, she saw only one old gentleman sitting near the altar. After she preached her sermon, she asked someone who the old gentleman was. "That is John Wesley, the founder of Methodism!" came the reply.

Remembering the dream, she consented to preach. Response was so favorable that she was persuaded to continue the meetings for six weeks. Seventy-five people were saved. In September 1868 she received an exhorter's license and on March 6, 1869, the quarterly conference of Stone Ridge, Ellenville, New York, gave her a local preacher's license.

Over the next thirty years, Van Cott traveled constantly — even after the General Conference of 1880 revoked all preaching licenses issued to women. Her converts were said to number 7,500. Her story is told in *The Life and Labors of Mrs. Maggie Newton Van Cott*, first published in 1872 with the help of John O. Foster. A later expanded edition is titled, *The Harvest and the Reaper: Reminiscences of Revival Work of Mrs. Maggie N. Van Cott*.

N. A. Hardesty

August 31
John Bunyan (1688)
See Common of Teachers, Saints

A puritan preacher and writer, Bunyan is best remembered for *The Pilgrim's Progress*, an extended allegory about the Christian pilgrimage.

Born into an Anglican family in 1628, Bunyan experienced a dramatic conversion when he married Margaret Bentley, a member of a Puritan sect, in 1648. Starting shortly after his conversion and continuing to the end of his life, he engaged in a ministry of preaching, teaching, and writing. After the restoration of the monarchy in 1660 following the English Civil War, his activities as a lay preacher landed him in jail on more than one occasion. During an early imprisonment he wrote his famous spiritual autobiography, *Grace Abounding to the Chief of Sinners*. Most scholars agree that much, if not most, of *Pilgrim's Progress* was also composed while he was in jail.

Good Calvinist that he was, Bunyan perceived the world on the grandest of scales, as the stage in which the overarching plot of divine providence unfolded amidst the numberless scenes of the struggle between the children of light and "the cosmic powers of this present darkness." His genius lay in his ability to cast that drama in terms that made it real to his contemporaries — and to us. His ear for vivid detail brought the mystery of sin and salvation into the room with his readers, making it part of their everyday experience.

Perhaps Bunyan's most lasting gift to us is his vision of the life of the Christian as an adventure upon which one must embark. Driven first by conviction of sin and later by hope of heaven, Christian, the central character in *Pilgrim's Progress*, is always on the move. His steps might falter, or they might for a time go astray, yet they do not stop. Along the way he encounters characters such as Worldly-Wiseman, Timorous, and the Giant Despair, all of whom try in their different ways to make him settle down. Yet Bunyan's Christian, who represents all of those who are called by that name, cannot settle down, at least not on this side of eternity. He has to keep pushing forward until at last he reaches that City which is his only true home.

There," said they, "is the Mount Sion, the heavenly Jerusalem, the innumerable company of angels, the spirit of the just...made perfect; you are going now," said they, "to the paradise of God."[182]

R. A. Ratcliff

September 3
Samuel Checote (1884)
See Common of Pastors and Bishops

Samuel Checote was born in the Chattahoochee River valley of the Creek Indian nation, in present-day Alabama. When he was ten years old, he attended the Asbury Manual Labour School, which had been established by Methodist missionaries with the agreement of the Creek tribal council. The school closed that year as the Creek Indians were forced by the federal and state governments to emigrate to the Indian Territory west of the Mississippi River.

In the new Creek nation, Samuel again attended mission schools, but by 1835, recurring tension between whites and Indians resulted in the expulsion of missionaries from Creek territory. When missionaries later returned to work among his people, Samuel converted to Christianity.

Checote's early days as a Christian were not easy. The Creek council banned the preaching of Christianity and imposed a punishment of fifty lashes on those who violated the ordinance. In an early expression of his life work as a statesman and Christian, young Samuel successfully interceded with the Creek chief to reverse the ban. By 1849, a Creek Methodist district was established where Christianity had once been prohibited.

Eager to bring Christianity into the homes of all his people, Checote worked to have the Bible translated into his native language, and he personally assisted in the translation of hymns into Creek. At the same time, he remained deeply proud of his Creek heritage, and was elected chief three different times. He also served as a licensed preacher, and conducted services in an arbor adjacent to the Council House when he was chief.

Samuel Checote saw division between races and regions destroy his native land twice, first in the disastrous removal of Indians from the Southeast, and again in the Civil War. Rather than let such turbulence defeat him, Checote looked for ways to bridge racial and cultural differences. He raised money for schools, homes, and churches for his people, and defended the rights of the Creek Nation in petitions to Congress.

As we struggle with dissension in our own lives, we remember the courage of Sam Checote who chose love over hate and faith over cynicism. "You may kill me," he was reported to have said, "but you cannot separate me from my Lord Christ."[183]

S. H. Hill

September 4
Albert Schweitzer (1965)
See Common of Healers, Teachers

A diversely gifted person, Schweitzer was born in 1875, the son of a German Lutheran pastor. Study at Strasbourg led to doctorates in philosophy, theology, and medicine. He was also an acclaimed organist and an acknowledged interpreter of Bach. The famous organist Charles-Marie Widor asked him to write a study of the life and art of the composer. The resultant book, *J.S. Bach: Musician-Poet* (1905) offered a view of the composer as a religious mystic attuned to the forces of the natural world.

In *The Quest for the Historical Jesus* (1906), Schweitzer debunked many contemporary attempts at writing a life of Jesus. By insisting on a view of Jesus that emphasized first-century eschatological thought, he changed the course of theological thought about Jesus.

By this time, he had decided to become a medical missionary in Africa. Building a hospital with the help of the local population at Lambarene in French Equatorial Africa (now Gabon), he equipped and maintained it with income derived from his books, lectures, concerts, and awards. After internment as an enemy alien during the First World War, he turned his attention to world problems. In his two-volume *Philosophy of Civilization* (1923), he espoused "reverence for life" as the only solution to the problems of the world. "Being good," he wrote, "is to preserve life, to promote life, to raise life to the highest level it can attain. Being evil is to destroy life, to injure life, to suppress life which could attain a higher level."[184]

In all he did, he endeavored to put his philosophy into practice: "My attitude toward my own life must be affirmative. That does not automatically imply that I am willing to continue my existence at any cost, but that I appreciate it as an awe-inspiring mystery."[185]

His success in that endeavor led to the 1952 Nobel Peace Prize. He promptly poured the prize money into the Lambarene complex.

G. L. Hayes

September 6
James Bradley Finley (1856)
See Common of Preachers, Evangelists

Finley was an eminent Methodist preacher and presiding elder in the early Western frontier. Born in North Carolina in 1781, the son of a Presbyterian minister, he was raised in the backwoods of Kentucky and was deeply troubled by his father's predestinarian teachings and guilt over his own sin. He went to the famous Cane Ridge revival in 1801, and during the preaching reported that "a peculiarly-strange sensation . . . came over me. My heart beat tumultuously, my knees trembled, my lip quivered, and I felt as though I must fall to the ground." Fleeing into the woods, he suffered under the conviction of his sins for a day until a German from Switzerland "who had experienced religion" prayed with him. Finley writes, "suddenly my load was gone, my guilt removed, and presently the direct witness from heaven shone full upon my soul. Then there flowed such copious streams of love . . . that I thought I should die with excess of joy." His wife convinced him to attend a Methodist meeting where he was "astonished beyond all expression" at the simple, common-sense religious testimonies he heard.[186] He joined the Methodists, became a class leader, and after some struggle felt a call to preach.

Finley, a gifted preacher, was received by the Western Conference on trial in 1809, serving large circuits in Ohio for seven years. After the success of John Stewart among the Wyandot Indians at Upper Sandusky, Ohio, Finley was appointed superintendent of the mission by Bishop McKendree. His work, described in his book, *Wyandott Mission* (1840), was highly successful. He sympathized with the Native Americans against white encroachment, and was heartbroken at the removal of the Wyandots to the West. Finley then served for three and a half years as chaplain of the Ohio penitentiary, writing about that in *Memorials of Prison Life* (1850). He was a delegate to the 1844 General Conference and was involved in the process of splitting the Northern and Southern churches.

Called the "Old Chief" by many for his conservatism, when in 1847 a congregation in Dayton decided to engage in the "promiscuous" practice of letting families sit together in the pews (rather than separating men and women), Finley was at first against it. After preaching there and being encouraged by the response, he surprised everyone when he said, "So long as the seats were free, I for one will make no serious objection."[187]

C. F. Guthrie

September 9
Mary Bosanquet Fletcher (1815)
See Common of Saints

Mary Bosanquet Fletcher (b. 1739) was a prominent lay preacher in the Methodist movement in England. After the great London revival of 1761-62, she returned to her hometown in Essex and opened an asylum for orphans and the poor. When John Wesley visited it, he said that it "appeared to him the only perfect specimen of a Christian family he ever saw." In 1781 she married John Fletcher, vicar of Madeley (see August 14). He lived only four years but she stayed on in the parish for more than thirty years supervising the building of chapels, entertaining traveling preachers, preaching herself, and overseeing diverse charitable works. Her journal provides interesting insights into Wesleyan spirituality of the time and her own understanding of it. She writes on October 8, 1776:

> I know the power of God which I felt when standing [preaching] on the horseblock in the street at Huddersfield: but at the same time I am conscious how ridiculous I must appear in the eyes of many for so doing. Therefore, if some persons consider me an impudent woman, and represent me as such, I cannot blame them. Again, many say, If you are called to preach, why do you not do it constantly, and take a round as a preacher? I answer, Because that is not my call. I have many duties to attend to, and many cares which they know nothing about. I must therefore leave myself to His guidance who hath sole right of disposing of me. . . . I think the Spirit of the Lord is more at work among the Methodists; and while I see this, though they were to toss me about as a football, I would stick to them like a leech. Besides, I do nothing but what Mr. Wesley approves; and as to reproach thrown by some on me, what have I to do with it, but quietly go forward saying, *I will be still more vile*, if my Lord requires it. Indeed for none but thee, my Lord, would I take up this sore cross. But thou hast done more for me. O do thy own will upon me in all things! Only make me what thou wouldst have me to be! Only make me holy, and then lead me as thou wilt![188]

K. K. McCabe

September 11
Isabella Thoburn and **Clara Swain** (1901 and 1910)
See Common of Evangelists, Healers

In her lecture, "The Law of Christian Service," Isabella Thoburn said, "When we only seek eminence and position, how few avenues are open! When we seek service, how many. . . ."[189] Thoburn goes on to speak of the work she and Clara Swain found on those avenues of service in India, the land of betel leaf, elephant, and 'zanana' — the life of virtual isolation in which India's women were kept. Because men were prevented from contact with women, James M. Thoburn (see November 28) perceived a need for women missionaries and wrote to his sister Isabella to encourage her to come India. Isabella and 'Doctor Miss Sahiba,' as Dr. Clara Swain was known among the native people, traveled together to India in 1870. They were the first women missionaries deployed by the newly formed Foreign Women's Missionary Society of the Methodist Episcopal Church.

Isabella always thought of herself primarily as a teacher. She established a school for girls, known as Lal Bagh or Ruby Garden, which doubled as a headquarters for women's missionary work. Isabella said many times to native preachers, "no people ever rise higher, as a people, than the point to which they elevate their women."[190] She opened the first Christian college for women in Asia in 1895. It was renamed for her after she died on this date of cholera in 1901.

The first qualified woman doctor in Asia, Dr. Clara Swain was appointed to Bareilly from 1870 to 1884, where she established India's first modern hospital for women and children. She treated close to 1,300 women and children in her first year. Seeing a demand for more women to be medically trained, she began her first medical class for women in March, 1870.

Isabella Thoburn's and Clara Swain's service was always directed toward the physical and spiritual welfare of India's secluded women. Upon reading the vision of the New Jerusalem and seeing comfort come to a grief-stricken Indian woman whose two-year-old son had just died, Dr. Swain wrote these words to her sister in America, "It was worth the journey to India to witness that poor mother's interest in what we read. We are praying . . . the light . . . in her heart may grow brighter and brighter unto the perfect day."[191]

H. P. Minor

September 13
Anthony Bewley (1860)
See Common of Martyrs

Bewley was a Tennesseean preacher who had moved to Missouri and been accepted into the Missouri Conference in 1843. For two years he served circuits in the extreme southwestern part of the state. When the rest of the Conference voted in 1845 to go with the Southern church, he refused and became presiding elder over the few members and preachers in the area who chose to remain within the Methodist Episcopal Church.

The continuing activity of Northern preachers in the area was resisted and they were warned to leave. Mobs threw stones at one of Bewley's coworkers and the Bewley children were excluded from schools. Many of the Northern Methodists in the area were eventually driven to move to free states.

Northern bishop Edward R. Ames, who aggressively pursued a policy of Northern Methodist incursion in the South, sent Bewley to Texas as presiding elder of the Texas Mission and its five circuits, but little was accomplished because of opposition. As the intolerance for Northern Methodists grew, rumors arose that Bewley and others were poisoning wells and burning entire towns in their abolitionist zeal. A letter was circulated, presumably false, implicating him in a series of crimes. Nevertheless, when reappointed in 1860, Bewley returned to Texas with his wife and his five children in 1860, but they soon fled north when serious threats were issued against Bewley's life. Along the way they found posted notices offering a $1000 reward for his capture and return to Texas. He was finally apprehended by a posse in Cassville, Missouri in early September.

Detained in Fayetteville, Arkansas, he wrote a final letter to his family: "Now, my feelings I cannot describe; but I know there is a God that doeth right." He was returned on the overland stage to Fort Worth and hanged on a tree. Southern newspaper accounts reported he had been given a fair trial while Northern accounts reported he had been murdered by a mob. It was said that he was buried in so shallow a grave that his bare knees protruded from the soil.

One Southern Methodist preacher said Bewley had a "self-willed, stubborn disposition." A sympathetic Northern writer argues that the witnesses were all false and that, "The whole and only charge against him was, that he was a sound member of the M. E. Church, and antislavery according to her principles and the teaching of Holy Scripture."[192]

C. F. Guthrie

September 14
Holy Cross Day

It is said that after Constantine's dream of victory under the sign of the cross and after achieving that victory, he sent for the bishop of Rome to come and baptize him. Following his baptism, Constantine sent his mother Helena with an army to Jerusalem to find the true cross of Christ and to build a church on the site at which it was found. After committing a man named Judas to a pit for seven days for refusing to answer her query, Judas prayed that God would reveal to him "with the sweetest scent of all precious perfumes"[193] the place where the cross was hidden. Digging at that place, three crosses were found. To determine which was the true cross of Christ, the body of a dead man was brought and laid next to each. When laid next to the true cross, he was raised from the dead.

Holy Cross Day commemorates two sets of events. The first set includes the discovery of the cross by Helena and the subsequent dedication of a church on the site of Calvary by Constantine in 335 when the cross was exposed for the veneration of the faithful. The pilgrim Egeria, whose diary of her travels in the late fourth century is available to us, reports vigils before the cross in this church throughout Holy Week. The second commemorates the exposition of the cross after it was recovered from the Persians, into whose hands it had fallen in 614, by Emperor Heraclius in 628. It became customary for those churches which had a portion of the cross to expose it for veneration by the faithful on September 14. This solemn ceremony was called the *Exaltatio*, or the "Lifting Up," of the Cross.[194]

The following prayer may be used today:

Holy and impassioned God,
    beneath the cross of Christ we are redeemed,
    in the glory of the cross we are delivered,
    by the cross lifted high in triumph we are led into the light of salvation:
May we daily take up the cross that by it we may proclaim your glory,
through Jesus Christ, who with you and the Holy Spirit, reigns in glory.
    Amen.

E. B. Anderson

September 18
Dag Hammarskjöld (1961)
See Common of Leaders

Dag Hammarskjöld was born in Sweden (c. 1905), the son of a prominent political family. He was descended from soldiers and politicians through his father, and through his mother from clergy and scholars. These two sides, active and reflective, were the poles around which his later life was built.

The second, and highly dynamic Secretary General of the United Nations (1953-61), he died on a mission of peace as the plane carrying him to meet with rebel leaders in the Belgian Congo (now Zaire) crashed in Northern Rhodesia (now Zambia). After his death, the publication of his journal *Markings* astonished the world communities who knew him as a cultured politician and agnostic humanist. Conscious of his highly public career and his status as a citizen of the world, Hammarskjöld had not committed to any church, yet his journal discloses a life of belief, of wonder, of responsibility, and of prayer.

I don't know Who — or what — put the question. I don't know when it was put. I don't even remember answering. But at some moment I did answer *Yes* to Someone — or Something — and from that hour I was certain that existence is meaningful, and that, therefore, my life, in self-surrender, had a goal.

Markings, which Hammarskjöld described as "a sort of a White Book concerning my negotiations with myself — and with God," is relentlessly self-critical. Yet he celebrated the vital connection, the "Yes" to God that frees one from self-obsession for loving involvement in the world.

The "mystical experience." Always *here* and *now* — in that freedom which is one with distance, in that stillness which is born of silence. But — this is a freedom in the midst of action, a stillness in the midst of other human beings.

In the tensions of his life and thought Hammarskjöld embodied the contradictions of his time, prosperity and a Cold War, unlimited progress and nuclear annihilation. In that age of anxiety, Hammarskjöld walked and worked along the outward road of power and negative forces, while traveling inward toward peace and a *Yes*.

For all that has been — Thanks!
For all that will be — Yes![195]

H. M. Elkins and G. Chien

Matthew

From the second century, the church held that the author of the first of the four gospels was the apostle Matthew. In Christian iconography, Matthew is depicted either as the Evangelist (a winged man) or as the Apostle (holding either the spear or sword as an emblem of his martyrdom, or a money-box as an emblem of his original profession as a tax-collector). This traditional distinction serves modern sensitivities well, for contemporary scholars hold that the apostle did not write the gospel attributed to him, but that it was written in the late first century by an anonymous second generation Christian. The later attribution to Matthew was most likely based on the fact that only the first gospel narrates the call of Matthew (contrast Mt 9:9-13 to Mk 2:13-17 and Lk 5:27-32 where the name Levi is used). For convenience sake, scholars continue to refer to the anonymous author of the first gospel as "Matthew," and it is this anonymous Matthew on whom we primarily reflect today.

As the relatively high number of allusions and quotations in early Christian writings show, Matthew was the early church's favorite of the gospels, probably because of its clear, ecclesiastical focus. A major feature of its structure supports this focus. The narrator has collected most of Jesus' teaching into five thematic discourses: the Ethical Discourse (i.e., the Sermon on the Mount, 5:1-7:27); the Missionary Discourse (10:1-42); the Parabolic Discourse (13:1-52); the Community Discourse (18:1-35); and the Apocalyptic Discourse (24:1-25:46). This organization lends itself well to catechetical use and is evidence that the author's primary intent was to organize the story of Jesus in a way that would most benefit the church.

Of these discourses, it is in the fourth that Matthew's ecclesiastical concerns are most apparent. Consider Jesus' instruction concerning how the community should deal with inner-community offenses:

> If another member of the church sins against you, go and point out the fault when the two of you are alone. If the member listens to you, you have regained that one. But if you are not listened to, take one or two others along with you, so that every word may be confirmed by the evidence of two or three witnesses. If the member refuses to listen to them, tell it to the church; and if the offender refuses to listen even to the church, let such a one be to you as a Gentile and a tax collector. (18:15-17).

O. W. Allen

Proverbs 3:1-6
Psalm 119:33-40 (*UMH* 842)
2 Timothy 3:14-17
Matthew 9:9-13

Gracious God of vocation, as you called Matthew from his occupation as a tax collector to be a disciple, so bid us to rise from our preoccupations to stay close to you, heeding your teaching and discerning the coming of the kingdom, through Jesus Christ our Lord, who lives and reigns with you and the Holy Spirit, one God, now and forever. Amen.

[DTB]

Good Lord, you taught in parables that the reign of God is like treasure hidden in a field.
Bring us, like your evangelist Matthew, to choose daily what will bring true joy and to yield all to be free to follow you. Amen.

[DTB]

September 25
Peter Cartwright (1872)
See Common of Pastors and Bishops

Influential circuit rider and great revival preacher of the Northwest territories, Cartwright was born in Virginia in 1785 but shortly moved with his family to Kentucky. His mother, a devout member of the Methodist Episcopal Church, encouraged and prayed for him until he became convinced of his own sinfulness at age 16. Shortly thereafter he received the assurance of his salvation at a camp meeting.

Just two years later he was appointed to be a Methodist traveling preacher. In 1812 he was made a presiding elder by Asbury, an office he held almost continually until his retirement, a total of over fifty years. He served circuits and districts in what are now the states of Kentucky, Tennessee, Ohio, Illinois, Wisconsin, and Iowa, but spent the majority of his ministry in Illinois. During his ministry he baptized 8,000 children, 4,000 adults, received another 10,000 people into the Church, and was elected to thirteen general conferences.

His life spent on the rugged trails of the Western circuits, Cartwright was a roughhewn character and a legend in his own day. Abel Stevens described him at the 1852 General Conference looking as if "he might wrestle with bears and come off conqueror, as I learn he really has heretofore. . . . He appears war-worn and weather-beaten. . . the integuments of his face wrinkled and tough, his eyes small and twinkling, and defended by a heavy pair of spectacles with green side glasses. . . and his hair — there is no description of that, it looks as if he had poked it into the bag of the Kilkenny cats, and had not had the time to comb it since its extrication."

In 1869, the Illinois Annual Conference held a celebration in honor of Cartwright's fiftieth year as a presiding elder. Cartwright, now 84, said to the assembled crowd,

> I no longer have the strength to labor as a regular traveling preacher. . . . And now I retire from the regular work, not because I do not like it, for I say to you one and all, to the young preachers and to the old, that with all the losses and crosses, labors and sufferings peculiar to the life of a Methodist traveling preacher, I would take. . . the same track over again with the same religion to bear me up, rather than be President of the United States. I ask your prayers that you will remember an old man who has spent a long life in the service of the Church, and would do it again. . . . Amen.[196]

L. H. M. Hoover

September 26
Freeborn Garrettson and
Catherine Livingston Garrettson (1827 and 1849)
See Common of Evangelists, Saints

Born in 1752 to a Maryland family of moderate wealth and named for his grandmother Elizabeth Freeborn, Freeborn Garrettson lost both this mother and elder sister before he was ten. At twenty-one his father died, leaving him land, property, businesses, and slaves. He had already come under the influence of Robert Strawbridge. On his way home from hearing Methodist preacher Daniel Ruff, he writes: "the enmity of my heart was slain, the plan of salvation was open to me . . . and I felt the power of faith and love that I had ever been a stranger to." Shortly thereafter, he was moved to free his slaves before he was "at liberty to proceed in worship."[197] Licensed to preach in 1776, he was among those who kept Methodism going during the revolutionary war. After the war, he traveled 1200 miles in less than six weeks, gathering sixty itinerant preachers for the Christmas conference of 1784. There he was ordained elder and was sent to Nova Scotia where he helped establish a Methodist conference.

Catherine was born (1752) to an immensely wealthy landowning family in Rhinebeck, New York. The suffering of the revolutionary war and a series of family deaths led her to question her comfortable life and study the bible. The subsequent death of a friend moved her to read the *Book of Common Prayer*, during which she experienced a deep conversion in 1787. When through her housekeeper she became attracted to Methodism, her Calvinist family was mortified; doubly so when Catherine fell in love with Freeborn Garrettson. Determined to wait for her family's approval, she dove deeper into her spiritual, even mystical, journey. They eventually married in 1793.

Though Freeborn's work meant constant travel, Catherine vigorously supported his ministry, sometimes traveling with him, but always in contact by letter. Asbury called the Garrettson home "Travelers Rest" and to it came all the leaders of American Methodism. Catherine exercised a remarkable ministry of hospitality, using her intellectual and spiritual vigor to meet the pastoral needs of her guests. Her ministries in this influential household were extensive, but included preaching, teaching, spiritual guidance, and leading worship.[198]

Freeborn served in many leadership capacities, going from conference to conference as needed. He was an opponent of slavery and questioned the extent of episcopal power which Asbury developed.[199] On several occasions he mediated disputes in the emerging denomination. He died on this date in 1827 after 52 years of ministry. Catherine died at 96 in 1849.

D. W. Vogel

September 27
John Dickins (1798)
See Common of Saints

Born August 24, 1747, and London educated, Dickins was the first Book Steward of the Methodist Episcopal Church. He had made America his home and joined the southern Virginia Methodist society by 1774. He was appointed to preaching circuits in North Carolina and Virginia in 1777. Within a year Dickins was describing himself as a "broken down preacher" — words probably reflecting his predisposition to melancholy. In 1780, he married Elizabeth Yancy and settled in Halifax County, North Carolina.

He and Francis Asbury soon became intimates. By 1783 Asbury had prevailed upon Dickins to fill the stational pastorate at Wesley Chapel (later called John Street Methodist Church) in New York City. Thomas Coke arrived at Dickins' parsonage in 1784 with word that John Wesley desired American Methodists to form an independent church. The Christmas Conference unanimously elected to follow Dickins' suggestion that the newly formed denomination call itself the Methodist Episcopal Church.

In 1789 the Methodist Episcopal Church named Dickins its first publisher or "Book Steward." He and his wife, Elizabeth, showed their commitment to publishing by contributing proceeds from the sale of their Halifax plantation — Elizabeth's dowry — to the fledging denomination's book concern. His revision of the first *Discipline*, which became the standard for subsequent editions of the publication, had already shown his writing abilities and won the approbation of his colleagues. He now moved his family to Philadelphia, the cultural and political capital of the newly formed United States, and set up the long desired Methodist book business. There he remained until death, publishing 114,000 copies of books and pamphlets. Among these publications was a pocket hymnal, the first Methodist periodical (the *Arminian Magazine*), the *Discipline*, and several books by John Wesley.

Dickins held the same commitment toward religious publishing as that expressed by the 1796 General Conference: "The propagation of religious knowledge by means of the press is next in importance to the preaching of the gospel. To supply the people therefore with the most pious and useful books . . . is an object worthy of the deepest attention. . . ."

Dickins died of yellow fever on this date in 1798. Asbury wrote, "What I have greatly feared for years hath now taken place, Dickins the generous, the just, the faithful, skillful Dickins is dead."[200]

T. J. Bell

September 27
Alejo Hernández (1875)
See Common of Evangelists

Hernández traveled an unlikely road to become known as the father of Hispanic Methodism. Born in 1842 in Mexico to upper-class Catholic parents, he abandoned his studies for the priesthood — as well as his faith — when the Church's hierarchy endorsed the 1862 French invasion of Mexico. While serving in the resistance army, Hernández stumbled upon a anti-papist tract. Instead of fortifying his atheism as he hoped, the pamphlet challenged him to read and interpret God's Word first-hand. The search for a copy of the scriptures took him to Brownsville, Texas where a sudden rainstorm drove him into the midst of a service of worship. His description of this life-changing moment is reminiscent of John Wesley's Aldersgate experience:

> I felt that God's spirit was there, although I could not understand a word that was being said, I felt my heart strangely warmed. . . . Never did I hear an organ play so sweetly, never did human voices sound so lovely to me, never did people look so beautiful as on that occasion. I went away weeping for joy.

In 1870, Hernández joined the church of a Methodist family who befriended him in Corpus Christi, and he soon began a career of sharing the gospel with his Hispanic brothers and sisters. He became the first Mexican ordained in the Methodist Church in 1871. After brief service in Texas, he was sent to Mexico City in 1874 where he organized the first Methodist church south of the U.S. border. Within 18 months, his missionary work was cut short by a debilitating stroke. He died on September 27, 1875.

The impact of Hernández' ministry far exceeds its brevity. In four years, this former atheist dramatized the spiritual needs of Hispanic people throughout the western hemisphere and energized the church to meet those needs. Bishop John Keener's eulogy underscores the character and legacy of Alejo Hernández:

> He was ready for any enterprise in the Master's service to go alone and on an hour's notice, if need be, to the ends of the earth. His conversion had satisfied every early desire, and it only remained for him to spend his life at the feet and in the work of his gracious Savior. He became in an instant a missionary then and for ever. How full must have been the flood of holy passion in the soul of this young man to diffuse itself, as it has, throughout our church![201]

T. Gildemeister

September 29
Michael and All Angels

Angels (literally "messengers," from the Greek *angelos*) are mentioned throughout the Bible; four are identified by name: Uriel, Raphael, Gabriel, and Michael. Michael is portrayed in the scriptures as the captain of the heavenly host, who leads the angels and aids humanity in the fight against the enemies of God. The Book of Daniel describes Michael as the "Prince," who functions as the patron angel of the Jews (10:13,21; 12:1). In the New Testament, the motif of Michael as patron angel is carried over into the new covenant so that Michael, along with his angels, appears as the guardian of the kingdom of Christ on earth (Rev 12:7). The only other scriptural reference to Michael is found in Jude 9, which refers to Michael disputing with the devil about the body of Moses.

The authority of Michael is further attested by early Christian writers. In *The Testament of Abraham*, Michael is portrayed as possessing power enough to rescue souls from Hell and to bring them to an eternal rest. This work may have been the inspiration for an offertory antiphon in the old Roman ritual of the dead which reads, "May Michael the standard-bearer lead them into the holy light, which you promised of old to Abraham and his seed." The *Shepherd of Hermas* describes Michael's authority over the people of God: "And the great and glorious angel is Michael, who has authority over this people and guides them, for it is he who puts the law into the hearts of those who believe. So he examines those to whom he has given the law to see if they have kept it."[202]

Christians have recognized Michael to be a protector, defender, intercessor, healer, and guardian on behalf of the people of God. Before the ninth century, Michael was the only angel in whose honor liturgical feasts were observed (called, in England, "Michaelmas"). Because of his popularity, numerous churches and shrines were dedicated to his patronage. In some Catholic areas, as well as among some of the churches of the Reformation, celebration of the work of other angels was combined with the more prominent feast of Michael.

K. B. Westerfield-Tucker

The following prayer may be used today:

Eternal, holy God, whose company of angels ever praise, honor, worship, and glorify you, may that company guard, protect, and defend us until that day when we stand with them before your throne ever singing, "Holy, holy, holy, Lord." Amen.

[EBA]

September 30
Jerome (420)
See Common of Teachers

Considered by many to have been the greatest scholar in early Latin Christianity, Jerome was born about 341 at Strido in Dalmatia. He experienced all the benefits of an upper class childhood and was educated in Rome where he studied Latin grammar, rhetoric, and literature. There he visited holy sights and became involved with a circle of Christian friends, and sometime after 366, was baptized.

But Jerome had an arrogant disposition and penchant for controversy that eventually led to his lack of favor among his friends. Leaving Rome, he traveled to Gaul, Italy, and eventually to Aquileia. It was here, under the influence of Christian ascetics, that he began to contemplate a monastic life.

Around 372, Jerome and several friends moved eastward to the city of Antioch. Arriving quite ill from their travels, two of Jerome's colleagues died. Overcome with both grief and sickness, Jerome had a dream of his own day at the judgment seat of God. Before the heavenly throne, God tells Jerome: "You are not a Christian, but a Ciceronian." The dream sent Jerome into the wilderness north of Antioch where he lived for several years as an ascetic studying the scriptures in Hebrew and Greek. As his knowledge of these languages increased, so did his writings. "To be ignorant of scripture," he proclaimed in one of his commentaries, "was to be ignorant of Christ."[203]

Returning to Rome in 379, Jerome served as a secretary to Pope Damasus. He then began his greatest scholarly project: a translation of the scriptures into Latin. Jerome's "Vulgate" translation would take him more than 20 years to complete. It become the central translation for the western church for several centuries.

His interest in the ascetic life continued while in Rome and he became an advisor to a group of wealthy women who shared his interest. In 385 they moved to Bethlehem and setting up one monastery for women and another for men. His relationship to this group of women was surrounded with controversy.

When he died around 420, he was buried under the Church of the Nativity in Bethlehem. Because of his association with books and scholarship, Jerome is the patron saint of students and librarians. In the middle ages he was portrayed as a cardinal, often pictured in art as wearing a red hat with a lion resting at his feet.

J. S. Hudgins

September 30
George Whitefield (1770)
See Common of Preachers, Evangelists

Early leader of the evangelical revival of the eighteenth century, George Whitefield was born in 1714 in Gloucester, England, the youngest son of Elizabeth Edwards and Thomas Whitefield, proprietors of the Bell Inn. Attracted to the stage as a youth, he was gifted with a strong, rich voice which, coupled with his extraordinary histrionic powers, was to make him by age twenty-five the most famous preacher of his time. He acquired a position as servitor at Pembroke College, Oxford, where he befriended John and Charles Wesley and became, except for the Wesleys, the most influential member of the "Methodist" Holy Club. He had a 'new birth' experience just before Easter in 1735 (or three years before Aldersgate). Ordained deacon in 1736, he followed the Wesleys to Georgia where he was popular among the colonists. He later founded an orphanage in Savannah.

Upon returning to England in December 1738, Whitefield was ordained a priest and resumed preaching in England, and, by January, found himself banned from every pulpit in London on account of his "enthusiasm." Churches in Bath and Bristol rejected him as well. Whitefield then broke with convention and began preaching outdoors to coal miners on the Kingswood Common near Bristol. Within months he had stirred a religious revival of unparalleled force throughout the region. Anxious to extend his work and return to Georgia and hearing of John Wesley's own conversion experience, Whitefield convinced him to come to Bristol to organize the throngs of people who were responding. Although reluctant at first, Wesley followed Whitefield's example and began preaching outdoors himself, with surprisingly successful results. In 1741 Whitefield wedded Elizabeth James and set up a chapel in Moorfields, Bristol.

In contrast to Wesley's Arminian theology, Whitefield's was Calvinist in doctrine. He publicly denounced Wesley's teaching, seriously straining their friendship. They later reconciled as friends though not as theologians. Through the patronage of Selina, Countess of Huntingdon, Whitefield opened a Tabernacle in Tottenham Court Road, London. This group of "Calvinistic Methodists" became permanently separated from the Wesleyan Methodists. He visited America seven times, itinerating up and down the Atlantic seaboard. His appearance in Philadelphia in November, 1739 reinforced the influence of Jonathan Edwards and marks a beginning point of the general American revival movement known as the Great Awakening.

R. Brooks

October 4
Francis of Assisi (1226)
See Common of Saints

Francis was born the privileged son of the rich textile merchant Pietro di Bernardone. Seeking glory as a young knight in Assisi's battles with neighboring Perugia, he instead landed in prison and fell seriously ill.

As a result of his long recovery and a series of encounters with lepers and beggers, he experienced a radical change of heart leading to his disavowal of wealth and an identification with the poor. Praying before a crucifix in the crumbling church of San Domiano of Assisi, he heard the voice of the Crucified Christ telling him, "Go and repair my house, which, as you see, is falling completely into ruin." This "Prayer Before the Crucifix" is traditionally associated with that experience and is indicative of Francis' simplicity of spirit:

Most high,
glorious God,
enlighten the darkness of my heart
and give me, Lord,
a correct faith,
a certain hope,
a perfect charity,
sense and knowledge,
so that I may carry out Your holy and true command.

Those who became followers of the *"Poverello"* (little poor man) were known as the Order of Friars Minor (little brothers) and were led by a simple rule approved by Rome. Franciscan spirituality is characterized by its identification with the sufferings of Christ (Francis was the first person recorded as having received the stigmata, or the wounds of Christ, which he carried on his body the last two years of his life) and a sacramental reverance for the whole of God's creation, eminently represented in Francis' "Canticle of Brother Sun."

Cannonized less than two years after his death by Pope Gregory IX, Francis is probably the most popular of all the saints; his love of creation, his total embrace of humility and poverty, and his charity towards the poor and outcast seem almost superhuman in relation to ours, yet at his death he is said to have remarked to his followers: "Let us begin, brothers, to serve the Lord our God for up to now we have made little or no progress."[204]

C. F. Guthrie

October 6
William Tyndale (1536)
See Common of Martyrs, Teachers

Tyndale has been lauded as the "father of the English Bible." Educated at Oxford and Cambridge, Tyndale became the tutor for the family of Sir John Walsh in 1521, serving also as pastor to the family and their tenant farmers. He was deeply influenced by Erasmus, who, in his *Handbook for the Christian Soldier*, stressed the importance of reading the Scriptures for growth in faith and correct doctrine. In debates with visiting priests who were entertained at the manor, he was struck by the clergy's ignorance of the Scriptures. He is said to have remarked to one priest: "if God spare my life . . . I will cause a boy that driveth the plough shall know more of the Scriptures than thou dost."[205]

It became his life's mission to make the Scriptures available to all his compatriots in their native tongue, that he might be "found faithful to my father and lord in distributing unto my brethren and fellows . . . their due and necessary food."[206] Unable to carry out this task by legal means, he left England, never to return. He visited Luther for some time, whose work left its mark on Tyndale's notes and prologues to the epistles. Tyndale brought forth the first complete edition of his New Testament in 1526 at Worms. Copies were smuggled back into England by the thousands through sympathetic merchants. Tyndale then set to work on the Hebrew Scriptures, distributing a translation of the Pentateuch. His work met with violent opposition, as copies of his New Testament — as well as many of his partners — were burnt by order of the king and his chancellor, Thomas More. Tyndale himself was finally arrested by agents in Antwerp and strangled at Brussels in 1536.

Tyndale was more than a translator. His prologues, as well as several tracts, show that he was also a theologian. He saw the reformation doctrines of justification by faith and the covenant relationship with God as the keys to Scripture, stressing obedience to God's law as the essential response to God's favor: "Remember that Christ made not this atonement that thou shouldest anger God again, neither died he for thy sins, that thou shouldest live still in them."[207] Tyndale's dedication to the Scriptures should encourage Christians, for whom the Word remains a most "necessary food," to read more eagerly and study more carefully what was made available at such cost.

D. A. deSilva

October 6
Jennie Fowler Willing (1916)
See Common of Teachers

Jennie Willing, born into a family instrumental in the founding of Canadian Methodism, spent most of her own life in the U.S. where she worked as a licensed preacher, educator, writer, and a leader in the Illinois suffrage movement. Ill health prevented her from receiving much formal education. That did not stop her from learning, however, or from teaching others. She worked as a local school teacher at the age of fifteen, and in 1874 became professor of English language and literature at Illinois Wesleyan University. She married William C. Fowler, a lawyer-turned-Methodist-minister working in Illinois and New York.

As a writer of devotional literature, Willing focused on practical concerns such as getting along in marriage, growing old, and "how to cure the blues." She often took controversial stands on issues such as the abolition of slavery and the role of women, leading one critic to label her writing "strong and mannish." Her devotional writings call on women to see their ordinary abilities and gifts as Christian ministry. In one remarkably contemporary sounding essay written in 1880, she credits women with the evangelization of Europe. There she retrieves the untold stories of the women who spread the Gospel in their roles as mothers, teachers, and advisors:

> During the dark ages, when a woman was a being to be treated with silly adulation or contempt, a plaything or a drudge, altogether unfit to be trusted with a knowledge of books or of affairs, even in those murky days, a woman was used for the evangelization of nearly every country in Europe ... Helena, the mother of Constantine the Great, made Christianity the religion of the Roman empire.... But time would fail to speak of all the great schemes that God has inaugurated through the smallest agencies.[208]

Jennie Fowler Willing stood convinced, based upon her reading of scripture, that those eras in the history of Christianity fostering disdain for women were times of "retrograde Christianity." "The Bible is a woman's Magna Charta," she wrote. "Women never had and never can have a firmer, better friend than the Son of Mary." This conviction about the value and standing of women came from her faith that both women and men are "coworkers with the Lord Jesus Christ." She practiced her convictions in her work as a leader in the movement for women's suffrage, as well as through her foundational roles in the establishment of the Woman's Foreign Missionary Society of the Methodist Episcopal Church, the Woman's Home Missionary Society, and the Woman's Christian Temperance Union.[209]

J. A. Mercer

October 7
John Woolman (1772)
See Common of Prophets

John Woolman — preacher, writer, mystic, and social reformer — was the fourth child and eldest son of thirteen children born to Samuel and Elizabeth Burr Woolman. As he was growing up on a Quaker plantation near Burlington, New Jersey, the Quakers were undergoing a trial "by favor and prosperity," finding, like their Puritan neighbors, virtue in worldly success and wealth.

Woolman's life and faith were profoundly shaped during his youth through his experience of God in nature's beauty on the Woolman plantation. As a youth he came to understand himself moved by an inward principle to love God, and by the same principle, to love all of God's creatures in the visible world.

Through his formal education was confined to a country Quaker school, his parents encouraged him to read and learn trades. Working as a clerk in Mount Holly during 1740-41, Woolman was stirred to begin a public ministry as he became aware of the conditions of others in the larger world.

Recognized as preacher in 1743 by the Burlington Quarterly Meeting, Woolman began that year his first of numerous preaching journeys. Beginning with his first preaching trip under the tutelage of Abraham Farrington, he began a long campaign against slavery, constantly traveling among the Quaker communities in defense of black rights. By 1749, as a property owner, a successful tailor and shopkeeper, he married Sarah Ellis. Their first child, Mary was born in 1750. The Woolman's only other child, William, died three months after birth.

Perhaps best remembered as a herald of the antislavery movement, some propose that the central evil Woolman opposed was the exploitation of labor, his ideal a society in which no person should profit by the degradation of another. His ministry of gentle yet forcible action was a liberation movement of influence, an appeal to the conscience of all professing Christians.

Woolman's mystical connection with God's inner light was seamlessly interwoven with a bold ministry of action aimed at freeing the spirit of persons from material bondage. He substantially decreased slave ownership, particularly among the Friends in Pennsylvania and New Jersey. He fought for equitable treatment of Native Americans. He revitalized the practice of pacifism among Quakers while restoring their dependency upon the Light within.

R. Brooks

October 15
Teresa of Ávila (1582)
See Common of Teachers

Teresa de Cepeda y Ahumada was born in 1515 into an aristocratic Castilian family. At seven, she and her brother wished for martydom in the land of the Moors. "I believe the Lord had given us sufficient courage for this . . . but our great hindrance seemed to be that we had a father and a mother." When her religious fervor waned in her youth her father sent her to be educated by Augustinian nuns. While recovering from an illness she decided to enter the Carmelite Convent of the Incarnation in Ávila.

Her health problems returned, however, and she moved back in with her family for treatment. Three years of sickness and the relative laxity of the convent led her to abandon prayer until her father's death in 1543. Her interior conversion and life as a mystic began in earnest in 1555 after her confessor encouraged her to pray and make more frequent communion. Teresa soon felt her first divine ecstasy and heard God speak, "I will have thee converse now, but not with men, but with angels."[210] Within a year she had a vision of the cherubim who pierced her heart with a spear of fire, leaving her aflame with God's love.

Against opposition, she began a series of Carmelite reforms, founding the Convent of St. Joseph at Ávila in 1562 in which a strict rule of poverty and service was followed. Her perseverance led to her collaboration and friendship with John of the Cross and a similar reform of the Carmelite friars. Eventually, her reformed (Discalced) Carmelite Order was officially recognized.

She began to record her spiritual conversations at age 47. Her writings include *The Book of Her Life* (1565), *The Interior Castle* (1577), and *The Way of Perfection* (1579). In *The Interior Castle,* Teresa shares her method of 'mental' prayer with her sister nuns, describing the soul as a castle and how the inward journy into it yields union with the incarnate Christ. Her greatest contribution to Western spirituality is her treatment of the entire journey of prayer, from meditation to mystical union. When Teresa's views came under criticism of the Inquisition, she fended off attacks writing, "Fix your eyes on the Crucified and nothing else will be of much importance to you."[211]

Teresa was canonized in 1622 by Pope Gregory XV and proclaimed the first woman Doctor of the Church by Pope Paul VI in 1970.

H. P. Minor

October 16
Thomas Cranmer (1556)
See Common of Pastors and Bishops

Cranmer was archbishop of Canterbury and first archbishop of the Church of England. He was pulled into the politics of the church by King Henry VIII to deal with Henry's displeasure with Rome. When consecrated as archbishop in 1533, he became one of Henry's primary instruments for the overthrow of papal supremacy in England. In 1534 Cranmer put into motion a translation of the Bible which resulted in the appearance of the Great Bible in 1539. As a result of his attempts to implement protestant reforms in England, he was tried for heresy and sentenced to imprisonment in 1544, only to be freed upon producing the signet of the King. Upon his freedom, he continued conversations with and sought some form of union with the reforming churches in Europe. Edward, who succeeded Henry, was more open to protestant reforms. But, after Edward's death and the ascension of Queen Mary, a Roman Catholic, in 1553, Cranmer was committed to the Tower. In 1554, as the result of his views on transubstantiation he was again declared a heretic and no longer a member of the church. Subsequent maneuvering in Rome resulted in Cranmer's excommunication and the official withdrawal of his bishopric. Finally, in 1556, he was sentenced to execution. Although he recanted on the eve of his execution, he retracted rather than confirmed this recantation of the day and was quickly led to be burned at the stake. It is said that at his burning, he held the hand with which he had signed his recantations into the fire crying, "This hand has written contrary to my heart."[212]

We remember Cranmer as the creator and author of the *Book of Common Prayer,* first issued in 1549, and then, in revision, in 1552. His legacy to us remains the liturgical language and structures of the prayer book which continue to shape the piety and spirituality of the Church of England, and by extension, the worldwide Anglican communion and those it has influenced. Perhaps no prayer remains more familiar to us today than Cranmer's Collect for Purity, which is included in contemporary form as the opening prayer in the "Service of Word and Table I," in *The United Methodist Hymnal* (6):

Almighty God, to you all hearts are open, all desires known, and from you no secrets are hidden. Cleanse the thoughts of our hearts by the inspiration of your Holy Spirit, that we may perfectly love you, and worthily magnify your holy name, through Christ our Lord. Amen.

E. B. Anderson

October 17
Ignatius of Antioch (c. 115)
See Common of Pastors and Bishops, Martyrs

Nothing is known of Ignatius' early life. He became the bishop of the influential city of Antioch around 69. During the reign of Trajan, the empire began a widespread persecution of Christians. They were targeted not on grounds of their behavior as such, but because of their unauthorized associations. If they recanted their faith when encountered by Roman authorities, they would be freely pardoned. Ignatius, like many of his fellow Christians, aggressively refused. He was arrested, placed under military guard, and condemned to death.

Most of what is known about Ignatius comes from his own writings while on his final journey from Antioch to Rome. He wrote seven influential letters urging the churches to unity, affirming the sacramental life of the church, exhorting obedience to the bishop, and citing Peter and Paul as preeminent founders of the Roman church. Four of these letters were written at Smyrna, where they were enthusiastically received by local Christians and their leader Polycarp.

The letters reveal a person discovering a new level of discipleship through suffering. Ignatius longed to be with Christ. To the Romans he wrote to discourage any attempt to rescue him from death: "I am now beginning to be a disciple; may nothing visible or invisible prevent me from reaching Jesus Christ."[213] And he encouraged the Christians at Ephesus, writing, "You are all fellow pilgrims, carrying with you God and His temple; you are bearers of Christ and of holy offerings, decked out in the commandments of Jesus Christ. And with this letter I am able to take part in your festivity, to be of your company, to share in the joy that comes from setting your heart not on what is merely human in life, but on God."[214]

When he arrived in Rome, he was taken to the Colosseum and thrown to the lions. Just before being fed to the lions, in a well known prayer, he described himself as "the wheat of Christ" reflecting his own sense of unity with Christ in death.

Ignatius has inspired many Christians with his steadfast commitment in the light of persecution. He also stood as a testimony in his own day to the power of Christ as manifest in the unity of the church.

J. S. Hudgins

Luke

I too decided, after investigating everything carefully from the very first, to write an orderly account for you, most excellent Theophilus, so that you may know the truth concerning the things about which you have been instructed. (Lk 1:3-4)

Here we have the clear intention of the writer of the third Gospel and Acts to be careful, comprehensive, and orderly as he sets out to narrate the story of Jesus and the early Christian community. Taken together, Luke-Acts comprises a full quarter of the New Testament, renders a fluid narrative of the rise of the Christian Church out of the life and ministry of Jesus, and gives Christians their most compelling and systematic picture of their origins. To see the importance of these books for Christian life and worship, it is necessary only to mention some of the stories which appear there but nowhere else: the Annunciation, the Visitation, the Christmas story of angels, shepherds and the stable, the Presentation, young Jesus teaching in the Temple, the good Samaritan, the prodigal son, Lazarus and Dives, Zacchaeus in the sycamore, the resurrection appearance at Emmaus, the Ascension, Pentecost, Peter's release from prison and his vision of the blanket let down from heaven, and details of Paul's journeys, his defense before the authorities, and his shipwreck and arrival in Rome. In many ways, the Church's story *is* Luke's story.

By the latter half of the second century, the writer of these remarkable books was widely identified as Luke the "beloved physician," a sometime companion of Paul (see Phlm 24; Col 4:14; 2 Tim 4:11), and a native of Antioch. Although this is difficult to prove, several passages in the later stages of Acts are written from the first person plural (the famous "we" passages), indicating that the writer may well have been an eyewitness to the events described there.

Luke's writings reveal recurring themes that appeal to contemporary spirituality: concern for the poor, the place of women in society, reconciliation between Jewish and Gentile believers, and an emphasis on liturgical prayer. The evangelist's symbol is the ox, perhaps a reference to the fact that the Gospel begins with Zechariah's sacrificial duty in the Temple. Luke is considered the patron of physicians and, because of an ancient apocryphal tale of his having painted an icon of the Virgin Mary, of artists.

C. F. Guthrie

Isaiah 35:5-8 or Ecclesiasticus (Sirach) 38:1-15
Psalm 147 (*UMH* 859)
2 Timothy 4:5-11
Luke 4:14-21

Almighty God, who inspired your servant Luke the physician to set forth in the Gospel the love and healing power of your Son: Establish the reign of this power and love among us and empower your whole church to be rich toward you in worship and service to the poor, through Christ our Lord. Amen.

[DTB]

Gift from on high,
come upon us in freedom and grace,
  that delivered from all entanglements
we may seek the lost,
  heal the sick,
  announce God's reign, and
  delight that our hearts know you in the breaking of bread.

[DTB]

James of Jerusalem

The James commemorated today is the person Matthew and Mark call one of Jesus' brothers, along with James, Joses (Mt: Joseph), Simon, and Jude (Mk 6:3; Mt 13:55). The meaning of the word "brother" (Greek *adelphos*) has been interpreted in a variety of ways: actual brother (i.e., a son of Mary and Joseph), stepbrother (a child of Joseph by a previous marriage), or cousin. The evidence of the New Testament and early Christian writings does not allow us to decide in favor of any of the above theories, although the third seems least likely.

Paul says that James was a witness to the Resurrection (1 Cor 15:7). In his letter to the Galations, he calls James one of the "acknowledged pillars" of the Jerusalem church, along with Cephas and John (Gal 2:9). Paul goes on to make clear to the Galatians that at his meeting with the leaders of the Jerusalem church, it was agreed that he was to preach to the Gentiles, while the other three were to preach to their fellow Jews. In later Christian literature, James is presented as the leader of the Jerusalem church, and the representative of Palestinian Jewish Christianity. It seems that during the century after the death and resurrection of Jesus, his relatives held positions of authority in Palestinian Jewish Christian circles: not only in Jerusalem, but also in the Galilean towns of Nazareth, Kokhaba, and (perhaps) Sikhnin.[215]

The New Testament contains no reference to the death of James. However, Eusebius includes in his *Ecclesiastical History* narratives from the second-century historian Hegesippus and the first-century Jewish historian Josephus concerning James' death. The two sources do not agree on the date, which probably fell some time around 75 C.E.

Jerome cites a story about a resurrection appearance of Jesus to James from the apocryphal Gospel According to the Hebrews, an account which witnesses to the authority and importance of James within the Jewish-Christian community:

> And when the Lord had given the linen cloth to the servant of the priest, he went to James and appeared to him. For James had sworn that he would not eat bread from that hour in which he had drunk the cup of the Lord until he should see him risen from among them that sleep. And shortly thereafter the Lord said: Bring a table and bread! And immediately it is added: he took the bread, blessed it and brake it and gave it to James the Just and said to him: My brother, eat thy bread, for the Son of man is risen from among them that sleep.[216]

G. S. Sperry-White

Acts 15:12-22a
Psalm 1 (*UMH* 738)
1 Corinthians 15:1-11
Matthew 13:54-58

God of Israel, you raised James the brother of Jesus to be a pillar of the church, and grafted many of us as branches upon the tree of Israel's faith: Grant us strength from our deep roots that we may prosper and yield fruit through Jesus the Messiah, who lives and reigns with you and the Holy Spirit, one God, from generation to generation. Amen.

[CFG]

We thank you Lord for leaders like James who
    rooted and planted in their Jerusalems
    live faithfully beyond their narrow familial bonds and
    have vision and hold power for the sake of those in the wider circle. Amen.

[DTB]

October 24
Sarah Crosby (1804)
See Common of Preachers

Little is known of the early life of the first woman preacher of Methodism, Sarah Crosby. Born in 1729, she joined a Methodist Society in 1750, and this was the fellowship that sustained her when her alcoholic husband abandoned her after seven years of marriage. She was a gifted teacher and counselor, as demonstrated by the circumstance that drew her into preaching. She had prepare to meet with her class of 30, and discovered over two hundred people had gathered to hear her speak.

Sarah immediately wrote to John Wesley, her spiritual mentor, for advice as the numbers continued to grow. In a time when women's public speaking was considered shameful and unnatural, Sarah Crosby discovered an inner peace and conviction of her call. John Wesley came to the defense of what he called the "extraordinary call" of her ministry as it grew from class meeting to open-air preaching. Her journal reveals the extraordinary schedule she kept, often preaching 2 to 3 times a day, beginning at 5 am. One male colleague wrote of her, "This apostolic woman was an *itinerant*, yea, a *field preacher*."

As women's religious leadership opportunities expanded, their influence on social patterns widened. Schools were founded, prison reform begun, medical help for the poor extended as women such as Sarah Crosby found their voice in the outpouring of the Spirit: "She used to begin prayer with the simplicity of a little child, and then rise to the language of a mother in Israel. Thus she prayed with the Spirit, and with understanding."

Within a decade of John Wesley's death, the recognition of the extraordinary ministry of women turned into repression. Women were barred from the ministry of preaching. Yet Sarah Crosby's letter of advice to a younger woman retains its prophetic power.

When we know we have our Lord's approbation, we should stand, like the beaten anvil to the stroke; or lie in his hands, as clay in the hands of the potter. Through evil report, and good, we pass, but all things worketh together for good, to them that love God. Speak and act, as the spirit gives liberty, and utterance; fear not the face of man, but with humble confidence, trust in the Lord; looking unto him who is able, and willing to save to the uttermost, all that come unto God by him.[217]

H. M. Elkins

Simon and Jude

Virtually nothing which can be substantiated is known of the lives of these apostles, outside of their listing in the catalogue of the apostles found in Matthew 10, Mark 3, Luke 6, and Acts 1. In ecclesiastical commemoration the apostles Simon and Jude have been traditionally coupled together in the West, probably due to a sixth century tradition that has them traveling together to Persia and suffering martyrdom there. This date may be the date on which their remains were translated to St. Peter's in Rome in the seventh or eighth century. In the East they are celebrated separately on May 10 and June 19, respectively.

Simon, is called either "the zealot" (Luke-Acts), or "the Cananaean" (Matthew and Mark). In Hebrew and Aramaic the terms would be equivalent. His emblem is a saw due to a tradition of his having met martyrdom by being sawn in two.

Jude represents an amalgam of at least three persons who appear in the scriptures: the apostle Judas, son of James (Luke-Acts) also called Thaddeus (Matthew and Mark); Judas, one of the brothers of Jesus mentioned in Matthew 13:55 and Mark 6:3; and Jude, the author of the short Epistle of Jude which ends with this well-known doxology:

Now, to him who is able to keep you from falling, and to make you stand without blemish in the presence of his glory with rejoicing, to the only God our Savior, through Jesus Christ our Lord, be glory, majesty, power, and authority, before all time and now and forever. Amen.

In John 14:22, "Judas (not Iscariot)" interrupts Jesus' discourse at the Last Supper to ask him, "Lord, how is it that you will reveal yourself to us, and not to the world?" Jesus answers that the difference will be in how people love him and how that love issues forth in obedience.

In more recent times, Jude has become popular as the patron of lost causes, prayers to him appearing regularly in newspaper classified ads. This connection is possibly due to the tradition that because his name is so similar to the Judas who betrayed Jesus, Jude was not very often invoked in prayer. Therefore, he can well sympathize with those who are encountering difficulty. His emblem is usually the club. Sometimes, however, Simon and Jude are pictured together as fishermen, Jude holding a ship and Simon a fish.

R. A. Reed

Isaiah 28:11-16
Psalm 116 (*UMH* 837)
Jude 17-24
John 14:18-24

Almighty God, your church is built on the foundation of the apostles and
prophets with Christ as the chief cornerstone: restore the whole church
to the foundation of your holy faith and cause it to persevere in the way
of prayer and mercy, through Christ our Lord, who lives and reigns with
you and the Holy Spirit, one God, now and forever. Amen.

[DTB]

God of all hopeless cases and lost causes,
as we commemorate Simon and Jude, cause us to trust you
in all that overwhelms,
with all that risks obscurity,
for all the disregarded. Amen.

[DTB]

All Saints

This is a day to remember the whole company of Christians of every time and place. "The saints" in New Testament usage refers to Christians collectively. We are made saints (i.e., holy), not because of our moral or spiritual attainments but by the free gift of God in Jesus Christ.

In the Apostles' Creed we affirm "the communion of saints." In our Eucharistic liturgy we pray: "And so, with your people on earth and all the company of heaven, we praise your name and join their unending hymn." Even when no one is visibly with us in our daily prayer we are invisibly joined by the community of saints.

In his journal, John Wesley repeatedly noted the special meaning All Saints' Day had for him. He called it, "a day of triumphant joy" (1748), "a festival I dearly love" (1767), "a comfortable day" (1788), and "a day that I peculiarly love" (1789). On Saturday, November 1, 1766 he wrote,

> God, who hath knit together his elect in one communion and fellowship gave us a solemn season at West Street, as usual, in praising him for all his saints. On this day in particular, I commonly find the truth of these words [by Charles Wesley]:

> The Church triumphant in his love,
>   Their mighty joys we know;
> They praise the Lamb in hymns above,
>   And we in hymns below.[218]

Traditionally a distinction has been made between the joint celebration of all the church's canonized saints on All Saints Day and the commemoration of persons whose names do not appear on any calendar of saints but whom we cherish as role models of the faith on 'All Faithful Departed' or 'All Souls' Day. Because The United Methodist Church does not officially recognize particular saints it is appropriate that we combine these emphases on a single day. So, on this day, each of us may well remember those of our family, friends, or congregation who have died, especially those who have died within the past year. Some congregations may choose to remember the living as well as the dead, and even reflect on the mystery of the generations yet unborn who will praise God's name. This is a day with not only a common meaning for the whole community of faith but also special and distinctive meanings for each one of us. We, each in our own way, may join Wesley in regarding this as "a day that I peculiarly love."

H. L. Hickman

Year A	Year B	Year C
Revelation 7:9-17	Ecclesiasticus 3:1-9	Daniel 7:1-3, 15-18
Ps. 34:1-10, 22 (*UMH* 769)	or Isaiah 25:6-9	Psalm 149
1 John 3:1-3	Psalm 24 (*UMH* 755)	or Psalm 150 (*UMH* 862)
Matthew 5:1-12	Revelation 21:1-6a	Ephesians 1:11-23
	John 11:32-44	Luke 6:20-31

God concealed in mystery and majesty,
    we have seen your glory and grace in the lives of men and women who
        followed Christ.
    You reveal yourself in their kindness and courage;
        we bless you for their fidelity to your purpose and way,
        through Christ, our Lord. Amen.

[DTB]

Jesus, baptized into your life, you have given us a vocation of justice and
    compassion, and
    you have joined us to a company beyond counting.
    Encourage us with this knowledge,
        and by the promptings and warnings of the Holy Spirit,
        bring us with all your saints to lives
        transformed in faith and service. Amen.

[DTB]

See *The United Methodist Book of Worship,* 74, 236, 413

November 2
Phoebe Palmer (1874)
See Common of Evangelists

Phoebe Palmer was the preeminent woman theologian and evangelist of the Holiness movement. She believed in and trusted the direct call of the Spirit and she believed that call strong enough to overturn society's proscription against women in the pulpit.

Phoebe was born in New York City in 1807 of Henry Worrell and Dorethea Wade who had become members of Methodist societies in England. She married physician Walter C. Palmer in 1827. Both came under the influence of the revival at Allen Street Methodist Church in 1832. She had an experience of sanctification on July 26, 1837 and soon became leader of the "Tuesday Meeting for the Promotion of Holiness" and a popular speaker.

Together, the Palmers conducted evangelistic meetings throughout the United States, Canada, and England. They extended their ministry through publishing their periodical, *A Guide to Holiness*. They also shared in suffering. The Palmers lost three of their six children in infancy and childhood, one child dying from a fire ignited by a candle which fell into her gauze-covered cradle.

Phoebe had a strong biblical faith. She believed that one must do what the Spirit commanded. When she felt called by the Spirit to testify, she was compelled to speak. Palmer found particular affirmation of the role of women in the writings and actions of the apostle Paul and John Wesley. But as she strongly insisted in a statement that might be thought of as her creed, "THE BIBLE, THE BLESSED BIBLE, IS THE TEXTBOOK. Not Wesley, not Fletcher . . . not Mrs. Phoebe Palmer, but the Bible."[219] She also claimed in the book *Promise of the Father* that she was not campaigning for women to preach. The burden of her message, however, was that one should follow the direct leading of the Spirit, wherever that may take one.

A near tragedy in her life exhibited the depth and relevance of Palmer's faith. Returning from a New England camp-meeting in an elegant steamer, the boiler burst. Phoebe was concerned because she felt many of the other passengers had no "preparation for eternity." Phoebe and her companions began singing hymns with themes such as, "We're going home to die no more." Finding strength from their faith, the other passengers urged them to sing more. By the time they had finished singing, the immediate difficulty was repaired and the boat proceeded on its way. "There are some Methodists here!" exclaimed one of the passengers as they arrived at their destination.[220]

I. A. Fisher

November 3
Richard Hooker (1600)
See Common of Teachers

Richard Hooker is best known for explicating that distinctively Anglican mode of theological and liturgical discourse known as "the via media" (the middle way). Educated at Corpus Christi College at Oxford, he served there as a scholar, fellow, and deputy professor until his marriage in 1584 necessitated his resignation from Oxford. After that, he served as a Master of the Temple in London and as rector of various English parishes. His most significant theological reflection was done during the years he was a parish priest.

Hooker faced a daunting theological challenge, that is, how does one answer God's call to reform the church while retaining Catholic creedal and liturgical forms? During the first century of the English Reformation that was no mere academic question. Puritans demanded the rejection of all liturgical forms and ecclesiastical structures that did not possess a direct biblical warrant. The memory of Mary Tudor's reign had given ample reason to suspect things Catholic.

Hooker's response to the Puritan critique is expressed in the eight books of *The Laws of Ecclesiastical Polity*, his most enduring contribution. In *The Laws*, he argued for a reformed theological method that honors antiquity while using the best of human reason. Hooker thus expressed that characteristically Anglican methodology which uses Scripture, Tradition, and Reason, upon which the much later Methodist "quadrilateral" (adding "experience") would be based. Book V of *The Laws* answered the Puritan critique of *The Book of Common Prayer*. He wrote there,

> Neither may we in this case lightly esteem what hath been allowed as fit in the judgment of antiquity and by the long continued practice of the whole Church, from which unnecessarily to swerve experience hat never as yet found it safe. . . . For the world will not endure to hear that we are wiser than any have been which went before.[221]

Hooker argued for a liturgical conservatism borne of humility and wisdom. His witness encourages Reformed thought — he acknowledged, for example, the need for sermons as well as the public reading of Scripture. At the same time, his legacy challenges that characteristically American error of assuming that one must reject ancient tradition for the sake of the missional imperative.

M. W. Stamm

November 10
Leo the Great (461)
See Common of Pastors and Bishops

Leo the Great, consecrated bishop of Rome in 440 and called the first pope, became the ecclesiastical leader of Rome at a time of decline for the empire and controversy for the Church. Given the obvious weakness of the Western emperor at this time, the Church increasingly emerged as the most powerful institution in Rome. When the city of Rome experienced barbarian incursions, the Church contributed its spiritual authority to Rome's defense. As Attila and the Huns marched on Rome in 452, Leo went forth in full ecclesiastical regalia in a successful effort to persuade him to spare the city. Three years later Leo attempted the same mission when Genseric menaced Rome, but he failed and Genseric pillaged the city for fourteen days. Leo thus witnessed the decline of the empire and, in part due to his courage and firmness, a corresponding growth in the power of the Church.

The Church too went through a period of crisis, however. In the Eastern half of the empire, theologians fought over questions about the divinity and the humanity of Christ, and their theological questions quickly became entangled with political intrigues. Leo's firmness again served him well. Against those who questioned the full humanity of Christ, Leo asked that they "show from what source they promise themselves hope of eternal life, which no [one] can attain without the help of the *man* Jesus Christ, the Mediator between God and [humanity]."[222] Leo was thus one of the principal architects of the Council of Chalcedon's formula that Christ is two natures in one person, one of the primary sources for subsequent orthodox reflection on the nature and person of Christ.

Leo's life is inseparable from the major events of his bishopric. Little is known about his youth or his personal life apart from it. Nonetheless, his letters do reveal his character. Leo was stern and practical at a time of crisis when people required firm leadership. In the city of Rome, his leadership took the form of a courageous appeal to barbarian invaders. Within the Church, he defended the humanity of Christ out of a profound sense of our need for a mediator with God. Even in our very different time, Leo's faith and courage can serve as models for us.

H. Hill

November 11
Martin of Tours (397)
See Common of Pastors and Bishops

Martin of Tours, bishop and monastic, is a patron saint of France and was one of the favorite saints of the Middle Ages. He was also one of the first non-martyrs to be commemorated in the church calendar. Much of Martin's fame can be attributed to the widely read account of his life and miracles written by his acquaintance, Sulpicius Severus.

Martin was born in present-day Hungary and joined the Roman army in which his father was an officer. Enrolled in the Christian catechumenate, Martin felt that he could not be both a soldier and a Christian and so was put jail for a time for his refusal to serve. It was shortly after this in 334 that Martin had his famous encounter with the poor man. After watching several people pass by a nearly naked man in the city gate, Martin was moved to mercy. Taking his sword, he divided his cloak and gave him half. Sulpicius states that Martin had a vision on the following night in which he saw Christ wrapped in the part of the cloak he gave away and in which he heard Christ say, "Martin, who is still but a catechumen, clothed me with this robe."[223]

Baptized in 337, he later came under the influence of Hilary, bishop of Potiers, and was given the office of exorcist. When Hilary was banished after defending Nicene orthodoxy against the Arians (who had gained power), Martin returned to Hungary. When Hilary returned triumphantly to Potiers in 360, Martin also returned and started a hermitage at Ligugé which became the first monastery in France. He gradually gained a reputation as a miracle worker. Against his wishes, he was made bishop of Tours in 372, but he continued his monastic life. As a bishop he dedicated himself to evangelism, particularly in the pagan countryside, and in the founding of an important monastery at Marmoutier. His miracle-working became more renowned, especially with the report that he had raised a man from the dead. He sometimes experienced conflict from clergy because of his high expectations of them and for his resistance to the execution of a Gnostic heretic.

Martin died on November 8 near Tours, but from an early date he was commemorated on this, the day of his burial.

L. Ruth and C. F. Guthrie

November 11
Søren Kierkegaard (1855)
See Common of Teachers

Born and living almost his whole life in Copenhagen, Søren Kierkegaard was a student, a prolific author, and, finally, a well-known and controversial figure in Copenhagen public life. Because of his inherited wealth, which lasted until a month before his death, Kierkegaard was able to devote his whole life to exploring the religious life and trying to persuade the established Danish church of its distance from authentic Christianity.

Kierkegaard was driven to "find the idea for which I can live and die."[224] Searching for that idea, he wrote his early philosophical works under various pseudonyms in order to deflect attention from himself. Kierkegaard detested all philosophical systems, particularly Hegelianism, and insisted that we face the responsibility of our individual struggle between good and evil. As such, he is the precursor to Existentialism.

An extreme introvert, Kierkegaard's melancholic religious disposition was formed in him by his father, whose death in 1838 prompted his initial explorations of the religious life. His guilt-ridden engagement with Regine Olsen also prompted discourses on the differences between the aesthetic, moral, and religious life, and studies on religious psychology in which he meticulously analyzed the experiences of dread, anxiety, fear, joy, love, and faith. He continued to have a great sense of his own unworthiness and of the mysterious nature of God's power and love: "God in Heaven, let me really feel my nothingness, not in order to despair over it, but in order to feel the more powerfully the greatness of Thy goodness."[225]

Kierkegaard underwent a period of extreme suffering and public humiliation by a series of attacks in the press. This, plus indignation at the way a comfortable established bishop was publicly praised as an authentically Christian "Witness to the Truth," moved him to become a vociferous critic of the Church of Denmark. Kierkegaard's attempt to reintroduce the strangeness of the Christian faith to self-assured Denmark was rebuked by others. The resulting stress led to his breakdown and death. He knew the pain of attempting to speak honestly to a people who were deluded into assuming that being a Christian was an easy and automatic work. Yet he also knew the inner peace of seeing his whole life surrendered to and surrounded by a God of unknowable power and love. When asked on his deathbed whether his sense of peace was based on confidence in God's grace, he replied, "Yes, of course, what else?"[226]

C. G. Lindquist

November 13
Sarah Peters (1748)
See Common of Saints

Sarah Peters was one of the early Methodists in London, a soul-friend of John Wesley. They would meet twice a week "to unbosom ourselves to each other." He wrote an "Account" of her last weeks of life, reprinted in the Arminian Magazine as a model and inspiration for believers.

She used to say, "I cannot rest, day or night, any longer than I am gathering in souls to God." Long before Elizabeth Fry, she visited condemned prisoners in Newgate prison. She would sing a hymn with them, read Scripture and pray. In October 1748 she visited John Lancaster, sentenced to death for stealing, among other things, some candlesticks and velvet from the Foundery (John Wesley's preaching place). Friends urged her not to go, as gaol-fever (typhus) was raging at the prison, but she insisted. She met with Lancaster and five or six others for three weeks until their execution. They were all converted, and Lancaster, going in the cart to his execution, exhorted the bystanders to repent and sang hymns, especially, "O remember Calvary, And let us go in peace", which Sarah Peters had doubtless sung with him.

Not surprisingly, Sarah contracted "a malignant fever" and died after ten days' illness. John Wesley testified to her character: "I never saw her, upon the most trying occasions, in any degree ruffled or discomposed, but . . . always loving, always happy." This was not the shallow happiness of a sheltered life. Her own experience of the love of God compelled her to go to "those who needed her most." She did not merely collude with an oppressive system of criminal justice by ministering to the prisoners, but "resolved to leave no means unattempted" to procure a pardon for John Lancaster, having petitions drawn up and going "to every part of the town, where anyone lived, who might possibly assist therein."

Sarah Peters lived out her faith in words and deeds. She took control of her own lifestyle, saying "I can live upon one meal a day, so that I may have to give to them that have none." She took up an activity in which women were expected to engage (visiting the sick and poor) and extended it in a new and challenging way. Her faith gave her the resources to meet these challenges: in John Wesley's words, "God endued her above her fellows, with the love that believeth, hopeth, and endureth all things."[227]

M. P. Jones

November 16
Margaret, Queen of Scotland (1093)
See Common of Saints

Margaret was born in Hungary in 1046, the child of an exile from the throne of England only to be exiled herself. Her family returned to England at the invitation of Edward the Confessor, but twelve years later when Edward died, William the Conqueror took the throne. Seeking refuge from William after the Battle of Hastings in 1067, Margaret and her brother fled from England, intending to return to Hungary. A storm set their boat on the coast of the Firth of Forth in Scotland. After being offered refuge and welcome in the court of King Malcolm Canmore, she so captivated him by her beauty, goodness, and accomplishment that they were married in 1070.

Margaret's deeds on behalf of Scotland were twofold: the tempering of Malcolm, in that she "rendered him one of the most virtuous kings ever to have occupied the Scottish throne,"[228] and the promotion of Christianity, education, and the arts of civilization for the country. Through Malcolm, she sought good priests and teachers, succeeded in reforming many abuses, convened synods to regulate the Lenten Fast and Easter communion, and founded a number of churches, most notably the Church of the Holy Trinity at Dunfermline. She also formed a guild among the ladies of the court to provide vestments and church furniture.

Margaret lived an austere, perhaps even ascetic life. She ate sparingly and slept little in order to have time for prayer. It is said that she "never sat down at her own table till she had waited upon nine little orphans and twenty-four poor people." In addition to keeping the fasts and disciplines of Lent, she kept Advent as a similar period of fasting and prayer. During these times she always rose at midnight and went to the church for Matins. On her return, she would wash the feet of six poor persons and give them alms.

Lying on her deathbed, she received the news of the death of her husband and eldest son on the battlefield. Raising her eyes and hands to heaven she replied, "I thank thee, O almighty God, because Thou has willed that I should bear so great trials at my departure; and because Thou has willed my purification, as I hope, from some sinful stain, by bearing them."[229] Margaret was canonized in 1250 and named patroness of Scotland in 1673.

E. B. Anderson

November 17
Philip William Otterbein (1813)
See Common of Pastors and Bishops, Leaders

Born on June 3, 1726, this German Reformed pietist was educated and ordained at the Herborn Academy. He pastored churches in Germany for three years and was then recruited along with five other young ministers in 1752 to preach in America. He was sent to a German Reformed congregation in Lancaster, Pennsylvania where he had an experience of personal assurance of God's grace. His ministry revitalized, he went on to three more successfully pastorates until in 1774 he became pastor of the German Evangelical Reformed Church in Baltimore on Howard's Hill. He served that congregation for thirty-nine years until his death.

Otterbein's pastorates were always marked by his vigorous preaching and by his organization of small pietist groups for Bible study and prayer. His theology emphasized the new birth made possible by God's grace. One of his few surviving writings is a sermon preached in 1760 on the "Glorious Victory of Jesus Christ over the Devil and Death":

Are you converted? Has Jesus delivered you from sin? Are you convinced on the basis of living experience of the work of grace in you? ... Have you sat — and how long have you sat — weeping with Mary at the feet of Jesus? Which sin in you has been put to death by Jesus? ...

There is a cost involved before one can come to peace with God. The new birth and its process does not happen without much pain. But so great also is the change brought about by grace in conversion. ... If your salvation means anything to you, join up with the prodigal son, for Jesus is waiting for you. The garment of salvation is already prepared. All is ready. Come.[230]

It was during an early pastorate at York, Pennsylvania that he attended a "big meeting" at nearby Long's Barn in the spring of 1767 to hear evangelical Mennonite Martin Boehm preach. Deeply impressed with the message and spirit of Boehm, Otterbein threw his arms around Boehm declaring aloud, "Wir sind Brüder!" or, "We are brothers!" Their relationship eventually grew into the German pietist movement known as the Church of the United Brethren in Christ. Otterbein was also a friend and contemporary of Francis Asbury, assisting in Asbury's consecration as Superintendent in 1784.

Martin Boehm's son Henry recalls that Otterbein was tall and had "a thoughtful open countenance, full of benignity, a dark bluish eye that was very expressive."[231]

T. A. Rand

November 18
Hilda (680)
See Common of Saints

Hilda, abbess of Whitby, was the daughter of Hereric and Berjuswida, members of the Northumbrian nobility. After spending her first thirty-three years in a secular life, she then followed her sister Heresuid into the monastic life, determined to leave her homeland behind. After a year she took up a monastic residence with a few companions. She became the abbess of Hartlepool (Heruteu) for several years and then at Whitby (Streaneshalch) in Yorkshire where she administered the monastery until her death at age 66.

The double monastery at Whitby, housing both monks and nuns, was known for its devotion to study. Hilda encouraged them all to spend much time studying the Scriptures and doing good works. She was admired for her wisdom and she advised both neighbors and kings. Five of the monks at Whitby went on to become bishops. Bede tells the story of how Hilda recognized in Caedmon, an old stable-worker, a divine gift for putting Scripture and doctrine into verse. She urged him to join the monastery, where she saw that he received full schooling in the Bible so that he might further apply his talents to the writing of religious poetry.

When a synod was held in the monastery of Whitby in 664 to resolve the differences between the Celtic and Roman traditions on the observance of Easter, Hilda participated in the synod. Although the abbess and her followers kept the Celtic observance, all at the synod agreed to conform to the Roman form.

In the monastic communities Hilda was known for her able administrative work and enthusiasm for regular discipline. She modeled for them a strict piety and taught them to follow the virtues, "particularly of peace and charity." Through seven years of illness she continued to praise God and give instruction to the nuns and monks. With relatively little known about her life and no written work of her own left to us, we can nevertheless hope to appreciate this woman called "Mother" by all who knew her. She was influential in the church of Northumbria, providing leadership and guidance to many as Christianity grew and spread. Her unique piety and grace were examples "to many who lived at a distance, to whom the fame was brought of her industry and virtue."[232]

A. Berry Wylie

November 21
Anna Oliver (1892)
See Common of Preachers

Anna Oliver was the first woman to graduate from an American theological seminary and a pioneer Methodist Episcopal Church preacher and pastor. She was born near New Brunswick, New Jersey in 1840. Baptized Vivianna Olivia Snowden, she changed her name in the early 1870s so as not to embarrass her family when she decided to enter the ministry. Educated in Brooklyn public schools and Rutgers Female College in New York City, Oliver began her career as a public school teacher in Connecticut. In addition to teaching, she took an active role in women's suffrage and temperance movements in her adopted state for the next eight years.

In 1868 she volunteered to teach black children in Georgia under the auspices of the American Missionary Association. Inadequate facilities, domineering male supervisors, and hostility from the southern white community tested her commitment. A year later, when she learned that the AMA paid female teachers less than men who did the same work, Oliver resigned. She rejoined her family in Connecticut for a time, resumed her interest in women's issues, and took up painting. She soon relocated to Cincinnati, partly to study landscape painting and partly because the Ohio women's rights movement was more advanced than in Connecticut.

Oliver's temperance talks in Ohio's town halls and churches encouraged her to think about becoming an ordained minister. In 1873 she enrolled in the Boston University School of Theology. Armed with a B. D. degree (1876) and a license to preach, Oliver assumed the pastorate of First Methodist Episcopal Church in Passaic, New Jersey, and later, Willoughby Avenue Church in Brooklyn. In 1880, Oliver led an unsuccessful campaign for ordination at General Conference. Without ordination she continued as pastor of the Willoughby Avenue congregation until 1883 when the church was abandoned. Oliver remained in Brooklyn and devoted much energy to temperance and suffrage, and dress reform and health care for women and children. She continued to preach her message of personal holiness and social responsibility until her death of 1892 in Greensboro, Maryland. By opening her home to a growing stream of women who were pioneering ministerial roles in Victorian churches, she became a respected mentor and model. Throughout her ministry her favorite text was Revelation 3:8 (KJV): "Behold, I have set before thee an open door, and no *man* can shut it."

K. E. Rowe

November 23
Clement of Rome (c. 100)
See Common of Pastors and Bishops, Teachers

According to the earliest episcopal lists, Clement was the third successor of Peter in the Roman church, holding that office during the last decade of the first century. As a young man, Clement reportedly was acquainted with Peter and Paul. He may be the Clement mentioned in Paul's letter to the Philippians (4:3), but this identification is uncertain. Little is known about Clement's life and faith, but an epistle written from the church in Rome to the church in Corinth in the late first century is unanimously ascribed to him. I Clement, as ancient as some New Testament documents, enjoyed high esteem in the early church, even being regarded as canonical for a time in Egypt and Syria. In addition to providing evidence of evolving church structure and the ascendancy of Rome, the epistle reveals some of the piety and thought of its author.

Dissension in the Corinthian church was the occasion of I Clement. A few members of that community had rebelled and expelled several elders from office. Clement appeals to the congregation, calling it an injustice to remove those who were duly appointed and had served the flock of Christ blamelessly and humbly. The schism had led many astray, cast many into discouragement and doubt, and caused grief for all. Repeatedly, Clement calls for "peace and concord." The actual details of the Corinthian controversy occupy a rather small part of the letter. Much more space is given to illustrative, homiletical, and liturgical material. Examples are drawn from Israel's past, the life of Jesus, and Christian martyrs, as well as nature, society, and even pagan folklore.

Clement's concept of the church was influenced by the spirit of Roman hellenism. As the Empire functioned best when peace and orderliness prevailed, so would the church of God. Throughout its history the church has appropriated models and concepts from the surrounding society, sometimes to its benefit, sometimes to its harm. Our chief inspiration, Clement reminds us, comes from another source: "For it is to the humble that Christ belongs, not to those who exalt themselves over his flock. The scepter of God's majesty, the Lord Jesus Christ, did not come with the pomp of pretension or of arrogance, though he could have, but rather being humble" (16:1-2).[233]

N. C. Croy

November 24
Eliza Garrett (1855)
See Common of Saints

Eliza Clark, born in Newburgh in 1805, married Augustus Garrett in 1825. They were plagued early in their marriage by debts and the deaths of their three very young children. They flourished, however, in the fluid frontier society of Chicago and grew wealthy as the outpost became a town. Augustus became the seventh and the ninth mayor of Chicago, as well as one of the wealthiest men in the town.

Eliza was an active member of the Clark Street Methodist Episcopal Church (which later became Chicago Temple). Augustus, however, appeared frequently to fall from grace, being converted twenty times. When he died in 1848, she wrote, "I had prayed and hoped that he would live to do some little good in this World before he should have been called to give up his account."[234] But she inherited half of his estate and began to think of how best to use it for the good of the church. The pastor of Clark Street Church, Peter Borein, had struggled to compensate for his lack of formal education. This helped awaken Eliza to the educational needs of Methodist clergy, and consulting with a group already planning Northwestern University, an active vision grew to found a biblical institute for Methodist clergy.

When John Dempster came through Chicago with plans to found a biblical institute further south, he was impressed by Garrett's vision as well as the prospect of her financial support and lent his influence to petition the 1854 General Conference. Garrett's gift came at a time when Methodists were still reluctant to have an educated clergy. But, as Abel Stevens records the reaction of the General Conference to the proposal, "that body saw that it could not disregard so remarkable a providential opportunity, so munificent an offering. It may well be doubted whether the session which accepted and approved her overture ... would not have rejected any less providential appeal to its opinions; and to Eliza Garrett, therefore, belongs the credit of turning the whole Church into this new career of ministerial improvement."[235] The Garrett Biblical Institute opened on January 1, 1855 with four students and three faculty.

Eliza provided the means and the vision to supply the expanding church with educated ministers. At the time, her gift was the largest ever given in America for higher education, and by giving her gift before her death she set a new model of philanthropy for the nation's wealthiest citizens.

I. A. Fisher

November 25
Isaac Watts (1748)
See Common of Musicians

Isaac Watts was born in 1674 of a dissenting schoolmaster and grew up in an atmosphere which restricted singing in worship to Psalms and their metrical paraphrases. About 1695, he returned home to complain about the psalms sung, judging them as lacking both beauty and dignity. His father challenged him to see if he could do better. The result was the first of some seven hundred and fifty hymn texts. In 1699 he began work as assistant to the minister of the congregational chapel at Mark Lane, London. In 1702 he became pastor of that congregation, a post he held until his death in 1748, although ill health limited his activity throughout his pastorate.

Known as the founder of English hymnody, Watts was convinced that Christian praise had to go beyond Scriptural texts; congregational song should include original expressions of devotion and thanksgiving. Furthermore, psalms needed to be "Christianized" for use in Christian worship. He set about providing hymn texts to meet these objectives, and set the standard for English hymns to come. His hymns are Christ-centered in focus, have congregational worship as their context, and are permeated with biblical language and references. The best of his hymns deal with the great themes of Christian experience "with a depth of conviction, a grace and dignity, and a cosmic range and sweep, which few hymn writers have equaled."[236]

Texts of such hymns as "O God our help in ages past," "Joy to the world, the Lord is come!," "I'll praise my maker while I've breath," "Jesus shall reign where e'er the sun," Alas! and did my Savior bleed," and "When I survey the wondrous cross" continue to speak to us and for us in our worship and our spirituality. Less well known is Watt's paraphrase of Psalm 19 which concludes:

> Great Sun of Righteousness, arise;
>   Bless the dark World with heavenly Light;
> Thy Gospel makes the Simple wise,
>   Thy Laws are sure, thy Judgments right.
>
> Thy noblest Wonders here we view,
>   In souls renewed and Sins forgiven:
> Lord, cleanse my sins, my Soul renew,
>   And make thy Word my Guide to Heaven.[237]

D. W. Vogel

November 26
Sojourner Truth (1883)
See Common of Prophets

With an unquenchable passion for equality and the courage to challenge injustice, Sojourner Truth was a legend in her own time, the conscience of nineteenth century evangelical reform. As a preacher and lecturer, she devoted her life to the antislavery cause, to helping freed slaves settle in the West, and to woman' suffrage and equal rights.

Born Isabella Bomefree, among the Dutch-speaking settlers of Ulster County, New York, she was freed in 1827 when New York abolished slavery. Although illiterate, she successfully sued for her son's return from Alabama where he had been illegally sold in 1826.

After her emancipation, she moved to New York City where she worked as a domestic. She began preaching at camp meetings and joined a utopian community in Massachusetts. In 1843 she changed her name to Sojourner Truth which described her new life as an itinerant preacher.

Although she is best known for speeches made on behalf of black women's right to be included in woman's suffrage, one of her most memorable statements came in reply to acclaimed abolitionist orator Frederick Douglass. As the abolition of slavery seemed more and more remote, Douglass rose in anger saying that only through violent revolt would the slaves be free. Rising from the audience, she challenged him with the question: "Frederick, is God dead?"[238]

During an audience with President Abraham Lincoln after he had signed the Emancipation Proclamation, she said, "I told him that I had never heard of him before he was talked of for president. He smilingly replied, 'I had heard of you many times before that.'"[239]

In spite of sickness and old age, she never tired of her calling:

I am above eighty years old; it is about time for me to be going . . .
I suppose I am kept here because something remains for me to do;
I suppose I am yet to help break the chain. I have done a great deal
of work; as much as a man, but did not get so much pay. I used to
work in the field and bind grain, keeping up with the cradler; but
men doing no more, get twice as much pay; so with the German
women. They work in the field and do as much work, but do not get
the pay. We do as much, we eat as much, we want as much."[240]

A. M. Israel

November 28
John Dempster (1863)
See Common of Saints

Born on January 2, 1794 in the town of Florida, New York, John Dempster carried on the pioneering spirit of his father, James, who was sent from England by John Wesley in 1774 to supervise the Methodist ministries in western New York. Known as a founder of seminaries, Dempster spent the early years of his ministry as an itinerant preacher, often preaching twenty-one times a week. His itineracy ended in 1836 when he was appointed by General Conference to the mission field in Buenos Aires. There he established schools to train native ministers.

After he returned to the U.S. in 1842, he became consumed with the prospect of establishing schools to provide for a better educated clergy in the Methodist Episcopal Church. Although many Methodists were against such a project, Dempster was able to establish in Newberry, Vermont in 1845 what was later to become the Boston University School of Theology. It moved two years after its founding to Concord, New Hampshire.

After seven years in Concord, Dempster moved to Evanston, Illinois, where, with the aid of the wealthy benefactor Eliza Garrett, he established Garrett Biblical Institute (now Garrett-Evangelical Theological Seminary). He served there as president until 1863. He died that same year as he was preparing to embark on yet another seminary planting trip to the Pacific coast.

Central to his understanding of the ministry was a deep affection for spirituality which he hoped to plant in young ministers:

What one function belongs to the ministerial office not demanding the deepest spirituality? The whole character calls for a high controlling piety — a living, energetic, all-conquering piety — one that imbues the heart, the life, the studies, the habits, the whole [person]. This principle must sway the minister with the power of a passion. [The minister] can have no substitute for this living, glowing spirit — for a heart throbbing and flaming with restoring love.[241]

T. A. Rand

November 28
James Mills Thoburn (1922)
See Common of Evangelists

James Thoburn was born in 1836 in Ohio to Irish-immigrant parents. After making the final payment on the Ohio family farm, his father gave a gold eagle to his wife to buy a new winter cloak. She added the eagle to another her husband had given as a thank-offering toward missions work with the remark, "I will turn my old cloak."[242] Thoburn's family environment helped lead him to leave his pastoral work in the Pittsburgh Conference and follow the call to become a Methodist missionary. He arrived in northern India in 1859 shortly after it had become a subject nation of the British Empire. Thoburn would serve the people of India whom he loved for fifty years.

Thoburn started his work at the resort of Naini Tal, establishing schools there for boys and girls and learning the local language. Frustrated by the limitations on evangelism inherent in comity agreements between competing denominations, Thoburn chose to relinquish the Mission Society's financial support of his work. Upon doing so, others donated funds enabling him to move out beyond northern India. He traveled to Calcutta, Rangoon, and Singapore (which he foresaw becoming a great metropolis). In 1888 he was elected Missionary Bishop of India and Malaysia. As such, he supported and encouraged the development of a self-governing Central Conference for Indian Methodists.

Finding a quill from a vulture's wing during a walk, Thoburn fashioned a pen and composed a letter to his sister, Isabella. He noted that only women missionaries could reach the secluded women of India, stated the need for a boarding school, and asked her to come. The letter helped spur the founding of the Women's Foreign Missionary Society and a profound ministry among India's oppressed women. He also lent his considerable influence to the growing deaconess movement.

Thoburn also used techniques of mass evangelism, including employing native lay preachers and house-to-house visiting. His simple method reached members of all castes, particularly those in the lowest castes considered untouchable. Thoburn had arrived in India to find only a small number of Methodists. When he retired in 1908 there were over 200,000.[243]

H. P. Minor

Notes

Introduction

1. Edith Wyschogrod, *Saints and Postmodernism: Revisioning Moral Philosophy* (Chicago: The University of Chicago Press, 1990), p. 3.

2. Austin Farrer, *A Faith of Our Own* (New York: World, 1960), p. 14.

3. For a very helpful and concise history of the development of the sanctoral see Kevin Donovan, SJ, "The Sanctoral," in *The Study of the Liturgy*, revised ed., ed. Cheslyn Jones *et al.* (New York: Oxford University Press, 1992), pp. 472-84.

4. Kenneth L. Woodward, *Making Saints: How the Catholic Church Determines Who Becomes a Saint, Who Doesn't, and Why* (New York: Simon & Schuster, 1990), p. 56.

5. Woodward, p. 68.

6. *Methodist Almanac* (New York: Lane & Scott, 1847-49). See also, Thomas Jackson, *Lives of the Early Methodist Preachers Told by Themselves*, 4th ed., 6 vols. (London: Wesleyan Conference Office, 1837-38), and L. F. Church, *The Early Methodist People* (London: Epworth, 1948) and *More About the Early Methodist People* (London: Epworth, 1949). It is also noteworthy that for many years the portraits of important Methodist persons appeared at the front of the *Methodist Magazine* or *Quarterly Review*.

7. Laurence Hull Stookey, "The Wesleys and the Saints," *Liturgy* 5.2 (1985-86), p. 78.

8. "A Collection of Forms of Prayer for Every Day in the Week," *The Works of the Rev. John Wesley, A. M.*, ed. Thomas Jackson (Grand Rapids, MI: Baker Book House, 1978), XI:225.

9. "The Office of the Saints," in *Devotions for Every Day of the Week, and the Great Festivals*, in *The Christian Library*, (London: J. Kershaw, 1826) XXV:434.

10. "The Office of the Saints," p. 435.

11. Geoffrey Wainwright, "Wesley and the Communion of Saints," *One in Christ* 27 (1991), pp. 332-45. For the place of saints in Charles Wesley's hymns, also see Stookey's article.

12. Quoted from Wainwright, p. 334. See no. 812 in *Hymns and Psalms* (London: Methodist Publishing House, 1983), and no. 709 in *The United Methodist Hymnal* (Nashville: The United Methodist Publishing House, 1989).

13. J. Ernest Rattenbury, *The Eucharistic Hymns of John and Charles Wesley*, American Edition, ed. Timothy J. Crouch, OSL, (Cleveland: OSL Publications, 1990), p. 70.

14. No. 96 in *Hymns for the Lord's Supper*, in Rattenbury, p. H-31

15. Wainwright, p. 339.

16. *The United Methodist Book of Worship*, 74, 413-15.

17. *John Wesley's Prayer Book: The Sunday Service of the Methodists in North America*. intro. James F. White, (Cleveland: OSL Publications, 1991), p. A1.

18. For examples of Wesley's objections to Roman enthusiasms surrounding the saints, see *Works*, 9:4 and 24, and 10:104, 105.

19. Wesley, "Popery Calmly Considered," III.3, *Works*, X:146.

20. Wesley, *Works*, III:123.

21. Wesley, "A Short Account of the Life and Death of the Rev. John Fletcher," *Works*, XI:365. See also, "Sermon Preached on the Occasion of the Death of the Rev. Mr. John Fletcher," *Works*, VII:431-449.

22. These are, in fact, not very different from the criteria now being used by the Vatican in determining who should and who should not be made a saint. For a thorough and interesting account of the evolution of saint-making in Roman practice, see Kenneth Woodward, pp. 50-86.

23. There is solid ecumenical precedence for waiting for other denominations to recognize their own saints. Woodward points out, for example, that when a group of Lutherans approached the Vatican seeking recognition of Dietrich Bonhoeffer as a saint, the Council replied that this honor should be done by the Lutherans themselves. See Woodward, p. 400.

24. Aidan Kavanaugh repeatedly recalls us to the saying of the Latin formula of Prosper of Aquitaine, *legem credendi lex statuat supplicandi*, "the law of worship constitutes the law of belief." See, for example, Kavanaugh's *The Shape of Baptism: The Rite of Christian Initiation* (New York: Pueblo Publishing Company, 1978), p. xii.
25. Quoted from Woodward, p. 403.
26. See Wyschogrod, pp. 155-62, and Woodward, p. 403.

Saints Days

1. Clement of Alexandria, "The Instructor," I.1 in Alexander Roberts and James Donaldson, eds, *The Ante-Nicene Fathers* (Edinburgh: T & T Clark, 1866-1872), II:209.
2. Thomas Merton, "Light in Darkness: The Ascetic Doctrine of St. John of the Cross," in *Disputed Questions* (London: Hollis and Carter, 1961), p. 214.
3. *The Missionary Pioneer, or A Brief Memoir of the Life, Labours, and Death of John Stewart (Man of Color)*, pub. Joseph Mitchell (New York: J. C. Totten, 1827. Reprinted in New York by the Joint Centenary Committee, Methodist Episcopal Church and Methodist Episcopal Church, South, 1918). Quotes from pages 15, 93.
4. Alice G. Knotts, "Thelma Stevens: Crusader for Racial Justice," in *Spirituality and Social Responsibility: Vocational Vision of Women in The United Methodist Tradition*, ed. Rosemary Skinner Keller (Nashville: Abingdon Press, 1993), p. 242.
5. From Thelma Stevens, "Thelma Stevens' 'Thorns That Fester': An Oral (Auto)biography and Interview," ed. Alice G. Knotts (New York: Women's Division, General Board of Global Ministries, The United Methodist Church, December 5-7, 1983).
6. Roberta B. West, "How Methodism Came to North Montana," *Methodist History*, 5 (April 1967), p. 21.
7. From Edward L. Mills, *Plains, Peaks and Pioneers* (1947), following p. 128. Quoted from Frederick A. Norwood, ed., *Sourcebook of American Methodism*, (Nashville: Abingdon Press, 1982), p. 350.
8. West, p. 26.
9. Robert W. Sledge, "Envisioning the Future of Our Society," *Methodist History*, 28 (January 1990), p. 141.
10. Excerpt from Thomas Taylor's Letter to Wesley (April 11, 1768), from *Sourcebook*, p. 31.
11. Quoted from Frank Baker, "Captain Thomas Webb, Pioneer of American Methodism," *Religion in Life* 34 no. 3 (Summer, 1965), p. 414.
12. See also the excerpt from John Pritchard, "Sermon Occasioned by the Death of the Late Capt. Webb. . . .", in *Sourcebook*, pp. 26-29.
13. Eusebius, *Ecclesiastical History*, trans. Kirsopp Lake, The Loeb Classical Library 153 (Cambridge, Mass.: Harvard University Press, 1980), II.1.1.
14. "Irenaeus Against Heresies," III.1.1, *Ante-Nicene Fathers* I:414.
15. Eusebius, *Ecclesiastical History*, VI.14.7.
16. Prudentius, *Liber Cathemerinon*, no. XII, lines 97ff, in *Aurelii Prudentii Clementis Carmina*, ed. M. P. Cunningham, *Corpus Christianorum, Series Latina*, No. 126 (Turnhout, 1966), pp. 68-69.
17. Severus, "Homily 64," in *Les homiliae cathedrales de Severus d'Antioche. Homilies LVIII a LXIX*, ed. Maurice Briere, *Patrologia Orientalis*, No. 8 (Paris, 1911), pp. 315-16.
18. Adolf Adam, *The Liturgical Year*, trans. Matthew J. O'Connell (New York: Pueblo Publishing Co., 1981), pp. 139-40.
19. Gilbert Haven, *National Sermons : Sermons, Speeches and Letters on Slavery and its War, from the Passage of the Fugitive Slave Bill to the Election of President Grant* (Boston: Lee and Shepard, 1869), pp. 22-23.
20. William Gravely, *Gilbert Haven: Methodist Abolitionist; A Study in Race, Religion, and Reform, 1850-1880*, Commission on Archives and History of The United Methodist Church (Nashville: Abingdon, 1973) p. 256.

21. Quoted in Samuel P. Spreng, *The Life and Labors of John Seybert* (Cleveland: Lauer and Mattill, 1888), p. 13.
22. Spreng, p. 26.
23. Spreng, pp. 396-97.
24. Margaret Fell, "All in One Dress and One Colour," *The Quaker Reader*, ed. Jessamyn West (New York: The Viking Press, 1962), p. 219.
25. William B. Gravely, "Hiram Revels Protests Racial Separation in the Methodist Episcopal Church," *Methodist History*, 8 (1970), pp. 13-20.
26. Hiram Revels, "We Ought not to Separate," quoted in Gravely, "Hiram Revels," p. 18.
27. Thomas Merton, *The Wisdom of the Desert* (New York: New Directions, 1960), p. 62.
28. Adam, p. 241.
29. Geoffrey Wainwright, "Ecumenical Spirituality," in Cheslyn Jones, Geoffrey Wainwright, and Edward Yarnold, *The Study of Spirituality* (New York and Oxford: Oxford University Press, 1986), pp. 541-42.
30. *Homily 5,* in *Pseudo-Macarius: The Fifty Spiritual Homilies and the Great Letter*, trans. and ed. George A. Maloney, S. J., The Classics of Western Spirituality (New York and Mahwah: Paulist Press, 1992), p. 73.
31. Paul Wesley Chilcote, "The Legacy of J. Ernest Rattenbury," *Doxology*, 3 (1986), pp. 15-22.
32. Quoted from Chilcote, p. 20.
33. David L. Taylor, "The Order of Saint Luke and the Versicle; A Resume: 1946-1961," *Doxology*, 3 (1986), p. 48.
34. J. Ernest Rattenbury, *The Eucharistic Hymns of John and Charles Wesley*, American Edition (Cleveland: OSL Publications, 1990), p. 106.
35. Helen Griffith, *Dauntless in Mississippi: The Life of Sarah A. Dickey, 1838-1904* (South Hadley, Mass: Dinosaur Press, 1965).
36. E. Stanley Jones, *A Song of Ascents, A Spiritual Autobiography* (Nashville and New York: Abingdon Press, 1968), pp. 26-27.
37. E. Stanley Jones, *Christ of the India Road* (New York: Abingdon Press, 1925), p. 26.
38. E. Stanley Jones in *Daily Christian Advocate*, 21, No. 25 (Tuesday, May 28, 1928), p. 641.
39. *Homilae in Acta Apostolorum* 30.3, *Patrologia Graeca,* ed. J.-P. Migne (Paris: 1857-66), LX:225.
40. *Ep. ad Olympias* 7.3, trans. Anne Marie Malingney, *Sources chrétiennes* (Paris: Editions du Cerf, 1947) 13bis:140-142.
41. Joseph Pieper, *The Silence of St. Thomas* (New York: Pantheon, 1957), p. 40.
42. C. Howard Hopkins, *John R. Mott* (Grand Rapids: Eerdmans, 1979). Quotes from pages 47, 430.
43. Philip Jakob Spener, *Pia Desideria*, ed. and trans. Theodore Tappert (Philadelphia: Fortress Press, 1964), pp. 87-122.
44. K. James Stein, *Philip Jakob Spener: Pietist Patriarch* (Chicago: Covenant Press, 1986).
45. Spener, p. 96.
46. William J. Reynolds, *Hymns of our Faith: A Handbook for the Baptist Hymnal* (Nashville: Broadman, 1964), p. 275.
47. Ann C. Lammers, "The Rev. Absalom Jones and the Episcopal Church: Christian Theology and Black Consciousness in a New Alliance," *Historical Magazine of the Protestant Episcopal Church*, 51.1 (March 1982), pp. 159-84.
48. Larry G. Murphy, J. Gordon Melton, and Gary L. Ward, eds., *Encyclopedia of African American Religions* (New York: Garland Publishing, 1993), p. 404.
49. Absalom Jones, "A Thanksgiving Sermon" (January 1, 1808), *Afro-American History Series,* ed. Maxwell Whiteman, pp. 19-21.
50. Frederick Douglass, *Narrative of the Life of Frederick Douglass, an American Slave, Written By Himself* (Boston: Bedford Books, 1993), p. 56.
51. *Minutes Taken at the Several Conferences of the Methodist-Episcopal-Church, in America, for the Year 1799* (Philadelphia: Printed by Henry Tuckniss and sold by

Ezekiel Cooper, 1799), p. 22. Quoted in James Penn Pilkington, *The Methodist Publishing House: A History* (Nashville: Abingdon Press, 1968), I: 125.

52. Abel Stevens, *History of the Methodist Episcopal Church* (New York: Eaton and Maines, 1994), III:132.

53. Lester E. Suzuki, "Life of Kanichi Miyama," unpublished manuscript. See also Lester E. Suzuki, "Persecution, Alienation, and Resurrection: History of Japanese Methodist Churches," in *Churches Aflame: Asian Americans and United Methodism*, ed. Artemio R. Guillermo (Nashville: Abingdon Press, 1991), pp. 113-134.

54. Quoted from Enzo Lodi, *Saints of the Roman Calendar*, trans. and ed. Jordan Aumann, OP (New York: Alba House, 1992), p. 61.

55. *The Golden Legend of Jacobus de Voragine*. trans. and adapted from the Latin by Granger Ryan and Helmut Ripperger (New York: Arno Press, 1941).

56. Amanda Berry Smith, *The Christian Standard and Home Journal,* 25, no. 33 (Aug. 13, 1891), p. 3.

57. *George Herbert: The Country Parson, The Temple*, ed. John N. Wall, Jr., The Classics of Western Spirituality (New York: Paulist Press, 1981), pp. 270-71. The poem is slightly abbreviated.

58. Robert Paine, *Life and Times of Bishop McKendree* (Nashville : Publishing House of the M.E. Church, South, 1922), p. 69.

59. Elizabeth A. Clark, *Women in the Early Church* (Collegeville, Minnesota: The Liturgical Press, 1983), p. 103.

60. *On Perfection*, in *Saint Gregory of Nyssa: Ascetical Works*, trans. Virginia Woods Callahan, The Fathers of the Church, No. 58 (Washington: Catholic University of America Press, 1967), p. 122.

61. Sarah H. Bradford, *Scenes in the Life of Harriet Tubman* (Auburn, New York, J. E. Beardsley, 1869), p. 74.

62. Ann Petry, *Harriet Tubman Conductor on the Underground Railroad* (Thomas Y. Crowell Company, New York, 1955).

63. Murphy, et al., eds, pp. 765-66.

64. Bradford, pp. 109-12.

65. *Sketches of the Life and Travels of Rev. Thomas Ware* (New York: Mason and Lane, 1839), pp. 29-30, 189.

66. Gregory the Great, *Pastoral Care*, trans. Henry Davis, S.J., Ancient Christian Writers, No. 11 (New York: Paulist Press, 1950), pp. 89-90.

67. Lucy Rider Meyer, *Deaconesses and Their Work: Biblical, Early Church, European, and American* (Chicago: The Deaconess Advocate, 1897), p. 19.

68. Isabelle Horton, "The Burden of the City" in *The American Deaconess Movement in the Early Twentieth Century*, ed. Carolyn De Swarte Gifford (New York: Garland Publishing, Inc., 1987), p. 146.

69. Quotations from *The Works of St. Patrick*, trans. Ludwig Bieler (Westminster, Maryland: The Newman Press, 1953), pp. 21, 24, 40.

70. *The Works of St. Cyril of Jerusalem*, Vol. I, trans. Leo P. McCauley and Anthony A. Stephenson (Washington, D. C.: The Catholic University of America Press, 1969), p. 93.

71. Quotations from Perry Miller, *Jonathan Edwards* (New York: W. Sloane Associates, 1949), pp. 5, 329-30.

72. "Reminiscences of Rev. Henry Boehm" in *The Patriarch of One Hundred Years*, ed. J. B. Wakeley (New York: Nelson & Phillips, 1875), pp. 12, 581.

73. Ida B. Wells, *Crusade for Justice: The Autobiography of Ida B. Wells*, ed. Alfreda Duster (Chicago: University of Chicago Press, 1970), p. 356.

74. *The Life Experience and Gospel Labors of the Rt. Rev. Richard Allen* (Nashville : Abingdon, 1960), p. 15.

75. Richard Allen, Hymn I "The Voice of Free Grace," verse 1; in *A Collection of Hymns and Spiritual Songs, from various authors* (Philadelphia: Printed by T. L. Plowman, 1801),

p. 3. Allen's first hymnal was reprinted by Mother Bethel A.M.E. Church, Philadelphia in 1987.

76. For a prayer of Richard Allen see *The United Methodist Book of Worship* (461).

77. John Booty, ed., *John Donne: Selections from Divine Poems, Sermons, Devotions, and Prayers* (New York: Paulist Press, 1990), p. 84.

78. G. R. Potter and E. M. Simpson, eds; *The Sermons of John Donne* (Berkeley and Los Angeles: University of California Press, 1953-62), VIII:403.

79. Potter and Simpson, III:253-54.

80. Booty, pp. 255, 272.

81. *The Journal and Letters of Francis Asbury*, ed. Elmer T. Clark (Nashville : Abingdon Press, 1958), I:4-5.

82. Martin Luther King, Jr., *Strength to Love* (New York: Harper and Row, 1963), p. 37.

83. From a typescript of *The Day Book of John Dreisbach*, trans. J. G. Eller.

84. William Law, *A Serious Call to a Devout and Holy Life* (Philadelphia: Westminster, 1955), p. 45.

85. John Wesley, "A Plain Account of Christian Perfection," in *Works*, XI:367.

86. "Reflections in a letter from Finkenwalde," January 1936, in Eberhard Bethge, ed., *Dietrich Bonhoeffer: A Life in Pictures* (Philadelphia: Fortress Press, 1986), p. 84.

87. Dietrich Bonhoeffer, *Life Together* (New York: Harper & Row, 1954), p. 77.

88. Bethge, p. 228.

89. Robert Moats Miller, *Bishop G. Bromley Oxnam: Paladin of Liberal Protestantism*, (Nashville: Abingdon Press, 1990), p. 316.

90. Willis J. King, *Methodist Church Mission in Liberia* (The Liberian Annual Conference of the Methodist Church, 1955), p. 35.

91. Robert Stupperich, *Melanchthon*, trans. Robert H. Fischer (Philadelphia: The Westminster Press, 1965), p. 62.

92. Clyde Manschreck, trans. and ed., *Melanchthon on Christian Doctrine: Loci communes, 155* (New York: Oxford University Press, 1965), p. 165.

93. *The Prayers and Meditations of St. Anselm*, ed. Benedicta Ward (London: Penguin Books, 1973), p. 91.

94. St. Anselm, "Proslogium," in *Basic Writings*, trans. S. N. Deane (La Salle, Illinois: Open Court, 1962), p. 53.

95. St. Anselm, "Cur Deus Homo," in *Basic Writings*, p. 223.

96. John Wesley, *Works*, I:379, II:290.

97. John Wesley, *Works*, XIII:518.

98. Carlton R. Young, *Companion to the United Methodist Hymnal* (Nashville: Abingdon Press, 1993), pp. 234-35.

99. John Wesley, *Works*, I:442.

100. Manuscript, *The Peter Böehler Autobiography*, in the Moravian Archives, Bethlehem, PA.

101. Catherine of Siena, *The Dialogue*, trans. Suzanne Noffke, O.P, The Classics of Western Spirituality (New York: Paulist Press, 1980), pp. 36, 365.

102. Oswald Eugene Brown and Anna Muse Brown, *Life and Letters of Laura Askew Haygood* (Nashville, Dallas: Publishing House of the M.E. Church, South, 1904), pp. 31, 72f, 102, 275f, 486.

103. Athanasius, *On the Incarnation* 9, *Patrologia Graeca*, XXV:112.

104. Athanasius, *Oration against the Arians* 3.3, *Patrologia Graeca* XXVI:328.

105. Athanasius, *On the Incarnation* 14, *Patrologia Graeca* XXV:120.

106. Letter of Thomas Coke, August 9, 1784, quoted in Norman W. Spellmann, "The Formation of the Methodist Episcopal Church," in *The History of American Methodism*, ed. Emory Stevens Bucke (Nashville: Abingdon Press, 1964), I:200.

107. Thomas Coke, *Four Discourses on the Duties of a Minister of the Gospel* (Nashville: Southern Methodist Publishing House, 1880), p. 312. Quoted in *Selections from the*

Writings of Thomas Coke, ed. Warren Thomas Smith (Nashville: The Upper Room, 1966), p. 27.

108. *The Confessions of St. Augustine* (Book 3, Chapter 11, par. 20), trans. John K. Ryan (Garden City, New York: Image Books, 1960), p. 91.

109. *The Confessions,* (Book 9, Chapter 10, par. 26), p. 223.

110. Quotations from *Julian of Norwich: Showings,* trans. with introduction by Edmund Colledge, O.S.A., and James Walsh, S.J. (New York: Paulist Press, 1978), pp. 183, 238, 279, 321, 342.

111. Gregory of Nazianzus, "The Fifth Theological Oration — On the Holy Spirit," in *Christology of the Later Fathers*, ed. Edward Hardy (Philadelphia: The Westminster Press, 1954), p. 199.

112. The information on William Nast comes from Carl Wittke, *William Nast: Patriarch of German Methodism* (Detroit: Wayne State University Press, 1959).

113. G. A. Raybold, *Reminiscences of Methodism in West Jersey* (New York: Lane & Scott, 1849), pp. 166-67.

114. Mary M. Bethune, "Girding for Peace," Mary McLeod Bethune Foundation Papers, Daytona Beach, Florida, n.d., p. 6. Quoted in Clarence G. Newsome, "Mary McLeod Bethune and the Methodist Episcopal Church North: In But Out," *Journal of Religious Thought,* 49 (Summer-Fall, 1992), p. 15.

115. W. E. Sangster, *Can I Know God? and other Sermons* (New York, Nashville: Abingdon Press, 1960).

116. Paul Sangster, *Doctor Sangster* (London: Epworth Press, 1962), pp. 220, 269, 90-91.

117. W. E. Sangster, *The Pure in Heart: A Study in Christian Sanctity — The Cato Lecture of 1954* (New York, Nashville: Abingdon Press, 1954).

118. *Bede's Ecclesiastical History of the English People,* Book V, Chapter XXIV, ed. B. Colgrove & R. A. B. Mynors (Oxford: Oxford University Press, 1969).

119. "Cuthbert's Letter on the Death of Venerable Bede" in *The Venerable Bede's Ecclesiastical History of England,* ed. J. A. Giles, 2nd ed. (London: Henry G. Bohn, 1849), pp. xx, xxi.

120. John Calvin, *Institutes of the Christian Religion,* trans. Ford Lewis Battles, Library of Christian Classics, No. 20, (Philadelphia: Westminster Press, 1961), pp. 35, 690.

121. "The First Apology of Justin," in *The Ante-Nicene Fathers*, I:185.

122. Eusebius, *Ecclesiastical History*, V.1.41, p. 427.

123. *The Letters of Saint Boniface,* trans. Ephraim Emerton (New York: Octagon Books, 1973), p. 84-85.

124. Chief Seattle, in *The Portable North American Indian Reader*, ed. Frederick W. Turner III (New York: Penguin Books/Viking Press, 1974), pp. 251-53.

125. Chief Seattle, "All Things Are Connected," in *Native American Testimony: An Anthology of Indian and White Relations, First Encounter to Dispossession*, ed. Peter Nabokov (New York: Thomas Y. Crowell), p. 108.

126. *Adomnan's Life of Columba*, par. 39a, trans. Alan and Marjorie Anderson (London: Thomas Nelson & Sons, 1961), p. 289.

127. W. Douglas Simpson, *The Historical Saint Columba* (Edinburgh: Oliver and Boyd, 1963), p. 65.

128. *The Unpublished Poetry of Charles Wesley, Vol. 2: Hymns and Poems on Holy Scripture*, ed. S. T. Kimbrough, Jr. and Oliver A. Beckerlegge (Nashville: Abingdon Press, 1990), p. 346.

129. Basil the Great, *On the Holy Spirit*, 15.36, ed. Philip Schaff and Henry Wace, A Select Library of Nicene and Post-Nicene Fathers of the Christian Church, second series (Grand Rapids, Michigan: Eerdmans, n.d.), p. 22.

130. Dana Greene, *Evelyn Underhill: Artist of the Infinite Life* (New York: Crossroad, 1990).

131. Evelyn Underhill, "What is Mysticism?," in *Collected Papers of Evelyn Underhill*, ed. Lucy Menzies (A. R. Mowbray & Co. 1936; rpt. London: Longmans, Green and Co., 1946), p. 107.

132. Found in the Underhill archives in London by Grace Adolphsen Brame, published in *The* Christian Century, Oct. 31, 1990, together with Brame's article, "Continuing Incarnation: Evelyn Underhill's Double Thread of Spirituality."

133. Printed at the end of "Introduction" by Lumsden Barkway, *Collected Papers of Evelyn Underhill*.

134. *The Venerable Bede's Ecclesiastical History of England,* pp. 3, 15.

135. Charles Thomas, *Christianity in Roman Britain to A.D. 500*, (Berkely & Los Angeles: University of California Press, 1981).

136. Ode 1, Canon 2 for Orthros in the Byzantine menaion for June 24. Translated by the author from a French translation by P. Dennis Guillaume (Rome: Diaconie Apostolique, 1988).

137. Irenaeus, *Against Heresies*, 5.1, in *The Christological Controversy*, trans. and ed. Richard Norris (Philadelphia: Fortress Press, 1980), p. 58.

138. Donald B. Smith, *Sacred Feathers* (Lincoln: University of Nebraska Press, 1987), p. 60.

139. St. Augustine, Sermon 295, "On the Feast Day of Sts. Peter and Paul," *Patrologia Latina,* ed. J. -P. Migne (Paris, 1844-64), XXXVIII:1348-1352, abbreviated.

140. *Report of the International Council of Women*, Assembled by the National Woman Suffrage Association, Washington, D.C., March 15 to April 1, 1888 (Washington, D.C.: Rufus H. Darby, Printer, 1888), p. 25.

141. Anna Howard Shaw, *The Story of a Pioneer* (New York: Harper & Brothers, Publishers, 1915).

142. Brenton Thoburn Badley, *The Making of a Bishop: The Life Story of Bishop Jashwant Rao Chitambar* (Lucknow: Lucknow College Publisher, 1942), pp. 25, 51, 7, and 52.

143. Sidney Benjamin Bradley, *The Life of Richard Whatcoat* (Louisville: Pentecostal Publishing, 1936), pp. 33, 59, and 168.

144. Quoted in Matthew Simpson, *Cyclopedia of Methodism* (Philadelphia: Everts & Stewart, 1878; rpt. New York: Gordon Press, 1977). pp. 935-36.

145. *The Letters of John Hus*, ed. Matthew Spinka (Manchester: Manchester University Press, 1972), p. 187.

146. "The Treatise on the Church," in *Great Voices of the Reformation*, ed. Harry Emerson Fosdick (New York: Random House, 1952), pp. 42-57.

147. *The Rule of St. Benedict in English* (1980), ed. Timothy Fry, O.S.B. (Collegeville, Minn.: The Liturgical Press, 1982), pp. 15, 18-19.

148. Robert Taft, *The Liturgy of the Hours in East and West* (Collegeville, Minn.: The Liturgical Press, 1986), p. 36.

149. Gregory of Nyssa, "The Life of Saint Macrina," in *Saint Gregory of Nyssa: Ascetical Works*, trans. Virginia Woods Callahan, The Fathers of the Church, No. 58 (Washington: The Catholic University of America Press, 1967), pp. 166, 181.

150. Carolyn L. Stapleton, "Belle Harris Bennett: Model of Holistic Christianity," *Methodist History*, 21, No. 3 (April 1983), pp. 131-142.

151. Paula Giddings, *When and Where I Enter* (Bantam Books, New York, 1984), pp. 18, 41, 49, 65.

152. Douglas Chandler, "Belle Harris Bennett," in *Notable American Women 1607-1950*, ed. Edward T. James (Cambridge, Mass: Harvard University Press, 1973), I:132-33.

153. R. W. MacDonell, *Belle Harris Bennett: Her Life Work* (New York: Garland Publishing, Inc., 1987), p. 46.

154. Susan Haskins, *Mary Magdalen: Myth and Metaphor* (London: HarperCollins, 1993), pp. 220-21.

155. Harold C. Gardiner, S. J., in Introduction to *The Imitation of Christ*, trans. Harold C. Gardiner, S.J. (Garden City: Doubleday, 1955), p. 10.

156. Quotations are from *The Imitation*, p. 92, p. 192, and p. 206.

157. Eusebius, *Ecclesiastical History*, II.9.2-3, p. 127.

158. Ralph H. Jones, *Charles Albert Tindley: Prince of Preachers* (Nashville, Abingdon, 1982).

159. Quotations from Charles Winfred Douglas, *Church Music in History and Practice* (New York: C. Scribner's Sons, 1937), p. 194.

160. Gail R. O'Day, "John," in *The Women's Bible Commentary*, ed. Carol A. Newsom and Sharon H. Ringe (Louisville: Westminster/John Knox Press, 1992), p. 299.

161. John Wesley, *Journal* (August 1, 1742), in *Works*, I:387-93.

162. Quoted in Richard P. Heitzenrater, *The Elusive Mr. Wesley* (Nashville: Abingdon Press, 1984), I:181.

163. F. L. Cross and E. A. Livingston, *The Oxford Dictionary of the Christian Church*, 2nd ed. (New York: Oxford University Press, 1983), p. 958.

164. *The Methodist Hymnal* (Nashville: Board of Publication of The Methodist Church, 1966), No. 99.

165. Ambrose: *De Officiis* I. 41; II.28, *Patrologia Latina*, XVI:84-5, 141. For a summary in English, see V. L. Kennedy, *The Saints of the Canon of the Mass* (Rome, 1963), p. 134-5, which is the account used here.

166. *Clare of Assisi: Early Documents*, trans. Regis Armstrong (New York: Paulist Press, 1988), pp. 67, 36.

167. Nancy Boyd, *Three Victorian Women who Changed Their World* (New York: Oxford University Press, 1982), p. 174.

168. Henry Moore, *The Life of Mrs. Mary Fletcher* (New York: J. Soule and T. Mason, for the Methodist Episcopal Church in the United States, 1818), p. 162.

169. John Wesley, "A Short Account of the Life and Death of the Rev. John Fletcher," *Works*, XI:365. See also, "Sermon Preached on the Occasion of the Death of the Rev. Mr. John Fletcher," *Works*, 7:431-49.

170. *The Works of John Fletcher*, ed. Joseph Benson (London: Edwards, 1806-1808), IV:232-33.

171. Diane Dewar, *The Saint of Auschwitz* (San Francisco: Harper & Row, 1982), p.74.

172. *Butler's Lives of the Saints* ed. Herbert J. Thurston, S.J. and Donald Attwater, with a forward by Cardinal Basil Hume, OSB. (Westminster, MD: Christian Classics, 1981), pp. 331, 334.

173. Francis John McConnell, *John Wesley* (New York: Abingdon Press, 1939), p. 131.

174. Francis John McConnell, *The Christlike God: A Survey of the Divine Attributes from the Christian Point of View* (New York: Abingdon Press, c. 1927), p. 241.

175. Bernard of Clairvaux, "On Loving God," in *Bernard of Clairvaux: Selected Works*, trans. G. R. Evans, Classics of Western Spirituality (New York: Paulist Press, 1987), pp. 186-87.

176. Frederick St. George de Latour Booth-Tucker, *The Life of Catherine Booth: The Mother of the Salvation Army* (London: Salvation Army, c. 1893), pp. 96, 394.

177. Helen Johnson, "Georgia Harkness: She Made Theology Understandable," *United Methodists Today* (October 1974), p. 55. Quoted in Rosemary Skinner Keller, "Georgia Harkness — Theologian of the People," in *Spirituality and Social Responsibility*, p. 206.

178. Eusebius, *Ecclesiastical History*, V.10.3.

179. "The Conferences of Cassian," I.1, in *Western Asceticism*, ed. Owen Chadwick, The Library of Christian Classics, Ichthus Edition (Philadelphia: Westminster Press, 1958), p. 195

180. "The Sayings of the Fathers," IX.4, in *Western Asceticism*, pp. 102-3.

181. Augustine, *The Confessions of St. Augustine*, 1.1, trans. John K. Ryan (Garden City, New York: Image Books, 1960), p. 43.

182. John Bunyan, *The Pilgrim's Progress* (London: Penguin Classics, 1986), p. 212.

183. Paul D. Mitchell, *From Teepees to Towers: A History of the Methodist Church in Oklahoma* (Verden, Oklahoma, 1947), p. 40.

184. Quoted by F. W. Kantzenbach in *Eerdman's Handbook to the History of Christianity* (Grand Rapids: William B. Eerdmans Publishing Company, 1977), p. 596.

185. Albert Schweitzer, "The Problem of Ethics in the Development of Human Thought." *A.D.*, February 1975, p. 23.

186. W. P. Strickland, ed., *Autobiography of Rev. James B. Finley; or, Pioneer Life in the West* (Cincinnati: Methodist Book Concern, 1853), pp. 167, 169, 178.

187. Frederick A. Norwood, "When They All Sat Together in Dayton," *Methodist History* 25, No. 1 (October, 1986), p. 35.

188. Henry Moore, pp. 115-16.

189. James M. Thoburn, *The Life of Isabella Thoburn* (1903; rpt. New York: Garland Publishing, 1987), p. 246.

190. Thoburn, p. 70.

191. Clara A. Swain, *A Glimpse of India, being a Collection of Extracts from the Letters of Dr. Clara A. Swain, First Medical Missionary to India of the Woman's Foreign Missionary Society of the Methodist Episcopal Church in America* (1909; rpt. New York: Garland Publishing, 1987), p. 150.

192. Charles Elliot, "Martyrdom of Bewley," *The Methodist Review,* 45 (October, 1863), pp. 626-45.

193. *The Old English Finding of the True Cross*, ed. and trans. Mary-Catherine Bodden (Cambridge: D. S. Brewer, 1987), p. 86.

194. Adolf Adam, p. 182.

195. Dag Hammarskjöld, *Markings*, trans. Leif Sjoberg and W. H. Auden (New York: Adlfred A. Knopf, 1965).

196. Abel Stevens, *Daily Zion's Herald*, May 11, 1852. Quoted in Theodore L. Agnew, "Methodism on the Frontier," *The History of American Methodism*, I:489, 491.

197. Nathan Bangs, *Life of Freeborn Garrettson* (New York, 1829), pp. 30-31, 34.

198. Information on Catherine Livingston Garrettson from Diane H. Lobody, "A Wren Just Bursting its Shell: Catherine Livingston Garrettson's Ministry of Public Domesticity," in *Spirituality and Social Responsibility*, pp. 19-38.

199. Ezra S. Tipple, *Freeborn Garrettson* (New York: Eaton and Mains, 1920), pp. 10-11.

200. J. P. Pilkington, *Methodist Publishing House: Beginnings to 1870* (New York: Abingdon Press, 1968), I:110, 115.

201. Alfredo Nanez, *The History of the Rio Grande Conference of the United Methodist Church* (Dallas: Bridwell Library of Southern Methodist University, 1980), pp. 43, 46.

202. Similitude VIII (69:3), *The Shepherd of Hermas*, trans. Graydon F. Snyder, The Apostolic Fathers, No. 6 (Camden, N.J.: Thomas Nelson & Sons, 1968), p. 119.

203. Jerome, *Commentary on Isaiah*, prologue, I; *Patrologia Latina*, XXIV:17.

204. *Francis and Clare: The Complete Works.* trans. Regis J. Armstrong and Ignatius C. Brady, The Classics of Western Spirituality (New York: Paulist Press, 1982), pp. 103, 3.

205. Brian Edwards, *William Tyndale: The Father of the English Bible* (Farmington Hills, MI: William Tyndale College, 1982), p. 61.

206. *The New Testament of Tyndale 1534* (Cambridge: Cambridge University Press, 1938), p. 3.

207. *The New Testament of Tyndale 1534*, pp. 317-18.

208. Jennie F. Willing, *Diamond Dust* (New York: Phillips and Hunt), 1880. not paginated.

209. *Notable American Women 1607-1950: A Biographical Dictionary*, ed. Edward T. James (Cambridge, MA: Belknap Press of Harvard University Press, 1971), III:623-25.

210. *The Life of Teresa of Jesus — the Autobiography of Teresa of Avila*, trans. and ed. E. Allison Peers (New York: Doubleay, 1991), pp. 66, 232.

211. *The Complete Works of Saint Teresa of Jesus*, trans. and ed. E. Allison Peers (New York: Sheed and Ward, 1957), II:346.

212. Martin Draper, comp. *The Cloud of Witnesses*, (London: Collins Liturgical Publications, 1982), p. 60.

213. Ignatius of Antioch, "To the Romans," 5, *The Fathers of the Church: A New Translation*, ed. Ludwig Schopp (New York: CIMA Publishing, 1947), p. 110.

214. Ignatius of Antioch, "To the Ephesians," 9, *The Fathers of the Church*, p. 91.

215. Richard Bauckham, *Jude and the Relatives of Jesus in the Early Church* (Edinburgh: T & T Clark, 1990), pp. 19-32, 131.

216. Jerome, *De viris inlustribus* ill.2. English translation in: Wilhelm Schneemelcher, ed., *New Testament Apocrypha*, rev. ed. English translation ed. by R. McL. Wilson, Vol. 1 (James Clarke & Co/Westminster/John Knox Press, 1991), p. 178.

217. Paul Wesley Chilcote, *John Wesley and the Women Preachers of Early Methodism*, ATLA Monograph Series, No. 25 (Metuchen, N.J., & London: The American Theological Library Association and the Scarecrow Press, Inc., 1991), pp. 94, 206.

218. John Wesley, "Journal," (November 1, 1766), *Works*, III:268.

219. Pheobe Palmer *Promise of the Father; or a Neglected Specialty of the Last Days* (New York: Foster and Palmer, Jr., 1866).

220. Richard Wheatley, *The Life and Letters of Mrs. Phoebe Palmer* (New York and London: Garland Publishing Inc., 1984), pp. 305-7.

221. Richard Hooker, *Of the Laws of Ecclesiastical Polity*, *The Works of Richard Hooker*, arranged by John Keble, Vol II, Book 5.7 (New York: Burt Franklin, 1888. Facsimile Reprint: Ellicott City, Maryland: Via Media, 1994), p. 30.

222. St. Leo the Great, *Letters*, trans. Brother Edmund Hunt (New York: Fathers of the Church, Inc., 1957), pp. 269-70.

223. "Sulpicius Severus on the Life of St. Martin," trans. Alexander Roberts, *Nicene and Post-Nicene Fathers*, ser. 2 (New York: 1894), XI:5.

224. *The Journals of Søren Kierkegaard*, ed. and trans. Alexander Dru (London: Oxford University Press, 1938), entry #22.

225. Perry LeFevre, *The Prayers of Kierkegaard* (Chicago: University of Chicago Press, 1956), p. 5.

226. Recorded by Kierkegaard's friend Emil Boesen, and transcribed in *The Journals*, p. 551.

227. John Wesley, "Some Account of Sarah Peters," *Arminian Magazine,* 5 (1782), pp. 128-136; see also *Works*, II:119-26.

228. *Butler's Lives of the Saints*, ed. Michael Walsh (Turnbridge Wells, England: Burns and Oates Ltd., 1991), p. 301.

229. James Augustine Stothert, *A Panegyric on Saint Margaret* (Edinburgh: Charles Dolman, 1850), pp. 13, 14.

230. Philip William Otterbein, "The Salvation-Bringing Incarnation and the Glorious Victory of Jesus Christ over the Devil and Death," in *Philip William Otterbein: Pastor, Ecumenist*, ed. Arthur C. Core (Dayton, OH: Board of Publication of the Evangelical United Brethren Church, 1968), pp. 77-90.

231. Henry Boehm, *Reminiscences*, ed. Joseph B. Wakeley (New York: Carlton & Porter, 1865), p. 391. Quoted from J. Bruce Beheney and Paul H. Eller, *The History of the Evangelical United Brethren Church*, ed. Kenneth W. Krueger (Nashville: Abingdon Press, 1979), p. 43.

232. *Bede's Ecclesiastical History of the English Nation,* trans. by David Knowles, 4.23 (London: J.M. Dent & Sons, 1910), pp. 202, 203.

233. Translation by author, N. Clayton Croy.

234. Eliza Garrett, "Brother and Sister Hamline," Letter (January 29, 1849). Quoted in Ila Alexander Fisher, "Eliza Garrett: To Follow a Vision," in *Spirituality and Social Responsibility*, p. 55.

235. Abel Stevens, *The Women in Methodism* (New York: Carlton and Porter, 1866), pp. 285-86. Quoted in Fisher, p. 57.

236. Norman Victor Hope, *Isaac Watts and his Contribution to English Hymnody* (Hymn Society of America, 1947), p. 9.

237. Isaac Watts, "Psalm XIX: Long Metre," *Psalms of David*, 14th ed. (London: J. Oswald, 1747), p. 42.

238. Nell Irvin Painter, "Sojourner Truth," in *Black Women in America, an Historical Encyclopedia*, ed. Darlene Clarke Hine (Brooklyn: Carlson Publishing, Inc., 1993), pp. 1175-76.

239. Olive Gilbert, *Narrative of Sojourner Truth, with a History of Her Labors and Correspondence, Drawn from Her "Book of Life"* (Battle Creek, Michigan, 1884), pp. 176-80.

240. Letter from Elizabeth Cady Stanton to *The World* in Elizabeth Cady Stanton et al., *History of Woman Suffrage* (Salem, NH: Ayer Co, 1985), II:926-28.

241. John Dempster, *Lectures and Addresses* (Cincinnati: Poe & Hitchcock, 1864).

242. James M. Thoburn, p. 13.

243. W. Richey Hogg, "The Missions of American Methodism," *The History of American Methodism*, III:77.

Contributors

O. Wesley Allen, Jr. is pastor of Forest Park United Methodist Church and a Ph.D. candidate in New Testament Studies at Emory University, Atlanta, Georgia. *Bartholomew; Matthew.*

E. Byron (Ron) Anderson is a Ph.D. candidate in Theological Studies at Emory University, Atlanta, Georgia. *Cyril of Jerusalem; John Mason Neale; Holy Cross Day; Thomas Cranmer; Margaret, Queen of Scotland.*

Irvin W. Batdorf taught New Testament and Biblical Theology at United Seminary, Dayton Ohio, 1946-86, retired. *Mark.*

Thomas J. Bell is a Ph.D. candidate in Historical Studies at Emory University, Atlanta, Georgia. *Hiram Rhoades Revels, Thomas Bowman Stephenson; John Dickins.*

Daniel Taylor Benedict, Jr. is Worship Resources Director of the General Board of Discipleship in Nashville, Tennessee. *Prayers.*

Amanda Berry Wylie has taught at Saint Paul School of Theology and Trenton State College and is currently an independent scholar in Elizabeth, New Jersey. *John Chrysostom; Hilda; Athanasius; Clare of Assisi.*

Brad R. Braxton is a Ph.D. candidate in New Testament Studies at Emory University, Atlanta, Georgia. *Frederick Douglass.*

Rick Brooks is the pastor of Decatur United Methodist Church in Decatur, Mississippi. *Florence Nightingale; George Whitefield; John Woolman.*

George Chien is a Ph.D. student at the Graduate School of Drew University, Madison, New Jersey. *Dag Hammarskjöld*

Bufford W. Coe is the pastor of First United Methodist Church, Hastings, Michigan. *Samuel Wesley; Thomas Coke; Susanna Wesley; William Wesley Van Orsdel (Brother Van).*

Timothy J. Crouch is the Executive Director of the Opportunity Parish Ecumenical Neighborhood Ministry (OPEN M). He also serves as Chaplain-General and Director of Publications for the Order of Saint Luke. *Prayers.*

N. Clayton Croy has a Ph.D. in New Testament Studies from Emory University, Atlanta, Georgia. *Clement of Rome; Thomas.*

David A. deSilva is an assistant instructor at Emory University, Atlanta, Georgia. *John Donne; William Tyndale; Clement of Alexandria.*

Steven K. Doyal is a seminary student at Candler School of Theology, Emory University, Atlanta, and a student pastor in the Holston Conference. *Laura Askew Haygood; William Edwin Robert Sangster.*

Heather Murray Elkins is Assistant Professor of Liturgics at the Theological and Graduate Schools of Drew University, Madison, New Jersey. *Perpetua and her Companions; Dag Hammarskjöld; Sarah Crosby.*

Toinette M. Eugene is Associate Professor of Christian Social Ethics and the Cross Cultural Consultant at Garrett-Evangelical Theological Seminary, Evanston, Illinois. *Absolom Jones; Harriet Ross Tubman; Belle Harris Bennett.*

Ila A. Fisher is pastor of Wellington Park United Methodist Church in Chicago, Illinois. *Phoebe Palmer; Eliza Garrett.*

Mary F. Foskett is a Ph.D. candidate in New Testament at Emory University, Atlanta, Georgia. *The Conversion of Paul; Cornelius the Centurian; Mary.*

Carolyn De Swarte Gifford is an associate editor of the *Historical Encyclopedia of Chicago Women*, and the editor of the Journal of Frances E. Willard. *Frances E. Willard*

Thomas Gildemeister is a chaplain with Emory University Affiliated Hospitals, Atlanta, Georgia. *Boniface; Francis Burns; Alejo Hernández; Maximilian Kolbe.*

Larry A. Goleman is a Ph.D. candidate at Emory University, Atlanta, Georgia. *Dietrich Bonhoeffer; Monica; Columba and Aidan; Bernard of Clairvaux.*

Andrew P. Grant is pastor of Alpine Community Church — United Methodist, Alpine, New Jersey. *John Ernest Rattenbury.*

Colleen C. Grant is a Ph.D. candidate in New Testament at Emory University, Atlanta, Georgia. *Mary Magdelene; Mary and Martha of Bethany; John.*

Alan P. R. Gregory is Assistant Professor of Church History at Episcopal Theological Seminary of the South-West, Austin, Texas. *George Fox; Patrick; Anselm; Andrew; Nicholas.*

Clifton F. Guthrie is a Ph.D. candidate in Theological Studies at Emory University, Atlanta, Georgia. *General Editor; Introduction; Prayers; John Wesley; William Nast; Mary McLeod Bethune; Richard Whatcoat; James Bradley Finley; Anthony Bewley; Francis of Assisi, Luke; Captain Thomas Webb; Martin of Tours.*

Nancy A. Hardesty is an independent scholar in Granville, S.C. Her Ph.D. in the History of Christianity is from the University of Chicago. *The Visitation; Anna Howard Shaw; William Booth and Catherine Mumford Booth; Maggie Newton Van Cott.*

Gregory L. Hayes is the asociate pastor of St. Mark's United Methodist Church, Charleston, West Virginia. *Fanny Jane Crosby; William Law; Thomas à Kempis; Albert Schweitzer.*

Hoyt L. Hickman served for 25 years with the Commission on Worship and the Section on Worship of the General Board of Discipleship. *Jacob Albright; All Saints.*

Harvey Hill is a Ph.D. candidate in Historical Studies at Emory University, Atlanta, Georgia. *Sarah Ann Dickey; Leo the Great.*

Sarah H. Hill is an independent scholar. Her Ph.D. is from Emory University, Atlanta, Georgia. *Peter Jones, or Kahkewaquonaby; Samuel Checote; John Stewart.*

Lorinda H. M. Hoover is an ordained elder in the Iowa Annual Conference of The United Methodist Church. *Agnes of Rome; Peter Cartwright.*

J. Scott Hudgins is the Director of the Baptist Studies program, Candler School of Theology of Emory University, Atlanta, Georgia. *Antony of Egypt; Dominic; Jerome; Ignatius.*

Adrienne M. Israel is Associate Professor of History at Guilford College in Greensboro, North Carolina. *Amanda Berry Smith; Martin Luther King, Jr.; Sojourner Truth.*

Margaret P. Jones is pastor of Wesley Church, Leigh-on-Sea, England and part-time Tutor at Wesley House, Cambridge, England. *The Venerable Bede; Alban; Sarah Peters.*

Alice G. Knotts is an independent scholar and co-director of Shalom Ministries in Portland, Oregon, an urban ministry of the Oregon-Idaho Conference of The United Methodist Church. *Thelma Stevens.*

Curtis G. Lindquist is an Assistant Professor of History at Reinhardt College, Waleska, Georgia. *Jashwant Rao Chitambar; Søren Kierkegaard.*

Kendall K. McCabe is Professor of Preaching and Worship at United Theological Seminary, Dayton, Ohio. *Peter Boehler; Philip and James the Less; Barnabas; John William Fletcher; Mary Bosanquet Fletcher.*

Juana Clem McGhee is an M.Div. senior at Candler School of Theology, Atlanta, Georgia. *Garfield Bromley Oxnam.*

Myron B. McGhee is an M.Div. senior at Candler School of Theology, Atlanta, Georgia. *Matthew Simpson.*

Joyce Ann Mercer is a Ph.D. candidate in Theology and Personality at Emory University, Atlanta, Georgia. *Lucy Rider Meyer; Chief Seattle; Jennie Fowler Willing.*

Hugh P. Minor III is the pastor of Pleasant Valley United Methodist Church in Monroe, Georgia. *Timothy and Titus; Isabella Thoburn and Clara Swain; Teresa of Avila; James Mills Thoburn.*

Bruce T. Morrill is a member of the Society of Jesus, New England Province, and is a Ph.D. candidate in Theological Studies at Emory University, Atlanta, Georgia. *Gregory of Nazianzus; Justin; Irenaeus*

Steven D. Olson is director of the Southern Institute for Business and Professional Ethics and a Ph.D. candidate in Theological Studies at Emory University. *Thomas Aquinas; John Calvin.*

Thomas A. Rand is completing a Master of Theological Studies at Garrett-Evangelical Theological Seminary, Evanston, Illinois. *John Seybert; John Raleigh Mott; Philip William Otterbein; John Dempster.*

Robert A. Ratcliff is Academic Books Editor at Abingdon Press, and an adjunctive professor of church history at Candler School of Theology, Atlanta, Georgia. *Gregory of Nyssa; Gregory the Great; John Bunyan.*

Roy A. Reed is Professor of Worship and Music and the Director of the Master of Arts in Liturgical Arts program at the Methodist Theological School in Delaware, Ohio. *Simon and Jude; Francis John McConnell; Augustine of Hippo.*

Kenneth E. Rowe is Professor of Church History and Methodist Librarian at Drew University Theological School, Madison, New Jersey. *Gilbert Haven; William McKendree; Richard Allen; Francis Asbury; Anna Oliver.*

Lester Ruth is a doctoral candidate in the liturgical studies program at the University of Notre Dame, South Bend, Indiana. *Martin of Tours; The Nativity of John the Baptist; Laurence; Stephen; The Holy Innocents.*

Don E. Saliers is Professor of Worship and Theology at Candler School of Theology, Emory University, Atlanta, Georgia. *Jonathan Edwards; The Annunciation; Benedict of Nursia.*

Grant S. Sperry-White is Visiting Assistant Professor of Church History at Saint Paul School of Theology, Kansas City, Missouri. *The Holy Name; The Confession of Peter; Polycarp; The Martyrs of Lyons; Basil the Great; James of Jerusalem; Ambrose of Milan; John of the Cross; Pseudo-Macarius of Egypt; The Presentation; Macrina the Younger; James the Elder; Abba Moses of Scete.*

Mark Wesley Stamm is the pastor of Trinity United Methodist Church in Roaring Spring and McKee United Methodist Church, Pennsylvania. *Eli Stanley Jones; Richard Hooker.*

K. James Stein is Jubilee Professor of Church History at Garrett-Evangelical Theological Semianary where he has taught since 1960. *Philipp Jakob Spener; Martin Luther; Philip Melancthon; John Hus.*

Lester E. Suzuki is the author of the history of Japanese United Methodist churches and a retired United Methodist minister with a service record of forty-two years living in Berkeley, California. *Kanichi Miyama.*

Emilie M. Townes is Associate Professor of Christian Social Ethics at Saint Paul School of Theology, Kansas City, Missouri. *Ida Bell Wells-Barnett; Georgia Harkness.*

Barbara B. Troxell is Assistant Professor of Practical Theology and Director of Field Education and Spiritual Formation at Garrett-Evangelical Theological Seminary, Evanston, Illinois. *Julian of Norwich; Evelyn Underhill.*

Chris E. Visminas is a liturgical artist and owner of the C. E. Visminis Co., Ltd., 812 Ivy Street, P. O. Box 10189, Pittsburgh, Pennsylvania, 15232. *Artwork.*

Dwight W. Vogel has served as Prior-General of the Order of Saint Luke and is the editor of The Daily Office. He teaches theology, liturgy, and church music at Garrett-Evangelical Theological Seminary, Evanston, Illinois. *Martin and Henry Boehm; Charles Wesley; George Miller, John Walter, and John Dreisbach; Charles Albert Tindley; Johann Sebastian Bach and George Frederick Handel; Freeborn Garrettson and Catherine Livingston Garrettson; Isaac Watts.*

J. Barton Weakley is pastor of Bethlehem United Methodist Church in Concord, Virginia. *Richard Watson; Ezekial Cooper; Thomas Ware; Olaf Gustav Hedström.*

Sara Webb Phillips is the Chaplain and an Instructor of Religion at Union College, Barbourville, Kentucky. *Catherine of Siena; Matthias; Joseph, Mary's Husband.*

Karen B. Westerfield Tucker is assistant professor of liturgical studies at The Divinity School, Duke University, Durham, North Carolina. *Nicholas Ferrar; George Herbert; Harry Hosier; Peter and Paul; Michael and All Angels*

James F. White is Professor of Liturgy, University of Notre Dame, South Bend, Indiana. *Charles Grandison Finney.*

Index of Saints and Dates

Ignatius, October 17
Irenaeus, June 28

James the Less, May 1
James of Jerusalem, October 23
James the Elder, July 25
Jerome, September 30
John of the Cross, December 14
John, December 27
Jones, Absalom, February 13
Jones, Eli Stanley, January 24
Jones, Peter, or Kahkewaquonaby, June 28
Joseph, Mary's Husband, March 19
Jude, October 28
Julian of Norwich, May 8
Justin, June 1

Kahkewaquonaby, or Peter Jones, June 28
Kierkegaard, Søren, November 11
King, Jr., Martin Luther, April 4
Kolbe, Maximilian, August 14

Laurence, August 10
Law, William, April 9
Leo the Great, November 10
Livingston Garrettson, Catherine,
    September 26
Luke, October 18
Luther, Martin, February 18

Macarius (Pseudo) of Egypt, January 19
Macrina the Younger, July 19
Margaret, Queen of Scotland, November 16
Mark, April 25
Martha of Bethany, July 29
Martin of Tours, November 11
Martyrs of Lyons, The, June 2
Mary Magdelene, July 22
Mary of Bethany, July 29
Mary, August 15
Matthew, September 21
Matthias, February 24
McConnell, Francis John, August 18
McKendree, William, March 5
McLeod Bethune, Mary, May 18
Melancthon, Philip, April 19
Meyer, Lucy Rider, March 16
Michael and All Angels, September 29
Miller, George, April 5
Miyama, Kanichi, February 22
Monica, May 4
Moses of Scete, Abba, August 28

Mott, John Raleigh, January 31
Mumford Booth, Catherine, August 20

Nast, William, May 16
Nativity of John the Baptist, The, June 24
Neale, John Mason, August 7
Newton Van Cott, Maggie, August 29
Nicholas, December 6
Nightingale, Florence, August 13

Oliver, Anna, November 21
Otterbein, Philip William, November 17
Oxnam, Garfield Bromley, April 11

Palmer, Phoebe, November 2
Patrick, March 17
Paul, June 29; *See also* January 25
Perpetua and her Companions, March 7
Peter, June 29; *See also* January 18
Peters, Sarah, November 13
Philip, May 1
Polycarp, February 23
Presentation, The, February 2

Rattenbury, John Ernest, January 19
Revels, Hiram Rhoades, January 16
Rider Meyer, Lucy, March 16

Sangster, William Edwin Robert, May 24
Schweitzer, Albert, September 4
Seattle, Chief, June 7
Seybert, John, January 4
Simon, October 28
Simpson, Matthew, June 18
Smith, Amanda Berry, February 25
Spener, Philipp Jakob, February 5
Stephen, December 26
Stephenson, Thomas Bowman, June 21
Stevens, Thelma, December 18
Stewart, John, December 17
Swain, Clara, September 11

Teresa of Avila, October 15
Thoburn, Isabella, September 11
Thoburn, James Mills, November 28
Thomas, December 21
Timothy, January 26
Tindley, Charles Albert, July 26
Titus, January 26
Truth, Sojourner, November 26
Tubman, Harriet Ross, March 10
Tyndale, William, October 6

Tubman, Harriet Ross, March 10
Tyndale, William, October 6

Underhill, Evelyn, June 15

Van Orsdel, William Wesley, December 19
Van Cott, Maggie Newton, August 29
Visitation, The, May 31

Walter, John, April 5
Ware, Thomas, March 11
Watson, Richard, January 8
Watts, Isaac, November 25
Webb, Captain Thomas, December 20
Wells-Barnett, Ida Bell, March 24
Wesley, Charles, March 29
Wesley, John, March 2
Wesley, Samuel, April 24
Wesley, Susanna, July 30
Whatcoat, Richard, July 5
Whitefield, George, September 30
Willard, Frances Elizabeth Caroline,
    February 17
Willing, Jennie Fowler, October 6
Woolman, John, October 7